Food Culture in
Italy

Food Culture in
Italy

FABIO PARASECOLI

Food Culture around the World

Ken Albala, Series Editor

GREENWOOD PRESS

Westport, Connecticut · London

Library of Congress Cataloging-in-Publication Data

Parasecoli, Fabio.
  Food culture in Italy / Fabio Parasecoli.
    p. cm. — (Food culture around the world, ISSN 1545–2638)
  Includes bibliographical references and index.
  ISBN 0–313–32726–2 (alk. paper)
  1. Food habits—Italy—History. 2. Cookery, Italian—History. 3. Dinners and dining—
Italy. 4. Italy—Social life and customs. I. Title. II. Series.
  GT2853.I8P37 2004
  394.1'2'0945—dc22   2004010671

British Library Cataloguing in Publication Data is available.

Library of Congress Catalog Card Number: 2004010671
ISBN: 0–313–32726–2
ISSN: 1545–2638

First published in 2004

Greenwood Press, 88 Post Road West, Westport, CT 06881
An imprint of Greenwood Publishing Group, Inc.
www.greenwood.com

Printed in the United States of America

The paper used in this book complies with the
Permanent Paper Standard issued by the National
Information Standards Organization (Z39.48–1984).

10 9 8 7 6 5 4 3 2 1

Illustrations by J. Susan Cole Stone.

The publisher has done its best to make sure the instructions and/or recipes in this book
are correct. However, users should apply judgment and experience when preparing
recipes, especially parents and teachers working with young people. The publisher ac-
cepts no responsibility for the outcome of any recipe included in this volume.

Contents

Series Foreword

The appearance of the Food Culture around the World series marks a definitive stage in the maturation of Food Studies as a discipline to reach a wider audience of students, general readers, and foodies alike. In comprehensive interdisciplinary reference volumes, each on the food culture of a country or region for which information is most in demand, a remarkable team of experts from around the world offers a deeper understanding and appreciation of the role of food in shaping human culture for a whole new generation. I am honored to have been associated with this project as series editor.

Each volume follows a series format, with a chronology of food-related dates and narrative chapters entitled Introduction, Historical Overview, Major Foods and Ingredients, Cooking, Typical Meals, Eating Out, Special Occasions, and Diet and Health. Each also includes a glossary, bibliography, resource guide, and illustrations.

Finding or growing food has of course been the major preoccupation of our species throughout history, but how various peoples around the world learn to exploit their natural resources, come to esteem or shun specific foods and develop unique cuisines reveals much more about what it is to be human. There is perhaps no better way to understand a culture, its values, preoccupations and fears, than by examining its attitudes toward food. Food provides the daily sustenance around which families and communities bond. It provides the material basis for rituals through which people celebrate the passage of life stages and their connection to divinity. Food preferences also serve to separate individuals and groups from each other, and as one of the most powerful factors in the construction of identity, we physically, emotionally and spiritually become what we eat.

By studying the foodways of people different from ourselves we also grow to understand and tolerate the rich diversity of practices around the world. What seems strange or frightening among other people becomes perfectly rational when set in context. It is my hope that readers will gain from these volumes not only an aesthetic appreciation for the glories of the many culinary traditions described, but also ultimately a more profound respect for the peoples who devised them. Whether it is eating New Year's dumplings in China, folding tamales with friends in Mexico or going out to a famous Michelin-starred restaurant in France, understanding these food traditions helps us to understand the people themselves.

As globalization proceeds apace in the twenty-first century it is also more important than ever to preserve unique local and regional traditions. In many cases these books describe ways of eating that have already begun to disappear or have been seriously transformed by modernity. To know how and why these losses occur today also enables us to decide what traditions, whether from our own heritage or that of others, we wish to keep alive. These books are thus not only about the food and culture of peoples around the world, but also about ourselves and who we hope to be.

Ken Albala
University of the Pacific

Acknowledgments

First and foremost, I want to thank my family, particularly my mother Carmela, with whom I learned to prepare and enjoy food. I hope the legacy will be handed down to my nephew, Flavio, and my niece, Grazia. *Vi voglio bene!*

I owe a debt of gratitude to Stefano Bonilli, the publisher of *Gambero Rosso*, who gave me the opportunity to expand my passion for food into a profession. I also want to express my gratitude to Annalisa Barbagli, the recipe wizard of *Gambero Rosso*, for being an inexhaustible source of culinary knowledge, and my colleagues at the magazine, all of them experts in different fields of food and wine.

I am especially grateful to Darra Goldstein, who was the first in the United States to bet on my writing, and to the Department of Nutrition, Food Studies, and Public Health at New York University, especially Marion Nestle, Amy Bentley, Jennifer Berg, Mimi Martin, Domingo Piñero, and Lisa Sasson. A big hug to Liz Young and Kelli Ranieri, who were my guardian angels during my first semester of teaching. The conversations and the amiable discussions with all the participants in the Feast and Famine seminary at NYU were precious.

Shout-outs to all my students, both past and present, in Rome and New York City. Many have become good friends. Working with them allowed me to explore the uncountable facets of Italian food. Above all, I give them credit for introducing me to the joys of teaching.

Special and affectionate thanks to the friends and colleagues who encouraged me during the writing process and supported me with their comments and observations: Linda Parkoff Davidson, Mitchell Davis, James Dunn, Shelly Eversley, Rachel Laudan, Robert Reid-Pharr, and Douglas Young.

It would be almost impossible to list all the people that one way or another contributed to my intellectual journey. Let me mention Roberta Albertotanza, Gary Allen, Leonard Barkan, Warren Belasco, Herman Bennett, Charlotte Biltekoff, Janet Chrzan, Carole Counihan, Dexter Davis, Netta Davis, Jonathan Deutsch, Lisa Heldke, Alice Julier, Ed Korry, Regina Kunzel, Alison Leitch, Carolyn Lesjak, Laura Lindenfeld Sher, Patrick McGovern, Kathrin Merkle, Jennifer Morgan, Robert O'Hara, Christopher Pavsek, Khary Polk, Krishnendu Ray, Matthew Trachman, and Amy Trubek. For the many wonderful individuals that have somehow escaped being mentioned, blame my mind, not my heart.

Last but not least, thanks to my editors, Wendi Schnaufer at Greenwood and series editor Ken Albala. Without your help and guidance, I might never have managed to publish a book in English.

Introduction

Even before the Mediterranean diet became famous, Italian food had already become quite popular in the United States and throughout the world. Generations of Italian immigrants maintained their customs even when, as happened in the United States in the first half of the twentieth century, their diet was considered poor, incomplete, and lacking in proteins. It was not unusual for well-meaning social workers to visit Italian immigrants and try to convince them that eating all those vegetables was not good for them. With time, food like pasta and pizza acquired the status of staples, and dishes such as sauce with meatballs or chicken *parmigiana* became pillars of an Italian-American culinary canon that survived unchallenged for decades. Today, many Americans, especially in urban environments, are exposed to different kinds of Italian cuisine. Sophisticated restaurant goers can now make subtle distinctions between Neapolitan and Roman-style pizzas, name several types of *prosciutto*, and discuss the pros and cons of traditional balsamic vinegar on ice cream. In the 1980s the so-called northern cuisine challenged the monopoly of Italian-American style, showing that there was more to Italian food than garlic and heavy tomato sauces. Then came the fad that saw Tuscan traditions move into the limelight, and now virtually every Italian region is represented on the restaurant scene of the United States. Meanwhile, traditional Italian fare is increasingly appreciated for its benefits in maintaining a healthy diet.

Food is one of the main reasons why many Americans travel to Italy. Yet, the fascination with Italian cuisine is not all about health or taste.

There is much more to it. Italian food is perceived and represented in the media as one aspect of a lifestyle: People are more relaxed; families are still important; communities are close-knit; and everybody takes his or her time to eat, drink, and share with friends. These representations are often based on romanticized ideas about Italy and the daily lives of Italians, who are supposedly stress-free, good-natured, and incredibly welcoming to strangers. Reality, of course, is more complex. Virtually all of the Americans that have spent any significant amount of time in Italy, while still raving about its inhabitants, its food, and its inevitable charm, would be able to point out the madness of so-called Italian red tape, the chaos of traffic congestion in big cities, and the glitches in transportation and in the mail system. Even if Italy is now one of the most industrialized countries in the world, it still maintains its seductiveness. The press and the books about Italian food seem often unable to keep it real.

There is no room in this idealized Italy for growing racism and intolerance toward new immigrants, for the *Mafia,* for corrupted governments, or for media tycoons that miraculously become prime ministers even with several pending trials against them.

Innate qualities are often attributed to Italians, blessed with genes that favor pleasant attitudes toward life. Italians are likely to be represented as happy-go-lucky people who are virtually impossible to understand, but who are to be envied for their innocent, though slightly uncivilized, way of life.

It is evident that this interest and these perceptions are not so much about Italians, as they are about Americans and what they more or less consciously feel they lack as a social body. These preconceptions express the longing for a sense of community, the connection with long-lasting traditions, a more intimate relationship with nature, and the absence of the fear of impending social upheavals. Somehow, magically, food embodies all of these qualities and makes them available for ingestion and incorporation, not only as a substance, but also as modality of consumption.

For their part, Italians deeply enjoy this new gaze on their country. After decades of poverty and disorder, here they are, the new arbiters of elegance and style, the people who start new fashions in clothes, cars, and furniture, whose food is envied and coveted all around the world. Not bad, as a morale booster. Furthermore, the growing interest in Italian food entails numerous economic benefits.

The goal of this book, as part of the Greenwood Food Culture around the World series, is to offer a wider, at times critical, perspective about Italy and the relation of Italians to food. When teaching Italian and foreign students about Italian culinary traditions and history, it is quite easy to realize that they nurture numerous preconceptions, usually well-meaning ones, about the subject. Italian society is not rural any longer, but it is not fully modern and industrialized either, despite what most Italians might think. It is a good position to be in, allowing Italians to enjoy the best of two worlds. Unfortunately, many Italians and foreigners alike are not aware of these subtle (and often not so subtle) changes, preferring to stick to the stereotypes. At a time when food is socially acknowledged as a fundamental part of Italian culture and identity, when the interest for disappearing culinary traditions and rare specialties is expanding, as are the economic interests involved, it is important to have a balanced approach to these matters.

Timeline

12th century B.C.E.	The Italic people in Italy: introduction of rudimentary agriculture techniques.
11th century B.C.E.	The Etruscans in Tuscany: probable arrival of olive trees and vines in Tuscany.
8th century B.C.E.	Foundation of Phoenician bases in Sardinia and Sicily, which become part of the food-and-product trade routes connecting the shores of the Mediterranean.
770 B.C.E.	Foundation of Pitecusa, the first Greek colony in Italy, and the arrival of olive trees and vines in southern Italy.
753 B.C.E.	Traditional date of the foundation of Rome.
ca. 575 B.C.E.	Etruscan domination over Rome, which adopts culinary customs from its dominating neighbors.
5th century B.C.E.	Celts infiltrate northern Italy: introduction of salt-based meat-curing techniques and greater appreciation for pork.
ca. 470 B.C.E.	Independence of Rome from the Etruscans, and foundation of the Republic.
241 B.C.E.	Rome defeats Carthage and occupies Sicily, which becomes a prime source of food for Roman society.
237 B.C.E.	Rome expands its power to Sardinia, reinforcing its role in the Mediterranean and exposing itself to new influences, including culinary ones.

210 B.C.E.	Rome imposes the cultivation of wheat in Sicily.
202 B.C.E.	Rome defeats Carthage again and expands its influence to Spain and northern Africa.
188 B.C.E.	Rome extends its power to Asia Minor (present-day Turkey) and begins to absorb the lavish and refined culinary customs of the East.
186 B.C.E.	For the first time, in the war against the Eastern king Antiochus, the Roman armies employ specialized personnel for the kitchen.
180 B.C.E.	Law limits the number of guests that can be invited for dinner.
171 B.C.E.	Foundation of the guild of bakers, formed by freed slaves.
129 B.C.E.	Rome forbids populations beyond the Alps from planting olive trees and vines, trying to limit the cultivation of cash crops to Italy.
37 B.C.E.	Varro begins his masterwork *De re rustica* about Roman agriculture.
30 B.C.E.	Rome conquers Egypt, which becomes the new major source of wheat.
14 C.E.	Death of Augustus, the first Roman Emperor.
48	Apostle Peter, in Rome, decides that Christians are not obliged to follow Jewish dietary laws, including Kashrut. Paul introduces Greek culture into Christianity.
129	Supposed date of birth of Galen, whose work defined dietary customs for centuries.
ca. 200	The Egyptian Athenaeus writes *Deipnosophistae*, describing the Greek and Roman culinary customs.
212	All the free men in the Empire acquire the title of Roman citizen.
260	The first German tribes settle in the Roman territory between the Danube and the Rhein, absorbing many customs from the sedentary populations, including food habits of Mediterranean origin.
313	Emperor Constantine imposes Christianity as the official religion of the Roman Empire.

395	The Roman Empire is divided between Rome and Constantinople.
476	The Goths, a Germanic tribe, depose the last Roman emperor.
552	Byzantine emperor Justinian conquers Italy, reinvigorating traditional agricultural products that had almost disappeared under Germanic influence.
603	Longobards, a Germanic tribe, occupy northern and central Italy: In these territories the Roman culinary legacy is almost eradicated, with the exceptions of monasteries. The Byzantines are left with most of southern Italy, where Mediterranean customs survive.
902	Muslims conquer Sicily, introducing products and culinary techniques from the Middle East and North Africa.
1095	First Crusade: The Western nobles come into direct contact with the Muslim civilization, including its culinary arts and table manners.
ca. 1101	Medical school of Salerno produces the first European dietary book.
1183	German Emperor Frederick I bestows political autonomy to the *comuni* of northern Italy in exchange for formal submission. There is a rebirth of the currency-based market economy, with a consequent diversification of diets.
1204	Fourth Crusade: Constantinople sacked on behalf of the Venetians, who take control of the trade of spices with the East and Asia.
1220	Frederick II, Norman king of southern Italy, is also crowned emperor. Palermo becomes a center for cultural exchange between East and West, including culinary customs.
1256	Mongols conquer Baghdad. Stability in Asia increases commerce in spice and other products.
1347	Black Plague rages for three years, drastically reducing Europe's population.
1453	Turks conquer Constantinople. Commerce with the East becomes extremely difficult, stimulating explorations to find new trade routes.

1457	Publication of the culinary works supposedly written by the Roman Apicius.
ca. 1464	Master Martino writes book on the art of cooking.
1470	Bartolomeo Sacchi, known as Platina, publishes *De Honesta Voluptate et Valetudine*.
1492	Spanish monarchy conquers the Muslim Kingdom of Granada. Explorer Christopher Columbus lands in the Caribbean, starting the Columbian Exchange, which transforms the European diet in a few decades.
1549	Cristoforo Messisbugo publishes *Banquets, Course Composition and General Preparation*.
1570	Bartolomeo Scappi publishes his monumental *The Works* about cuisine in papal Rome.
1571	Venice, Spain, and the papal troops defeat the Turks. Coffee is introduced to Venice.
ca. 1606	Chocolate becomes popular in Italy.
ca. 1629	Economic recession hits Europe. Plague strikes northern Italy.
1672	Sicilian Francesco Procopio moves to France. He will found the first coffeehouse in Paris.
1760	Austria introduces modernizing reforms in Lombardy: agricultural development follows.
1766	Publication of *The Piedmont Cook Perfected in Paris*.
1815	After Napoleon, the Congress of Vienna reestablishes the status quo in Europe.
1860	Expedition of 1,000 men led by Giuseppe Garibaldi topples the Bourbon Dynasty and delivers southern Italy to the Savoy king Vittorio Emanuele II, who becomes king of Italy. Northern soldiers are exposed to southern dishes such as pasta with tomato sauce.
1870	Italy becomes a unified kingdom under the Savoia. Culinary traditions from different parts of the area travel with soldiers and internal migrations.
1891	Pellegrino Artusi publishes *Science in the Kitchen and the Art of Good Eating*.

1915	Italy enters World War I against Austria and Germany. Victuals granted to soldiers, such as coffee, dried pasta, and cheese, become everyday necessities for the whole population.
1917	Olindo Guerrini publishes *The Art of Using Leftovers*.
1922	Benito Mussolini and the Fascist Party seize the government.
1926	National Agency for the Scientific Organization of Work is founded.
1936	Mussolini proclaims economic self-sufficiency in Italy.
1940	Italy enters World War II on the side of Germany: a time of scarcity and the black market.
1943	King of Italy imprisons Mussolini and signs a truce with the Allies. The Germans occupy Italy.
1945	U.S. troops land in southern Italy. Together with local resistance groups, they defeat the Germans and Fascists.
1946	With a referendum, Italy becomes a republic, marking the beginning of the reconstruction, followed by an economic boom.
1963	Introduction of regulations establishing Controlled Denomination of Origin for wines.
1992	European Union establishes Protected Designation of Origin and Protected Geographical Indication.
2003	European Union admits new products to be registered as Protected Designation of Origin. Parma is chosen as the seat for the European Food Security Authority.
2004	The first four-year university program in gastronomy starts in Pollenzo (Piedmont), organized by Slow Food.

1

Historical Overview

Italian food traditions are becoming more and more popular with the American public. The general perception is shifting from a predominance of Italian-American classics to a more in-depth knowledge of regional and local cuisines. Starting in the 1980s, many restaurants chose to launch what was to become known as northern cuisine, a label that does not make much sense, especially in Italy where each town is extremely, even belligerently, proud of its own dishes. This attitude is called *campanilismo*, from the word *campanile*, or "bell tower": It points to the passion for whatever falls within the shadow of the local church bell tower. The reference to a supposedly homogeneous northern cuisine had the clear goal of differentiating these restaurants from the usual Italian-American fare, considered by most people as typical of southern Italy. More recently, many chefs have started introducing regional cuisines that reflect local distinctions, allowing Americans to get acquainted with new and unusual dishes. The freshness and authenticity of ingredients are now heavily emphasized, and many products are imported from Italy on an almost daily basis. These developments in the representation of Italian cuisine, boosted by magazines and other media, have spread bucolic fantasies about Italy, its connection with local roots, the abundance of its food bounty, and the endless pleasures and convivial warmth awaiting any visitor who might happen to wander into any God-forsaken village. Reality is quite different. Furthermore, these idealized images are historically inaccurate. Until the 1960s, when industrialization grew, many Italians left Italy, where rural populations often lived in harsh conditions, obliged to sell the best of their agricultural and herding output or give it to the landowners as a form of rent. With the exception of the vast plains along the river Po, most of the Italian territory is hills and mountains. This geographical configuration makes agriculture hard and energy consuming. Historically, Italy was far from being a land of plenty, even if in urban environments excellent and sophisticated food had always been available, with the exception of times of famine and war.

How did this happen? What are the historical reasons behind these phenomena?

THE ORIGINS

Despite its rich and long-lasting culinary traditions, the territory that today is called Italy made a late appearance in food history. It is likely that the original population had adopted a hunting and gathering lifestyle. The technology and the seeds necessary for a sedentary life moved from East to West, slowly conquering new territories to agriculture. The populations in western Europe were relatively slow in absorbing the new domesticated plants and animals that had become common in the Near East and that were making the Egyptian and Sumerian civilizations thrive: primitive forms of wheat, called *emmer* and *einkorn*; cereals such as barley and rye; pulses like chickpeas, lentils, and peas; and livestock, such as sheep, goats, cows, and chickens. Once the local populations shifted to agriculture and herding, they started domesticating local wild herbs until they developed new crops like poppy seeds and oats, probably between 6000 and 3500 B.C.E.

We have little knowledge of what Italy was like until the twelfth century B.C.E., when it was inhabited by a wave of migratory peoples collectively known under the name of Indo-Europeans, some of which had already invaded Greece and Turkey, destroying the Mycenaean culture that had been flourishing in that area. They penetrated Italy from the north, probably displacing the previous inhabitants. They spoke a group of similar languages and shared a common culture, mostly based on herding and a limited agriculture. These populations were organized in tribes sparsely settled in the peninsula, such as the Samnites, the Umbrians, and the Picens. They were to be known with the general name of *Italici* in Latin or *Italioi* in Greek, a name that might derive from the word *italòs*, or "young calf," an expression the Etruscans probably adopted to deride their less cultured neighbors. These Italic peoples were divided between those who lived in small towns and those who inhabited the countryside, basing their subsistence on a kind of traveling herding called *transhumance* or *transumanza,* a phenomenon that has almost disappeared now, but was still very visible until the 1970s. In winter, shepherds would lead their sheep and goats from the higher mountains in Abruzzo and Molise to lower altitudes in Puglia and then back when summer got warmer. This activity implied a political organization that was not based on territorial control, so that different tribes could go through alien land without provoking conflicts. The *transumanza* determined the importance of sheep and goat meat in the mountain peoples' diets, a habit that has lasted till today. In Abruzzo, in the villages on the Gran Sasso mountain, locals would add sheep meat to tomato sauce for pasta, or they would cut tiny pieces of castrated mutton and roast them on little wooden skewers called *arrosticini.*

ETRUSCANS AND PHOENICIANS

With time, new populations moved into Italy, forcing the Italics to the interior, toward the hills and mountains that did not allow for efficient agriculture. A peninsula located in the middle of the Mediterranean Sea, Italy was exposed to frequent migrations from central and northern Europe and from the sea. Between the eighth and the third centuries B.C.E., various cultures—including the Etruscans, the Phoenicians, the Greeks, and the Celts—interacted with the Italics. Since the beginning, Italy was not a monolithic block, but a fragmented territory that gave birth to an original civilization. Maybe its identity lies precisely in its diverse origins, in the waves of different populations that inhabited it, and in the persistence of its local traditions.

The Etruscans probably arrived some time around the eleventh century B.C.E., on the shores of what is today called Tuscany. For many years archeologists could not interpret their language, written in a script derived from the Phoenician alphabet (the base for our modern alphabet). Despite many material traces of their presence (such as buildings and tombs), their origin stayed shrouded in mystery until recently, when linguists succeeded in deciphering many inscriptions and documents. They noticed many similarities to Lydian, an ancient Indo-European language that was spoken in an eastern area of present-day Turkey by a population that tried to settle on the coast of Egypt and then was pushed toward the coast of Italy. They would be the Tyrsenoi or Tyrrenoi mentioned in Greek texts, and they can further be identified with the Turuscia, one of the sea people that the Egyptian pharaoh Ramses III chased from his territory in the twelfth century B.C.E. Because of their origins, the Etruscans were highly susceptible to Eastern influences, and from the time Greece became the cultural center of the Mediterranean in the eighth century, the Etruscans absorbed many elements from it, transmitting them to the neighboring populations. Around the sixth century B.C.E., the Etruscans became a strong sea and land power: They controlled Italy from the Po River to Campania, including Rome. Etruscan society was structured around an aristocracy that controlled both the use of the land and the political life. The Etruscans never formed a unitary state; each city kept its independence within the frame of a loose federation. Their land was very productive for the standards of that time, especially compared to the low outputs of their Italic neighbors and Rome. It is quite likely they were the first in Italy to use crop rotation: One year they would plant a field with grains, the following year with pulses or grass for cattle. This technique implies that property was not communal, so every owner could plan his own production over a few years. Because of the richness of their territory, the Etruscans were considered decadent and excessive in their consumption habits. They had two full meals a day, while most of the other populations only had one; furthermore, as we can see in many frescoes and sculptures found in the tombs of the nobles, their women would take part in banquets and official meals, a habit that appeared to demonstrate their unrestrained behaviors. Unfortunately, as often happens, we have very scarce information about the life of the lower classes. Nevertheless, we have a pretty clear idea about what the Etruscans produced, consumed, and traded. The main staple was barley, and together with wheat, *farro*, and millet, barley provided most of the carbohydrates. Grains were usually ground into a rough flower that was used in gruels similar to grits, called *puls*, or made into dough shaped into flat breads and cooked on hot stones or in the oven. Cereals were added to pulses and vegetables, which also played a very important role in the everyday diet: Peas, chickpeas, lentils, and fava beans were consumed in great quantities, especially in soups. Meat was available, but not abundant, especially in non-festive meals and for the less affluent social strata. Pork and chicken would be the most common, since sheep and cows were more useful alive. The Etruscans also grew fruits such as hazelnuts, figs, olives, and grapes. They developed a famed production of olive oil and wine, although it is not clear whether they borrowed their techniques from the neighboring Greeks or if they knew these techniques at the time of their migration from Western Asia. At any rate, during the sixth century B.C.E., they started exporting their goods throughout the Mediterranean, creating a certain competition with the other two merchant populations whose ships where riding the sea, the Phoenicians and the Greeks.

The Phoenicians were seafarers and merchants. Starting from their native towns scattered along the coast of present-day Lebanon, they expanded their commercial network throughout the Mediterranean. They became famous for their glass, all kinds of luxury objects (jewels, vases, and such), and the famed purple fabrics, dyed with a substance extracted from a sort of conch. We do not have much information about the Phoenician diet, but it is likely they traded in many products from neighboring Mesopotamia and Egypt. Besides olive oil and wine, they probably exported figs, dates, almonds, pistachios, pomegranates, and persimmons to western Europe. Some of these fruit trees adapted to their new habitats and became quite common. A particular type of onion, the scallion, got its name precisely from the Phoenician town of Ascalon. The Phoenicians established trading bases all along the coasts of the Mediterranean and beyond the Gibraltar Straight, on the Atlantic coast of Spain. In the eighth century B.C.E., they also founded a few bases in Italy, like Sulci, Bithia, and Cagliari in Sardinia, and Mozia, Palermo, and Lilibeo in Sicily, from which they controlled much of the commerce with northern Africa and Spain. The most important of the Phoenician trade posts was Carthage, in present-day Tunisia, which became a colony and then an independent sea power that developed its own network of trade posts in Sardinia. Inevitably, this led to a clash with the other populations that were trading over the sea: the Etruscans and the Greek colonies in southern Italy.

GREEKS AND CELTS

Starting from the eighth century B.C.E., Greece developed an original civilization that would provide much of the foundation of Western culture as we know it. It never became an unified country, but each city kept its own political organization and social traditions, while recognizing a common cultural and religious background centered around cult places like the Delphi oracle or gatherings such as the Olympics. The cities, which were often at war with each other, were nonetheless able to team up in case of danger, as when the Persians tried to extend their influence over Greece. The Greeks were deeply aware of the cultural divide that differentiated them from the neighboring populations, for whom they invented a term that would enjoy great fortune, *barbaroi*, the barbarians. This feeling of superiority seeped through all aspects of everyday life, including food habits. Some products were identified as signs of civilization, such as wheat, olive oil, wine, all deriving from sedentary agriculture. On the other hand, milk and meat, and, above all, game, were synonymous with nomadic life and hence were frowned upon. Furthermore the barbarians were believed to eat together in the most uncouth ways, unable to enjoy social conviviality and prone to consume raw food. On the contrary, in Greece banquets played a very important role in reinforcing social connections between adult males, who would lie on their sides enjoying the various dishes and often close with a special ceremony called *symposion* (literally, "drinking together"). All these habits and beliefs were part of the cultural heritage Greeks brought to the new colonies they founded all over the western Mediterranean, including in southern Italy and eastern Sicily. Starting from the eighth century B.C.E., many cities saw their populations grow fast, causing problems of unrest among the younger generations that often were not able to make a living on the limited land available for agriculture. To solve this problem, the city leaders would send part of their youth to found a colony elsewhere, providing them with ships, food for the journey, and seeds to start agriculture wherever they decided to land. It seems the Delphi oracle played an important role in deciding where the ships would head to: The temple priests could use the abundant information they gathered from the numerous pilgrims visiting from all over the Mediterranean. The Greeks brought advanced techniques to grow olives, grapes, cabbage, and onions to southern Italy.[1] They also introduced their traditional alimentary principles—above all, the appreciation for wheat, olive oil, and wine. The new colonies would also maintain the motherland's political and social structure, acknowledging solid cultural ties with it. The first Greek colony in Italy was Pitecusa, founded in 770 B.C.E. on the island of Ischia, off the coast of Campania. Other important Greek outposts were Cuma, Taranto, Sibari, Crotone, Siracusa, Agrigento. Unfortunately, these cities also adopted the habit of going to war with each other to ensure control over the commercial sea traffic. They also got involved in long and bloody conflicts with neighboring sea powers such as the Etruscans and the Phoenicians. In these fights, they often employed the services of mercenary warriors from all over the known world.

Some of these came from across the Alps: They were Celts, who inhabited a territory spreading from modern-day Austria and southern Germany to eastern France. The mercenaries traveling to Italy probably transmitted news of the local riches to the tribes beyond the mountains, as a result, starting from the fifth century B.C.E., small groups of the northern population infiltrated the Po River plains. In the following decades, a great wave of Celtic immigrants settled in those areas, forcing themselves on the Etruscans and pushing them back into Tuscany. The Celts even launched a few attacks on central Italy, temporarily occupying the city of Rome in 386 but successively retreating to their strongholds beyond the Appennines. The Celts were organized in tribes ruled by an aristocracy of warriors, who gave great importance to courage and personal connections. They introduced in Italy many luxury objects imported from their northern brethren, such as swords and jewels. They also brought with them their advanced techniques for extracting salt from under the earth and using it to preserve food. Their salting abilities, together with their passion for swine, gave birth to one of the most famous culinary traditions in Italy: *prosciutto*. It is not by chance that today some of the best cured pork products are still produced in an area that had important Celtic settlements: Parma.

THE EXPANSION OF ROME

The cultural and ethnic plurality that had been the main feature of Italy between the eighth and the fourth centuries B.C.E. had to come to terms with the expansion of a new power: Rome. Started as a humble federation of villages dwelling on top of the hills around the river Tiber, Rome was under Etruscan influence for many years, as indicated by the presence of kings named Tarquinius—that is to say, from Tarquinia, one of the most powerful Etruscan strongholds. The Roman diet was quite similar to that of the neighboring Italic and Latin tribes. It consisted of cereals like barley and *farro*, often ground into the *puls* we have already mentioned or added to soups. The *puls* was so important that anything else would be defined as *pulmentarium*, or an accompaniment, a simple addition to the basic staple food. Grains were roasted for better storage or even chewed raw. Romans also ate pulses, wild herbs gathered in the fields, vegetables, and a small quantity of meat, which they obtained from courtyard fowls, pigs, and sheep, while cows, used mainly for agriculture, were sacrificed and consumed only on religious feasts or important celebrations such as weddings and births. Cheese and honey integrated this meager diet. In Roman households storable food, also known as *penus*—cured pork (probably borrowed from the northern populations), cheese, honey, and, starting in the fourth century, olives—was so important that it gave its name to the gods that protected the home, the *Penates*. These ancient beliefs were maintained even when a new fire goddess, Vesta, became popular, and other protective gods like Larii or the Genius (representing the father's generative power) acquired importance; the Penates still kept their place in the kitchen. In the first centuries, Romans ate a single main meal, *coena*, usually consumed at midday, consisting of *puls* with vegetables or pulses. As mentioned, meat was quite rare. In more affluent families, the *coena* would start with some appetizers, *gustatio* or *pro-mulsio*, such as eggs, mushrooms, oysters, and salads, often followed by wine mixed with honey. This drink, called *mulsum*, was considered a good way to cleanse the palate for the main dishes, usually meat and vegetables. The rich *coena* would end with desserts, called *secundae mensae*, such as figs, fruits, and nuts. Breakfast, or *ientaculum*, would consist of a flat bread with side dishes like cheese, dried fruits, eggs, or honey. Dinner, called *ves-perna*, was also very light, usually consumed before going to bed. With time, the Romans started adopting food and uses from neighboring peoples: wine (always diluted with water) and olives came from the Greeks; meat-curing methods came from the Celts; and the habit of eating while reclining on one's side came from the Etruscans, who had themselves absorbed it from the Greeks.[2]

During the third century B.C.E., Rome extended its political hold over all of Italy, starting from the south and expanding to the Etruscan territories. They defeated the Celts, who had settled in the northern part of the peninsula. Although all of these territories became part of the same political system, they often maintained their own languages, cultures, and social structures. We can reasonably suppose the subjugated peoples somehow guarded their food traditions, thus explaining the resurgence of local differences when the empire crumbled in the fifth century C.E. The relations between the Romans and their subjects were not easy, especially because the conquered peoples had to pay taxes and provide soldiers for Rome's wars without getting any political representation in exchange. They were deprived of their land, which became public property and was redistributed to Roman citizens, especially the richer ones, who began creating *latifundia*, very extended agricultural properties. Furthermore, new Roman cities were founded in the midst of the conquered territories. These cities were called *colonia* (plural, *coloniae*), from which the English word *colony* is derived. Integration would not be unproblematic.

The rapid expansion in Italy inevitably led Rome to clash with Carthage, the other power that had extended its control over the sea routes in the western Mediterranean, and fighting against the Greeks from Sicily. Originally a Phoenician outpost, Carthage quickly became independent from its founding city, Thyre, occupying most of northern

Africa and establishing several colonies in Spain. Rome waged war against Carthage several times: During a first round of war, Rome occupied Sicily, then Sardinia, and then Corse. To fight against Carthage, Rome built its first fleet. The war was fierce and long. The Carthaginian king Hannibal invaded Italy in 218 B.C.E., crossing the Alps with African elephants and provoking a widespread rebellion among the Italic population that had been submitted to Rome. Rome eventually succeeded in defeating him and then destroyed Carthage and its sea empire.

From its enemy, Rome learned many farming and herding methods of African and Asian origin. All 28 books composing the *Agriculture* by the Carthaginian author Mago were translated into Latin, and the impact of his theories was so long-lasting that such famous writers as Cato and Varro quoted them in their own works. The new conquests made wheat, produced in large quantities in Sicily and northern Africa, more available. Bread became a very important item, assuming a central role in the cultural identity of the Romans, who were increasingly susceptible to the influences of the Hellenistic Greek kingdoms born from the fall of Alexander the Great's empire. Rome found itself more tightly integrated in the Mediterranean, creating commercial outposts on its eastern shores and establishing a monetary system based on the denarius, the Roman currency that became a very efficient trading instrument. In less than two centuries, Rome conquered Spain, Greece, the Middle East, France, and Egypt. The Romans came to call the Mediterranean *mare nostrum*, our sea. An uninterrupted flood of goods and money from the new provinces increased the standard of living in Italy, where the process of integration of the Italic populations into the Roman state grew stronger. The increase of international trade stimulated the development of speculative agriculture in many *latifundia*, aimed at producing commercial crops like olives (Puglia and Basilicata), grapes (Lazio, Campania, and Tuscany) and wheat (Sicily and Sardinia). New products penetrated the Roman market: cherries, quinces, peaches, and apricots and fowls like guinea hens and peacocks. Spices started to flow from the East, creating a connection with kingdoms as far as China.

In the vast and ever-expanding properties belonging to the rich Romans, slaves were the real forces behind all productive activities. Their number increased with each conquest, because many enemies were enslaved when defeated. While some worked in the mansions as cooks or maids, most of them lived near the fields, while their masters lived in elegant and often luxurious villas that were meant to display the conspicuous affluence and power of the owners. The new economy provoked a deep crisis in the traditional rural social structures. Small farmers often could not keep up with the commercial crops grown in the *latifundia:* Many of them sold their properties and became laborers or emigrated to the provinces to start a new life.

Despite the growing wealth, until the spread of Christianity the ideology that underpinned food habits remained largely the same. Romans classified their products as *fruges,* the output of agriculture, and *pecudes,* the cattle that grazed on wild land and the game provided by hunters. Although the *fruges,* considered the symbol of civilization, were held in higher esteem, the *pecudes* were absolutely necessary as victims for sacrificial ceremonies and banquets, which were paramount to the well-being of social life and to the relationship with the gods. At any rate, only domestic animals tended by men, especially cows but never game or fish, could be used for sacrifices, and they were butchered in a special market called *forum boarium.* Other markets were the *forum piscarium,* which specialized in fish, and the *forum olitorium,* where vegetables were sold. Although food consumption was increasing, frugality was still considered a virtue, but generosity toward guests was highly appreciated. Moral or political corruption was often depicted in terms of gluttony and alimentary decadence. Nonetheless, there was a clear contradiction between admiration for frugality and widespread behaviors that boosted food consumption. To slow this trend, in the second century sumptuary laws were introduced that were aimed at curbing excesses. In 180 B.C.E. a law was passed that limited the number of guests one could invite for dinner, followed by several laws that restricted spending on occasions such as weddings and festivals. In 78 B.C.E. the consumption of exotic animals from the new eastern provinces was drastically limited.

THE EMPIRE IN THE MEDITERRANEAN

During imperial times, the midday meal changed its name and content. Lunch, now called *prandium,* became lighter, consisting of bread, cheese, and cold cuts left over from dinner. The main meal, or *coena,* moved to the evening, still maintaining its tripartite structure: appetizers, main dishes, and desserts. High-class families had their meals in a dining room called *triclinium,* named for the bed in which they reclined. In older times the Romans often dined in an open space close to the kitchens, called an *atrium,* from the word *atrum* indicating the black of soot. Later these spaces were closed and often placed on the second floor. Banquets became social occasions with numerous meat dishes, considered the symbol of abundance and power of the host. One of the best records of these feasts is Petronius's *Satyricon*, which describes in detail some outrageous parties and the dishes served. We can gather information about the food consumed by the upper classes from the collection of recipes known as *De re coquinaria*, attributed to Marcus Gavius Apicius, who lived under the emperor Trajan (first century C.E.), but probably compiled between the second and fourth century. Fish became fashionable, and in many villas landowners built huge artificial ponds so their fish was always fresh. The ones in the outskirts of Naples were particularly famous, especially for their oysters.

Supper remained a light meal for the lower classes, still consisting mainly of *puls* and vegetables. Bread become more common, especially because, under the emperor Augustus, a special office, the *annona*, had been founded to ensure stable grain prices, even if the best white flour, called *siligo*, was meant for the exclusive consumption of the rich. Under certain circumstances, the *annona* would distribute grain for free, especially in Rome and other large cities, to avoid social unrest. As a matter of fact, the living conditions of the urban poor were often hard: They lived crammed in huge buildings called *insulae*, usually without kitchens for fear of fires. The poor often ate out in taverns called *tabernae* or in shops that sold cooked meals such as warm sausages, cheese, bread, wine, and nuts. *Tabernae* were extremely common: More than 200 *tabernae* were found in the ruins of Pompeii alone. Often they were places for gambling and prostitution, as the painted advertising on the outside clearly stated. At any rate, it was fairly common for wealthier citizens to have a light lunch on the street: Covered stalls called *lixae* sold drinks, sausages, and sweets. Anyone who could afford it would have slaves following them with a meal prepared in the kitchens of one's palace.

The imperial system worked very well until the end of the second century C.E., a long period of time when the Roman emperors ruled over a multiethnic world that, despite the apparent wealth, had many weak elements in it. The slave system that allowed the exploitation of the vast farms belonging to rich families remained the main economic structure. Commerce never attained the same importance as agriculture. Even rich merchants tended to invest their profits in land acquisitions. Most state tax income was supposed to derive from the vast *latifundia* properties, but the owners had often very close connections to the local and central government and enjoyed massive exemptions. The Empire was founded on slavery and conquest. When the military stopped providing war booties, the state found itself in a financial quagmire and had to increase taxation.

Inflation skyrocketed, and commerce almost disappeared altogether. As a result, rich landowners abandoned the cities and took refuge in their country dwellings. Each large farm became virtually independent and self-sufficient. Furthermore, the use of slaves did not stimulate technological progress and efficiency, because they constituted a very convenient source of cheap labor. The old aristocracy gave way to a new class connected to the military, often of humble origins, that had a scarce sense of the state. The internal crisis allowed the neighboring populations, especially the Germans beyond the northern borders, to occupy Roman territories. They were often acknowledged as federate peoples, or *foederati,* and entrusted the defense of the frontier. Permanent armies were gathered to defend the Empire, resulting in greater power for the generals, who started fighting among themselves. Heavy taxes had to be levied to pay the soldiers, who otherwise would drain resources directly from the territories under their control when they did not get their salary on time (*salary* is a word that derives from the Latin word *sal,* salt, that constituted an important part of the military pay). Long wars and epidemics ravaged the whole empire, causing frequent famines, while new waves of Germans continued to pour over the borders. Agriculture became increasingly less productive, and population decreased both in the countryside and in the cities. Urban culture decayed, causing a deep crisis in monetary exchanges and a return to an economy often based on barter.

In 395 C.E. the emperor Theodosius divided his empire between his two sons: the eastern part, with Constantinople (present-day Istanbul) as its capital, would enjoy a much-longer life, developing a culture derived from the Greek heritage of the city. The western part became increasingly weak. Eventually, in 476, Odoacer, king of a German tribe call the Goths, deposed Romulus Augustus, the last Roman emperor.

THE GERMAN MIGRATIONS: BYZANTINES, LONGOBARDS, AND FRANKS

Germans found themselves at the margin of the Roman culture, both attracted to its refinement and proud of their own traditions. They often used the Roman administrative structures, but at the same time they maintained tribal traditions, based on the personal loyalty between the king and his closest followers. *Latifundia,* virtually independent from the central powers, were still the most important economic structures: Roman landowners often accepted the presence of German soldiers as a form of protection, while German nobles often started their own *latifundia* and were increasingly assimilated with their Roman peers. Peasants, both Roman and German, were still heavily exploited. They were referred to as *servus terrae*, servants of the land, and they were inherited and exchanged with the plots they worked on.

The lack of a central authority and the crisis of commerce and long-distance exchanges stimulated the resurgence of local cultures, which in Imperial times had been crushed and forced to adopt Roman ideology.

The Germanic populations that settled in the countryside introduced seminomadic herding habits together with a subsistence agriculture, mainly cereals like rye and barley. Barley was also used to make beer, still produced without hops. This fermented drink, considered a barbaric abomination, was loathed by the Roman population, who continued to appreciate wine, even when it had become less and less available. Traditional foods like pulses, olive oil, and orchard vegetables were partly substituted with products prevalent in Germanic traditions, such as butter, lard, game, and wild berries. Bread was made with cereals like millet, *farro*, and rye, which were easier to grow than wheat. All of these elements were already present in Imperial times but were ideologically excluded from the wine-oil-bread triad that embodied the Roman conception of agriculture, geared toward urban consumption and fundamentally alien to the inhabitants of woods and remote villages. In times of scarcity, Roman and Germanic peasants all had to learn how to employ diverse resources, resorting to both agriculture and gathering activities, and exploiting *ager* (cultivated land) and *saltus* (wild territories). Meat became the symbol of power: It was considered necessary to acquire physical strength and fighting stamina. Warriors were supposed to eat meat abundantly in order to affirm their prowess. Only monasteries maintained their allegiance to the Roman alimentary traditions and to the preeminence given to the bread-oil-wine triad, which had become crucial also for Christianity: Wine and bread were used in Holy Communion, while oil was employed as a symbol of strength and endurance in many sacraments.

The German tribes that had swept away the western part of the Roman Empire never reached the eastern part, the Byzantine Empire. For centuries, its capital city, Constantinople, was to remain the richest and most advanced heir of Roman and Greek culture. In the first half of the sixth century C.E., after a 20-year-long war against the German Goths, the emperor Justinian conquered part of Italy. The new territories were called Romania, a word from which the modern region Romagna derives its name. Only a few decades later, though, the Longobards, a Germanic tribe that had never been exposed to Roman culture, invaded Italy. The only areas left to the Byzantines were Sicily, Sardinia, Puglia, Calabria, the Esarcate

(Ravenna and neighboring territory), and the Pentapolis (the word means "five cities," located on the eastern coast). For almost two centuries Italy was divided between the Byzantines and the Longobards, which took to the extreme the contrast between the Roman-Greek and the Germanic cultures. In the Greek-controlled areas traditional production structures such as *latifundia* were reestablished. Cultures such as grapevines and olive trees were partially reintroduced, together with skilled peasants that could teach the basic agricultural technologies to the locals. At the same time, at least when they first arrived, the Longobards tried to destroy all vestiges of Roman heritage: the remnants of the administrative and judicial structures, *latifundia*, and monasteries. Locals were not considered citizens, and they were prohibited from carrying weapons. The Longobards founded new small villages, called *farae*, to distinguish themselves from the rest of the peasant population, which was heavily exploited. Under their rule, agricultural output dropped to an all-time low, while hunting and gathering ensured the survival of the local farmers.

In 751 C.E. the Longobards conquered the Byzantine territories of the Esarcate and the Pentapolis. The Pope, who had already chosen Rome as his seat, called the Franks, another Germanic tribe which had settled in present-day France and converted to Christianity. The Franks invaded northern Italy and conquered most of the Longobard possessions, bestowing the Esarcate and the Pentapolis on the Pope, giving him the basis for the future State of the Church. In return, in 800 C.E. the Pope crowned the Frank king, Charles the Great, as emperor of the Holy Roman Empire, acknowledging him as the heir of Rome and at the same time the defender of Christianity. Only a few territories were left to the Longobards in the interior of southern Italy. The Byzantines retained their control over Puglia, Calabria, Sicily, and Sardinia, where the *latifundia* continued to be the most common economic structure. Local landlords were often closely connected to the representatives from Constantinople, who often levied heavy taxes that weighed mainly on the peasants.

FEUDALISM

The Franks introduced feudalism, a new social, political, and economical system that was based on their tribal traditions but also influenced by the legal habits inherited from Rome. The emperor assigned the management of his territories to his closest followers, called *comites* (from which the English word *count* is derived), who had both civil and military functions. The border areas, called *marcae*, were entrusted to marquises, who were usually military generals. Personally tied to the emperor by tribal bonds of allegiance, counts and marquises could exploit the lands to which they were personally entitled. On the other hand, they were required to send a part of the income from their territories to the emperor. They were also expected to serve their lord in war and to defend him in case of danger. On the other hand, the emperor often sent members of his court to peripheral areas in order to control the local powers. These functionaries were known as *missi dominici*, which means "sent by the master." This political system was integrated with the remnants of the previous *latifundia* economical and social structures, from then on known as *manors*. The landowner exploited the land around his dwelling, the *pars dominica* or demesne, which often included the oil press, the wheat mill, the tannery, the bread oven, the wine vats, and the cellars. Many artisans lived in quarters located close to the residence of the lord, providing him with their services. The rest of his land, the *masi* or *pars massaricia*, was toiled by peasants who were obliged to give part of their produce and free labor to the landowners. They were often considered almost like slaves: They were neither free to leave the land they worked on, nor to change jobs. All the meager surplus output produced by peasants was used by their lord for war or his own personal consumption. Because of the lack of stored food due to the low agricultural productivity, the slightest change in weather or any turmoil would cause heavy famines. Hunger became a common phenomenon, playing an important role in art, religion, legends, and literature.

Almost no resources were available for investment or commerce. Long-distance exchange virtually disappeared, being limited to luxury items like jewelry or spices for the most affluent strata of society. Merchants were considered sinners and profiteers because of their connection to money, increasingly rare in an economy that had almost totally regressed to barter. Society also despised other jobs connected to commerce, to entertainment (tavern owners, actors, prostitutes), to magic arts, and to blood (butchers, surgeons, barbers) and impurity (tanners, cooks).

Despite all of these difficulties, starting from the eighth century the Italian population started to show a certain increase, probably boosted by the availability of abandoned lands that were not submitted to any landowners and that peasants could cultivate to supplement their diet. Yet it is necessary to make a clear distinction between the foods consumed by the rich, the nobles, and the warriors, and the peasants. In this period both diet and table behaviors became a complex code that expressed class and cultural distinctions. For the nobles, who were mostly of Germanic descent, hunting had an almost ritual value, emphasizing courage and ability. In feudal courts, game and meat were usually roasted or grilled and constituted the main elements—if not materially, ideologically—of the nobles' diet.[3]

Feudal lords gave great importance to social gatherings around abundant meals as instruments to reinforce solidarity and class identity: Banquets and feasts were often organized on the occasions of succession ceremonies, weddings, and victory celebrations. During these gatherings, guests would consume huge amounts of alcoholic beverages, provoking the churchmen's criticism and the peasants' envy. In Italy, wine regained preeminence over beer and cider after a few centuries when the Germanic populations had somehow imposed their traditional drinks. Wine, often very strong and not very well made, was usually drunk mixed with water to soften its taste. At the same time, wine made water safer, disinfecting it from many bacteria.

Nevertheless, banquets were not frequent. The nobles' ordinary food was not much different from that of their humbler counterparts. Peasants based their diets on cereals, pulses, and vegetables grown in small orchards that were not submitted to taxation. Cabbage, beets, carrots, fennels, leeks, and onions were often used in soups that would cook all day on pots hanging in the hearth, to which they would also add pieces of dried or salted meat. Fresh cuts were considered a luxury. Cured pork had become popular. From the available iconography it appears that pigs were smaller and hairier than today's, probably more closely connected to wild boars. Beef was rare, because oxen were employed to pull ploughs in the fields, and cows were milked to produce cheese, which was a very important source of protein.

In monasteries, meat consumption was extremely limited for religious reasons: Many days on the liturgical calendar were consecrated to fasting, or at least to abstinence. Nevertheless, in many monastic communities a very refined cuisine developed, based on fish and eggs, while monks largely used wheat bread, just as the nobles did. Peasants, on the other hand, kept on making bread with other cereals such as rye or barley, especially in the northern part of the peninsula. In the south, and in certain areas such as Florence and Siena, wheat was still widely used.

The feudal system was the main political, social, and economic structure in northern and central Italy until the eleventh century C.E. While in southern Italy the Byzantine empire struggled to maintain control over its provinces, the Frank imperial territories south of the Alps became independent from Germany and France: It is the beginning of local states that would in time become nations in the modern sense of the term. Also the State of the Church was trying to affirm its autonomy from the imperial authority, provoking a political tension that would last for centuries.

THE MUSLIM AND THE NORMAN EXPANSION

During the ninth century C.E., a new phenomenon altered the political situation in the Mediterranean: the Islamic expansion. After the death of the Prophet Muhammad in 632, the Muslims conquered large territories with amazing speed. In a few years, northern Africa, large parts of the Byzantine Empire, and central Asia fell under their control. In the Mediterranean they occupied Corse, Sardinia, and the island of Pantelleria. The Franks stopped their expansion in northern Spain at Poitiers in 732, and 20 years later the Chinese did the same at the Talas River in central Asia. In 827 the Islamic state based in present-day Tunisia attacked Sicily and other Mediterranean towns. In 846 they raided Rome, then Puglia, and even southern France. In 902 they completed the occupation of Sicily, conquering the city of Taormina on the eastern coast of the island.

The Muslim governors lightened the burden of the heavy taxation imposed on the peasants by the Byzantines, while distributing vast *latifundia* to smaller landowners. Agricultural output was increased by the introduction of new techniques and crops. Some of these, such as cotton or sugarcane, would disappear shortly after the Muslims left the island, while others were integrated into the local diet: eggplant, spinach, melons, apricots, rice, saffron, and, above all, citric fruits. Lemons, sour oranges (the sweet ones would be introduced later, in the sixteenth century), and limes—known as *lumie*—would become an important part of the Sicilian landscape. Many of these new crops expanded slowly into the rest of Italy, because they required advanced agricultural skills, they were not easily adaptable to the feudal production system, and they were often perceived as Muslim and hence to be avoided.

Sicily became part of an extremely lively commercial network that connected most of the known world. Spices became largely available, giving Sicilian cuisine its particular flavor. Christians and Jews were allowed to profess their own faith, and many kept their occupations as merchants and artisans.[4] Palermo became one of the most important cities in the West, a center for art, culture, philosophy...and cuisine. Numerous Islamic elements were absorbed, giving birth to a new culinary tradition. The presence of sugarcane allowed the production of candied fruits, marzipan, and sorbets. These were already popular in Middle Eastern courts, but in Sicily they reached unprecedented heights of taste and refinement. Dried nuts and fruits such as almonds, raisins, pistachios, and dates would also play an important role in the local pastry industry, together with techniques coming from the eastern section of the Muslim world. Sweet and sour dishes, creamy textures, pâtés and jellies, and the technique of frying meat in olive oil are still prevalent in Sicilian cuisine.

The Muslim culinary tradition survived in Sicily even when the island was conquered by the Normans at the beginning of the eleventh century. These descendants of Scandinavian warriors and seafarers had settled in northern France around the year 900, in the region that would be named Normandy after them. In 1066 they had occupied Britain by defeating the Anglo-Saxons at Hastings. During that time, some Norman families also settled in southern Italy as mercenaries, and they soon became the defenders of the Pope against Islam and the Byzantines. In 1091 Robert of Alteville expelled the Muslims from Sicily, while his son Ruggero extended his dominion to the whole of southern Italy. The Norman kings introduced a new, centralized political organization, employing Greek and Muslim functionaries. Unfortunately, many commercial crops such as sugarcane almost disappeared for lack of specialized labor, while others such as oranges, eggplants, or almonds became part of the local agricultural landscape. Only during the thirteenth century did Frederick, who was both king of Sicily and Holy Roman Emperor, try to revamp the cultivation of crops such as indigo and sugar. He hired specialized farmers from the Muslim countries and tried to employ the remnants of the local Muslim communities who had submitted politically. His attempt was doomed to failure.

THE URBAN LIFE: THE COMMUNES

The rest of Italy, still under the Holy Roman Empire, was engaged in an ongoing power struggle between the emperor and the Pope, who had become virtually independent. Political instability did not hinder the economic and demographic growth that, starting from the eleventh century, affected the whole of Europe. Peasants deforested, reclaimed, drained, and toiled large stretches of wilderness outside the customary control of local lords to increase the arable land necessary to feed the growing population. Many new plots were used to grow wheat, with a consequent increase in bread consumption. In the twelfth century, Sicilian nobles introduced in Italy the use of wheat to make dried pasta, a product they had probably absorbed from the Muslims. While making fresh pasta and boiling it was a custom going back to the Greeks (they called it *laganon*), dried pasta appears in Muslim texts for the first time around the tenth century, under the name of *ittrija*. Two centuries later, we find pasta manufacturers in Naples, and smaller ones in Genoa, Florence, and Puglia.

In the same period, metallurgy technologies improved, and iron became more and more common. Blacksmiths were able to forge new tools such as the heavy moldboard plow, which oxen were attached to by a front yoke that allowed them to work better. At the same time, productivity increased following the introduction of the three-field crop rotation system, which replaced the old method of a two-year rotation (cereals and fallowing). Now fields were successively planted with fall crops (wheat), spring crops (pulses, barley, rye), and fallowing plants. Better agricultural outputs boosted commerce, which in turn stimulated the rebirth of urban life, often developing around the market where local peasants were able to sell their surplus. With time, many landowners moved to the cities, attracting artisans and artists who were now able to sell their work. The expansion of demand in urban centers provided further stimulation for the whole economy, for agriculture, and, above all, for trade. Money was circulating again, and landowners were investing capital in commercial ventures managed by a new class of merchants, who would profit from the growing business. These activities led to the development of banking and credit instruments such as credit letters, which allowed merchants to move capitals from place to place.

In northern and central Italy, the growth of cities led to increasingly intense political friction with the emperors, who were not willing to grant financial autonomy and self-government to the new urban centers, called *comuni* (communes). The tension often exploded into wars that lasted well into the thirteenth century. In southern Italy, under the Norman rule, there was no space for any kind of autonomy. Coastal cities, such as Venice, Pisa, Genoa, or Amalfi, were able to gain independence based on their commercial power, constituting the trade link between Europe and the Islamic territories. The presence of a strong power in central Asia, the Mongol Empire, made traveling and commerce (spices and luxury items) with the Far East much easier. The tales of Marco Polo introduced Europe to the marvels of China.

The development of agriculture, trade, and craftsmanship changed alimentary habits all over Italy. The richer classes were able to afford frequent and more abundant banquets, while refinement and elegance acquired importance for landowners and lords. Guests would share, in pairs, a bowl, a goblet, and a trencher, usually a slice of bread or a piece of wood where solid food could be placed. A spoon would be available to get soup from the common bowl or food from the serving dishes. Guests would use their fingers to eat solid food, and they would clean them on the table-cloth. It was considered impolite to suck one's fingers clean, to put back the food taken from the serving dish, or to spit close to the table.

The old ideal of the Germanic gargantuan warrior who displayed his physical prowess with his enormous ingestion of food was outmoded. Diet was a sign of distinction, and table manners did not exclude luxury and ostentation. Dishes would incorporate expensive spices such as cinnamon, ginger, and pepper. During the Crusades (the expeditions that the Christian kingdoms led against the Muslims who had conquered the Holy Land and Jerusalem), the influx of Eastern products rekindled the interest for Eastern styles of cookery, even when the Islamic culture was despised: Saffron was used to give golden hues to food, while sugar—also considered a spice—was employed in decorations and to enrich many dishes.

On tables of the well-to-do, game was served side by side with poultry, pork, and mutton. Meat was often poached before roasting in the pan. Pork fat became the most common condiment, especially in southern and central Italy, while in the north butter was prevalent. Olive oil, often considered a luxury product and often culturally identified with the Islamic world, was produced mainly in southern Italy, under Norman rule, and in Tuscany. Vegetables and pulses were still considered too heavy for the delicate stomachs of the nobles.

Monasteries also increased in size and power, thanks to frequent donations from landlords. Labor was hired to work the fields, while monks would manage the production and often the commercialization of their crops. For many monasteries, the most important harvest was grapes. Vineyards became a common feature of both the urban and the rural landscape, planted also by lay landowners and rich farmers. Wine was likely to be found on all kinds of tables, assuming the role that it still maintains in the Italian diet. The monks' diets became more abundant and varied, similar to that of the nobles even if they still respected the fasting periods, and they consumed more vegetables and fruit than the upper classes.

In the burgeoning cities, new professions connected with food production and sale acquired more acceptance, and, in some cases, even prestige. Tavern keepers and butchers, who in the past had been almost considered sinners, were allowed to form their own guilds under strict control from the city authorities. Butchers, often located outside the city walls, left the less noble aspects connected with their activities to others, like tripe vendors and the so-called *lardaroli* or *salaroli* (lard and salami makers). Tavern keepers thrived on the intensification of trade, selling wine, bread, and cheese (and less often, cooked meals) to travelers. Other categories of food professionals that acquired a growing respect were flour millers, oven owners, and bread makers, who prepared breads and cakes with the flour provided by their clients and then had the goods baked. The bread makers from Piacenza, for instance, were so highly thought of that they financed one of the pillars of the local cathedral, and images of their activities are sculpted on its capital.

CRISIS AND RENAISSANCE

By the end of the thirteenth century, the economic and demographic expansion that had stimulated Europe for two centuries began to slow down. The climate became colder, with heavier rains and bitter freezing periods, causing frequent famines. The terrible epidemics of the Black Plague, which struck in 1347, caused thousands of deaths. Frequent wars and the transit of mercenary troops made the whole situation even worse. Many arable lands and even whole villages were abandoned, while the decrease in food production hit urban populations heavily. It became more and more difficult for landowners to find labor to work in the fields. Some of them started renting plots of land to farmers who owned cattle and tools, and sharecropping became common. The poorest peasants, nevertheless, were exploited even more cruelly. The consequence was a long series of riots and rebellions that worsened the state of uninterrupted belligerency, especially in southern Italy, where a French noble, Charles of Anjou, seized power after the end of the Norman dynasty, only to be ousted out of Sicily—but not from the rest of his kingdom—by the local nobles who chose a noble from the Hiberic peninsula, the king of Aragon, as their lord. In the south, French and Spanish nobles colluded with the local landowners, establishing a hard rule over the local farmers. Over the same period, in the central and northern part of the peninsula, the communes kept fighting to affirm their independence, while artisans tried to acquire greater decision-making powers in the management of city affairs. The peasants that lived in the territories surrounding the cities did not have any political rights and were heavily exploited, just as in the south. The general state of unrest led many communes to hire professional leaders, called *potestà*, who would manage the city and try to find a balance among the different factions. Even *potestàs* were soon not able to manage the continuous state of crisis, and several cities preferred to give up democracy and self-government, hoping to obtain political stability. Various forms of autocracy became common, such as *signorie* (when an individual seized power and the commune recognized his position) and *principati* (when the new lords were, at least in the beginning, representatives of higher powers, such as the emperor or the Pope). The new political developments made wars between different cities even more frequent, while foreign powers such as France and Spain were trying to establish their influence all over the peninsula. In this climate of ongoing instability, from the fifteenth century Italian culture underwent a deep transformation: Classic Roman and Greek arts, literature, and philosophy were rediscovered and became the basis for what would be known as Renaissance.

In this period, the upper classes' diet was quite similar all over Europe, with little regional variations. A certain differentiation was more evident in the peasant's eating patterns, which was more dependent on local crops and seasonal changes and had not changed much since the eleventh century. On the other hand, urban environments in northern and central Italy became centers of conspicuous consumption, even when food was difficult to obtain. The differences in diet between the peasants and the upper classes were interpreted as a physical reflection of spiritual distinctions, closely connected with social status. Noble natures were to consume lighter and more refined food, while workers and countryside dwellers could digest heavier products like black bread or wild grass. So choices in diet were not acknowledged as a consequence of economics, but rather as the expression of innate instincts that revealed different spiritual structures.[5]

A certain degree of refinement had spread among well-off households, both noble and bourgeois. One scholar argues that forks were employed on distinguished tables starting from the end of the fourteenth century. By the sixteenth century, the new tool was adopted also by the less affluent classes, turning out to be a perfect tool for consuming the different kinds of pasta that were becoming increasingly popular.[6] Guests would also be presented with an individual dish and a napkin to clean their mouth. Even on fasting periods (Wednesdays, Fridays, and many holiday eves), great care was given to copious and sophisticated menus. Banquets were not structured in a more or less codified series of savory or sweet dishes, as they are today, but would form a certain number of successive services made of several dishes laid on the table at the same time. It was up to guests to taste what they wanted or, more often, what they were closer to. Great importance was given to presentation, so that, for instance, a fowl would be served dressed in its own feathers and mutton in its own skin. At the beginning of meals, it was not unusual to see services of fresh fruits or salads, often seasoned with oil and vinegar, which were considered helpful to prepare the stomach to receive more substantial dishes.

The Renaissance culture made banquets an important form of entertainment, acknowledging the social and aesthetic importance of food, in the frame of a renewed interest in the sensual aspects of man, often neglected during the previous centuries.[7] The rediscovery of classic literature texts attracted attention to the works of the Latin gourmet Apicius, but there is no direct connection between the publishing of his book in 1457 and the renaissance of culinary arts. Cookbooks had been available long before then. The first known example, *Liber de coquina (The Kitchen Book)* dates to the end of the thirteenth century, probably written in the area of Naples. Tuscany was also an important center of production for this kind of book. From that time on, those who could afford it would hire professional cooks. The first cookbooks, diffused both as parchment scrolls and bound books, listed recipes either by ingredient (vegetables, meat, and so on) or by class of dishes. These early cookbooks were written either in Latin or in the vulgar languages that would successively become the various Italian dialects. The former were clearly meant for well-educated readers, probably the lords who could use them to choose dishes and give orders to their domestic staff. However, there also existed books in vulgar language for the upper bourgeoisie, such as the *XII Gentili Homini Giotissimi (The 12 Very Gluttonous Noblemen)*, which included recipes that could be made at home. Cooks, on the other hand, would mostly use the books in vulgar languages: Recipes would include practical directions regarding ingredients, cost, preparation time, or utensils. Nevertheless, these cooks were at least able to read, which indicates their significant status. Probably the most famous in the early Renaissance was Master Martino, whose *Liber de Arte Coquinaria (Book on the Art of Cooking)* became a classic. Born in what today is Italian-speaking Switzerland, in the middle of the fifteenth century, he worked in Milan as the cook for the Sforza family, the lords of the city, and then in Rome, a position that put him in very stimulating cultural milieus. There he met another important writer, Bartolomeo Sacchi, also known as Platina, a food connoisseur and librarian at the Vatican. In his book, *De Honesta Voluptate et Valetudine (Honest Pleasure and Health)*, Platina, who was trained in the study of classic literature, stressed the cultural aspects of dishes and products, giving cuisine a new status.

THE NEW WORLD REVOLUTION

While the new cultural winds of the Renaissance swept Italy, many Italians played an important role in the explorations that European kingdoms such as Portugal, France, Spain, and England financed from the end of the fifteenth century. These explorations were aimed at securing commercial outposts in regions where precious products, including spices, were grown. The arrival of the explorers in the Americas gave way to the biggest ecological revolution in history, known as the Columbian Exchange.[8] A wave of new products hit the colonies from Europe, while the same phenomenon occurred in the opposite direction. Some of these crops were immediately successful in Italy. The most popular was certainly corn, especially in northern Italy, where peasants would grow it in their orchards without having to pay taxes on it or to give part of the harvest to the landowners. Thanks to its similarities to already known cereals, corn was easily integrated into the local diets in the form of *polenta*, quite similar to grits. At the same time, other cereals were adopted in the North, like buckwheat, which was often ground and mixed with corn polenta, and rice, which so far had been used mainly as a drug in medicine or ground to thicken sauces and soups. Hard wheat (*triticum turgidum*) replaced most of the softer varieties, making storage and transportation easier.

American beans quickly supplanted the older local types, among which, only one, the black-eyed pea, survives today. The same happened with pumpkins: The new, bigger American varieties almost totally replaced the local long and thin *lagenaria*. Other plants, like tomatoes and potatoes, went through a much longer process of adaptation.[9] Tomatoes were considered toxic at first, and only in the eighteenth century did southern populations start eating them fried or in salads. Finally, from the beginning of the nineteenth century, tomatoes were used to make red sauces for pasta, and this pairing spread from the south to the whole peninsula, especially after the unification of the country in 1870.

Potatoes were not integrated into Italian foodways until the seventeenth century. On the other hand, sweet and hot chili peppers were easily accepted, and spiciness became a feature of many southern Italian dishes. The arrival of new crops also favored the diffusion of plants that had been known for a long time but had not been widely appreciated, such as eggplants, fennel, and artichokes.

The only animal from the Americas that enjoyed immediate success was turkey, which at first was called "Indian chicken."

COURTLY LIFE

The opening of new markets all over the world, with the subsequent increase of commercial and banking activities, brought abundance throughout Europe. Even if the Italian principalities and kingdoms were not directly engaged in colonization, many merchants from the peninsula were heavily involved in the new world economy, lending money to princes and lords. Courts all over Italy reached a very high level of refinement in art, architecture, and culture. Banquets became an occasion to display power and sophistication, and great attention was dedicated not only to food and service, but also to presentation and manners, heavily influenced by books about etiquette, such as *Galateo* by Giovanni della Casa and *Cortigiano* by Baldassarre Castiglione. Guests were expected to restrain from showing any sign of gluttony or from conversing openly about taste and flavors (with the exception of wine). Hosts would do their best to stun their guests with abundance, creativity, and originality. Banquets were still organized as a series of so-called services, but different styles appeared. The Italian style consisted of an alternation of so-called kitchen services, prevalently warm dishes, and sideboard *(credenza)* services, consisting of lighter or cold dishes. The meal usually began with a sideboard service and included at least two kitchen services. In German-style banquets, services were planned for smaller tables, seating eight to ten guests, where each dish was served on a large platter placed in the middle of the table, favoring conversation and conviviality. The French style was structured around the sequence appetizer—cooked dished—fruit, but on fasting days, when meat was forbidden, meals were reinforced with fried food, usually vegetables and fish. According to Domenico Romoli, author of *La Singolar Dottrina* (*The Unique Doctrine*, 1560), this was also the model for everyday meals in well-off households. Wine was highly appreciated in all social classes, but in banquets only the best quality was offered: The bottler, or *bottigliere*, was in charge of choosing, buying, and pairing wines with the various dishes, while a cup bearer, or *coppiere*, would serve them. Numerous personnel were involved in these extraordinary meals, from the cooks, considered as low labor, to the cutters, or *trincianti*, in charge of cutting meat in front of the guest, usually directly from the spit and with spectacular moves, to the *scalchi*, a sort of *maitre d'* who would actually plan the sequence of the meal and every single dish.

Most cookbooks published in this period are written by *scalchi*, such as the already mentioned Romoli, and Cristoforo Messisbugo, who wrote *Banchetti, Composizione di Vivande, et Apparecchio Generale* (*Banquets,*

Course Composition and General Preparation, 1549): The only notable exception is *Opera* (*The Works,* 1570) by Bartolomeo Scappi, a monumental book in which the author, a cook in the Pope's palace, explains all the methods and recipes to prepare each ingredient that were then available in the markets of Rome, both local and imported. Reading these books, it is evident that there was no break with the previous culinary tradition, but rather an integration and a conscious and slow transformation of classic recipes to adapt them to the current times. Furthermore, foreign dishes were the expression of a circulation of techniques and ideas between the professionals working in the courts of Europe. Italian cookbooks contained Spanish olla podrida or Middle Eastern couscous, showing a certain curiosity on the part of cooks. It is difficult to establish the precise influences of one cuisine over another: Many scholars contest the theory that in 1533 the arrival in France of Caterina dei Medici as wife of the future king, together with a cohort of cooks from Florence, determined an Italian influence over French culinary arts starting from the sixteenth century. As a matter of fact, French gastronomy developed independently only from the second half of the seventeenth century, creating the basis for modern *haute cuisine.*

A few elements were introduced into Italian courtly cuisine, such as a larger use of fish (including cod, sturgeon, and caviar), cheese, butter, beef, and offal (brain, ears, and even eyes). Scappi mentions goose *foie gras,* which the Jews in Rome were still making when it had disappeared in the rest of Europe. Sauces were still based on bread crumbs and acid juices like lemon and sour orange. Spices, increasingly available on the market and hence affordable, were still abundantly employed but slowly lost their character as a status symbol in high-end cuisine. This goes against the common belief that spices were popular in the Middle Ages because they helped to preserve food, especially meat. As a matter of fact, the same people who could afford spices were able to buy the freshest meat and game, which needed no conserving. The taste for sweet dishes lasted longer in Italy than in the rest of Europe, especially in the southern sections of the peninsula, probably more influenced by the Islamic heritage. Sugar was omnipresent. There was a popular saying at the time: Sugar never spoils a soup. Transmitting the heritage of Islam to the rest of Europe, Italians were expert in producing jams, candied fruits, jellies, and all kind of confections. Triumphs, or decorative sculptures made of sugar, were in fashion. Venice and Genoa would import and refine sugar from the new Portuguese colonies of Brazil and Madeira and would export it all over Europe.[10]

The diet of the lower classes is much less documented. We can suppose that it did not change much from the past. As the population started to grow again, hunger spread all over the country, where local states and foreign powers, Spain and France in particular, waged frequent wars. *Ravioli* were a popular way to recycle leftovers, as was *pasticci*, two layers of hard dough containing all kinds of filling, which was used as a tool to cook food directly on the embers in the hearth. *Torte* and *crostate* were similar to *pasticci*, but the dough was thinner and had butter or lard kneaded into it to make it edible. Scappi mentions *torte* in Naples that were not thicker than half an inch and were not covered: They were clearly the progenitors of pizza.

THE SEVENTEENTH AND EIGHTEENTH CENTURIES: ITALY UNDER FOREIGN INFLUENCE

While trade and finance were developing at a fast pace, the more traditional economic activities such as agriculture and manufacturing were still trapped in ancient habits, hindered by guilds in the cities and by aristocracies in the countryside. Output levels stagnated, to the point that recession hit Europe around 1620, with high inflation, famines, and epidemics that caused a deep demographic crisis. Urban and rural riots shook all of southern Italy, where the fiscal pressure of the Spanish dominion had become unbearable. Frequent episodes of unrest also exploded in the northern areas of the peninsula, where the burgeoning bourgeoisie often took sides with the lower class to fight against the traditional status quo.

In this stagnating economic situation, starting from the seventeenth century, Italian cuisine saw an increasing prevalence of local traditions over the unitary approach that was shared by cooks like Platina or Scappi. Even when these cooks identified dishes as Tuscan, or Roman, or Neapolitan, their frame of reference was still the *haute cuisine* that was more or less common to all Italian courts. Also cookbooks become regional, as the Neapolitan *La Lucerna de Corteggiani* (*The Lamp of Courtesan*, 1634) by Giovan Battista Crisci and *Scalco Alla Moderna* (*Modern Banquet Direction*, 1692) by Antonio Latini, which analyzed all the local products of the southern areas of the peninsula.

Eventually, the economy improved and famines were made less harsh by the widespread adoption of products like potatoes and tomatoes that so far had not been able to penetrate the peasants' diets. In the plain of the Po, under Austrian control, intensive investments in agriculture permitted the introduction of new machinery, the use of modern growing techniques, and the privatization of lands, which deprived many peasants of their traditional use rights but at the same time made the exploitation of the soil more efficient. The transformation of agrarian structures and the increase in outputs set the basis for industrial development: Many displaced peasants were available to move where the productive activities were located, and they were compelled to buy the new industrial items, thus stimulating production. The Austrian authorities implemented a major tax reform, eliminating many hindrances to free exchange. Similar policies were adopted in Tuscany, during the reign of the Lorraine family, who were related to the Austrian Hapsburgs. In the rest of Italy, landowners were still using old methods, getting their profit not from investments but from the exploitation of peasant labor, especially in the papal territories and in the south, under the Bourbons, who were closely related to the Spanish kings. As a consequence, output was limited and the economy stagnated, limiting the growth of industrial activities.

The new bourgeoisie developed specific culinary tastes. Suspicious of complicated and expensive dishes considered heavy, they were attracted to the simple and often strong flavors of popular traditions. Of course, lower-class dishes went through a process of refinement and elaboration before getting to the bourgeois table. At the same time, as Italy became increasingly subordinated to foreign powers, national cuisine was heavily influenced by the French tradition: the so-called French-style service, in which a first course of soups and appetizers was followed by another composed of several main dishes and then by desserts, became popular among the bourgeoisie. The new French preference for fresh ingredients and for simpler sauces and more distinct flavors, without excess in the use of spices or mixtures of sweet and savory, slowly seeped through in Italy, where at any rate local traditions had never really been influenced by courtly styles and had remained faithful to simple ingredients. Around the end of the eighteenth century, cookbooks showcasing local recipes and ingredients were published, such as *Cuoco Piemontese Perfezionato a Parigi* (*The Piedmont Cook Perfected in Paris*, 1766), *Cuoco Galante* (*The Gallant Cook*, 1786), and *Apicio Moderno* (*Modern Apicius*, 1790) by Francesco Leonardi. For the first time, chefs dealt with the issue of culinary identities and the existence of diverse traditions in Italy that, precisely in those years, had finally fully accepted and integrated new world products such as potatoes, tomatoes, and corn, undergoing radical transformations.

The bourgeois also affirmed their identity in new fads, such as coffee and chocolate. The Venetians, who had learned about coffee from the Turks, first imported it into Italy. The first coffeehouses opened in the end of the sixteenth century, but the drink became a craze only in the following century. Chocolate had been introduced to the Spanish court in 1528 by conquistador Hernan Cortés, but it was prepared with sugar instead of spicy hot substances, as was the custom in Central America. Regular loads arrived in the Netherlands, then a Spanish territory, starting in 1580; cocoa drinks became fashionable, even if the preparation was kept a secret. In 1606 Antonio Carletti, a Florentian, was able to steal the recipe, but in the beginning chocolate was adopted only by physicians as a tonic. It took another century for chocolate to become fashionable in Italy, spreading from the cocoa houses in Venice and Florence and following the French fashion. On the other hand, a new craze started from Italy and invaded Europe: the passion for sorbets and ice creams, also inherited from the Muslim tradition and perfected in Sicily since the twelfth century.

THE ITALIAN POLITICAL UNIFICATION AND ITS CONSEQUENCES

A major change in diet accompanied the unification of Italy, led by the Savoy kings of Piedmont starting in 1848. The last territory to be annexed to the new kingdom of Italy was Rome. In 1870 Italian troops walked into what would shortly after become the capital, leaving the Pope only the tiny Vatican State, located in the heart of the city. Even if Italy now existed as a country, with a more or less defined identity, it was not the case for the population. Most of the countryside's population and large groups of urban dwellers were illiterate, let alone able to speak Italian, a language close to Tuscan and Roman. People still spoke their dialects and were proud of their local traditions and written literature. Social and political systems were radically diverse, so that the central government had to fight for years to establish its authority over Sicily and most of the South, where bands of supposed outlaws continued to resist, often backed by both noble and lower-class locals. Many scholars see in these events one of the causes for the birth of the criminal organizations that would later be known as Mafia in Sicily, Ndrangheta in Calabria, Sacra Corona Unita in Puglia, and Camorra in Campania. Few dishes enjoyed a national diffusion. The most famous case was pasta with tomato sauce, which was discovered by the troops advancing toward the south. The dish rapidly spread north.[11]

The central government made conscious attempts at unifying food habits all over the country, primarily using the school system and the military service. Some of the victuals granted to soldiers, such as coffee, dried pasta, and cheese, became everyday necessities for the whole population, because the men that went back home from the barracks had developed a taste for them.

Paradoxically, it was precisely when the country was finally united that cooks and chefs showed greater interest in local traditions. When in 1891 Pellegrino Artusi published his famous *La Scienza in Cucina e l'Arte del Mangiar Bene (Science in the Kitchen and the Art of Good Eating)*, a cookbook that is still largely used in Italy, he still had a quite confused approach to regional cooking. While he acknowledged the local origin of many dishes, he freely mixed them, with the result that he almost single-handedly created a new nationwide vocabulary for food, which till then had been quite fragmentary.

With the new century, regional food became the object of scholarly interest and anthropological research, while the first regional cuisine cookbooks started being published. In some cases, it was a full-blown case of the invention of a tradition, because many authors had little or no idea of the relatively recent origins and transformations of the dishes they considered as unchanged for centuries. These books were geared not so much toward chefs, but rather to the cooks and maids in bourgeois households, and housewives themselves when they could not afford to hire staff.

From the point of view of the table service, a new style known as "Russian" became popular, in which dishes were presented in a succession, to all the guests at the same time, so that all of them could enjoy every dish. The usual order, both in restaurants and private homes, was *antipasto* (appetizers), *primo* (usually a soup, or a pasta dish, less often rice), *secondo* (meat or fish) with *contorni* (side dishes, often vegetables), and dessert at the end. Antipasti were only for special occasions, but in the south it was normal to keep finger food on the table before the meal or between meals: olives, slices of salami, and bits of cheese. The meal structure is more or less the same today, even if the everyday meal is now less complex, and people tend to choose either a *primo* or a *secondo*.

The host was able to decide the content and the timing of the meal. He could control the quantities of food, all the while showing his refinement and, if he wanted to impress, his munificence. Every family, in some way, tried to transform the Sunday meal into a special occasion, a minor version of an important banquet. During the week, though, meals were much simpler, and recipes that allowed for leftovers were appreciated.[12]

The structure of the festive meal was adopted by restaurants, a new kind of establishment that had been created in France and that ensured jobs for cooks and chefs that the nobles were not able to afford any longer. Many of these professionals also found placements in hotels, another kind of establishment that followed the birth of mass tourism. Both hotels and restaurants were attuned to the spending power of the bourgeoisie. Those who could not afford elegant meals would still patronize *osterie* or *trattorie*, often located on the outskirts of cities, where simpler meals were offered or where people could bring their own food and limit themselves to buying wine.

The diet of lower classes was still pretty much the same as in the eighteenth century and would not change until after World War II. Cereals, pulses, and vegetables provided most of the calories, with meat and fish being just an integration or the main ingredients for festive meals. Famine and undernourishment were widespread, especially in the northeastern areas and in the south. Many decided to abandon their homeland and to immigrate, mostly to the United States, Canada, and South American countries such as Venezuela, Brazil, and Argentina.

The twentieth century brought major changes, with the introduction of canned food and, in general, industrial products. Canned vegetables acquired immediate popularity. They were available year round, to the point that they often replaced fresh, more expensive items in many dishes. Canned tomatoes and dried pasta constituted a fast and relatively cheap meal for many Italians, especially in urban environments where fresh produce was hard to find. The food industry published its own recipe books, which advised the use of canned food. Meanwhile, new stoves were introduced that allowed for easier preparation of food, at first burning coke coal, then gas. Besides being easy to use, these stoves helped to keep kitchens cooler and cleaner than ever before.

Food was scarce during World War I, but at the same time the war brought together men from all over the country, exposing them to different kinds of food. For the first time, Italians participated in a conflict as a unified country: The war events played an important role in the construction of the national identity. The 1917 book by Olindo Guerrini, *L'Arte di Utilizzare Gli Avanzi della Mensa (The Art of Using Leftovers)*, is representative of the food culture of the period.

In the 1920s and 1930s, during the Fascist era, a new interest in the scientific aspects of cooking became relevant, following the example of the home economics movement in the United States. Women were taught so-called modern culinary habits and new, more efficient, ways to cook, to the point of jeopardizing the transmission of traditional or local recipes.[13] The Fascist state made enormous efforts to enhance the national identity and to connect ideologically with the glorious past of imperial Rome. For this reason dialects were repressed, and so were many local traditions, including culinary ones, that were often considered backward and unworthy of a modern powerful nation. New products were introduced on the market, such as concentrated meat stock, instant chocolate, and baking powder.

In 1926 the National Agency for the Scientific Organization of Work was founded, aiming at rationalizing households, including kitchens where electric stoves, electric boilers, aluminum pots and pans, clocks, scales, and other appliances were introduced. A very Italian piece of machinery was invented: a mechanical kneader operated with a crank, in which dough would be pressed between metal cylinders, becoming thinner and thinner. This is an implement that can still be found in households where pasta is handmade, at least for special meals or weekends. Refrigerators were still rare, while many households had iceboxes.

The passion for modernity was expressed by a new art style, Futurism, embodying a deep fascination for machinery and speed. The artists belonging to this movement proposed a new kind of diet that refused all traditions, including pasta, which was compared to some sort of oppressive religion. The recipes they proposed were mostly daring assemblages, with frequent sexual or belligerent innuendoes, which were quickly forgotten.

With the beginning of World War II, the Fascist state made a call for economic self-sufficiency (autarchia), an attempt to exclusively use nationally produced food. Benito Mussolini showed up at harvest season on many wheat fields, where he would be filmed while, shirtless, he helped the workers. War inevitably brought hunger, especially in big cities, while in the countryside it was easier to find food. The situation got even worse when the Italian government ousted Mussolini and made peace with the Allies: The Nazis occupied most of northern and central Italy, making food virtually impossible to get. Some items could only be found on the black market, available to a tiny minority of the population. The government distributed food stamps that could be redeemed for basic products such as pasta, sugar, and some canned foods, but the system did not work properly, with many shop owners hiding their provisions to sell them on the black market at much higher prices. With the arrival of the Americans in the south, and then in the rest of the country, condensed milk, cookies, chocolate, coffee, and other victuals became available, while food was again brought from the countryside into the cities.

AFTER WORLD WAR II

During the reconstruction fuelled by the investments organized in the U.S.-sponsored Marshall plan, and later in the 1950s, when the raging

Cold War made Italy the battleground of international political interests, most Italians were still sticking, often willy-nilly, to what would be later glamorously known as the Mediterranean diet. At the time it was nothing fancy. Most farmers, and many urban dwellers, could only afford what a still-underdeveloped food distribution system could bring to the table at an affordable price. Especially in the southern and central parts of the country, these products were mostly fresh vegetables and fruit from the neighboring countryside, pasta, eggs, and the occasional fish or piece of meat. In the north, the consumption of animal fats was higher. Nevertheless, in the mid-1950s, the average per capita consumption of meat was not more than 30 pounds a year.[14] Besides, people led a more active life: For many, even taking the bus stretched their budget, and a bicycle was often considered quite a luxury. Famous movie makers, known as Neorealists, such as Roberto Rossellini, Vittorio De Sica, and Luchino Visconti, immortalized this whole situation of penury in somber or comical tones in many of their works, often exaggerating the admittedly hard reality for political reasons.[15]

Life did not become any easier for workers, even when, in the 1960s, the country underwent the so-called economic boom. Rapid industrial growth induced a major wave of internal migration from south to north, from villages to towns, from the hinterland to the coast. This phenomenon gave rise to deep social changes, displacement of important sections of the population, crises in the family structure and in the traditional values, which came to be questioned in an unprecedented way. Many agricultural workers decided to abandon their farms to work in factories, which secured more stable and substantial revenues. The inherited know-how of artisans, which ensured the production of many local specialties now considered gourmet food, risked being lost, and in some cases was lost. (In recent years, though, young producers have been rediscovering almost-lost food traditions, and many of these products are now highly appreciated and protected.)

The fresh immigrants all but wanted to forget their past, and many of the dishes they grew up with started to be considered unfashionable, if not despicable. Women, who in the past were usually in charge of cooking, often had to leave their homes and find jobs, dedicating less time to meal preparation. Furthermore, the rise of the feminist political consciousness pushed many women out the kitchen, considered a place of exploitation.

The displacement of major sections of the population, nevertheless, allowed regional or local food to become known in other parts of the county. While this interregional exchange had always existed for the higher classes, peasants and artisans had always tended to eat what was produced around them, finding local food more familiar and affordable. Now southern communities in the north craved certain products, creating the commercial demand for food that otherwise would have never traveled: This is the case of buffalo-milk mozzarella, sun-dried tomatoes, olive oil, and certain types of salami.

The 1980s witnessed a progressive interest in foreign food, and *nouvelle cuisine* extended its influence to Italian tables. It become fashionable to eat pasta with fresh cream and salmon and to serve lemon sorbet between courses of elegant banquets. Chefs and housewives were eager to try brave new stuff, often with debatable results. At the end of the 1980s, hordes of yuppies would try anything that sounded fancy and allowed them a display of conspicuous consumption. At the same time, fast food—namely McDonald's—made its appearance in Italy.

CONTEMPORARY ISSUES

Not much was left of the agricultural and pastoral traditions that had survived for centuries. Unexpectedly, though, the whole situation radically changed in the late 1980s: Food suddenly became the object of political and cultural interests.[16] The sense that local foodways and ingredients were increasingly threatened by mass production, globalization, and other contemporary trends spread among many Italians. A growing interest in issues connected with food started to spread also at the level of cultural and political institutions.

The magazine *Gambero Rosso*, founded in 1986, soon became the arena for a newly founded organization, Arcigola, in which *Arci* was an acronym for Recreative Association of Italian Communists, and *gola* ironically referred to both food and gluttony. The association had been founded by Carlo Petrini, a leftist militant from the Piedmont region, and had (and still has) its headquarters in Bra, a small town in the Langhe wine area. The scope for the work of Arcigola included the protection of the environment and the defense of consumers, but these missions were to be seasoned with a nice dose of conviviality, good living, enjoyment, and pleasure. *Gambero Rosso* and Arcigola thought that in Italy quality wine was not sufficiently explored and appreciated, so they started a new *Wine Guide*, ten thousand copies of which were first published in 1988. All sold out. Now the guide determines the wine market in Italy. Whoever receives the Tre Bicchieri, or Three Glasses, award given to the best producers often experiences an increase in sales from one day to the next.

The interest in both *Gambero Rosso* and Arcigola grew fast. On November 9, 1989, at the Opera Comique of Paris, representatives of the participating countries of the international movement for the Defense of and the Right to Pleasure—Slow Food—signed the register to mark the movement's official birth. Its manifesto was an open invitation to oppose the fast life and embrace sensual pleasure and slow, long-lasting enjoyment. The name itself—Slow Food—was chosen to express a strong opposition to Fast Food, and the movement gained momentum as a form of protest against the opening of the first McDonald's restaurant in Rome, near the historical Spanish steps.

Both *Gambero Rosso* and Slow Food helped to establish a cultural trend that considers food not only through categories of fashions, market trends, or economics, but also within a conceptual frame in which collective enjoyment, sharing, and community become the main points of reference. In this kind of approach, food allows individuals to get together, to rediscover their bonds to a vital tradition, to create relationships, to take their time in a world that moves at an increasingly fast pace.

Increasingly larger audiences are now able to appreciate the role of local communities and traditions, the manual skills and know-how of food producers, and their ties to a historically determined material culture. These elements were connected with labor, territory, and a more humane approach to time, as opposed to the obsessive rhythm of a modern capitalist economy that deprives us of our leisure time. This approach, especially strong in Slow Food, has been sometimes defined as Culinary Luddism, the goal of which is "to turn back the flood tide of industrialized food in the First World, and to prevent such foods from engulfing traditional ethnic foods elsewhere."[17] This criticism points to the real and present danger that the rediscovery of tradition could be captured within a conceptual framework built on conservative moral values and a patriarchal society, reconstructing the ideological myth of a time that knew neither disruptions nor crises.[18] The appeal of tradition has already been largely exploited in this sense by the advertising industry: In Italy, especially in the 1980s and the 1990s, many products were marketed as associated with the so-called good old days. We can mention Mulino Bianco cookies, which in the commercials were consumed by an ever-smiling family dwelling in a beautiful old mill in an uncontaminated countryside, or Antica Gelateria del Corso, an ice cream that claimed its origin in an imaginary *fin-de-siècle* parlor as two examples.

The cultural attitude toward food had changed profoundly. *Micromega*, a very prestigious political journal, dedicated an issue to the subject of food as culture. While in office as Prime Minister, Massimo D'Alema (a member of the former Communist Party, now called the Leftist Democrats) would invite the most famous chefs to cook at official receptions and was not embarrassed to hang out with them. This shift came to public consciousness in December 1998, when Minister of Culture Giovanna Melandri, also from the Leftist Democrats, missed the opening of the Opera season at the Scala Theater in Milan in order to attend the annual gala dinner organized by Gambero Rosso food magazine. Slow Food has also gathered a certain following among food and wine lovers in the United States, where several groups, called *convivia*, have been founded, following the Slow Food principles of enjoyment; a cultural appreciation of food traditions; and the defense of ecology, sustainable development, and biodiversity. Every other year food events like Salone del Gusto in Turin, organized by the Slow Food association, attract thousands of people from around the world.

Although the future of Italian food, both artisanal and industrial, has never looked more promising, the largest supermarket chains, such as Metro or Carrefour, are increasingly owned by foreign companies from other European countries. The distribution system at that level is now characterized by some concurrent phenomena: a strong concentration in the phase of purchase of the goods, which makes distributors stronger in the negotiations with producers; a strong concentration in the distribution, which allows larger profits; and a supranational development of mammoth supermarket and hypermarket chains. These companies could easily expand in Italy, because since the 1960s the local agricultural and, above all, meat production has been insufficient to meet the growing demands of a society that has become more and more affluent. However, the traditional sector caters to specific needs, ensuring higher-quality or registered products without particularly suffering from the competition waged by the large distribution companies. They actually meet different needs for the same consumer. Italians thus find themselves at the hinge of different distribution systems, trying to make the best of both and, above all, enjoying both.

THE EUROPEAN BATTLEFIELD

This rekindled interest in wine and food, in culinary traditions and local produce, promoted and exploited by the press, is reaching new heights just as western Europe is undergoing major political changes aimed at increasing integration between the member states, not only administratively but also economically. The nation-states that after the French Revolution had become a tool of self-promotion and enhancement for the economically dominant bourgeoisie are renouncing many of their traditional prerogatives. The process is not painless, and it is often clear how different countries are trying to reaffirm their power and their dominant role in the new political order. Food is not excluded from this phenomenon. Many countries are trying to gain advantage from systems that derive from the one France invented in 1855 to exert state control over its agricultural production: a registration that ranked 60 wine makers (or château) on the basis of their wine price and quality. In the 1930s, the system developed into the Controlled Appellation of Origin (AOC, or in Italian, *Appélation d'Origine Controlée*). Each area had to create rules to discipline the production of local wines. Wine makers had to meet specific requirements in order to receive the coveted denomination, which was perceived as a sign of higher quality and had become since the beginning a very effective marketing device. Regulations were enforced defining the grape varieties that could be used, their proportion in the mix, the aging methods, and so on. The system paid off. Wine quality was actually enhanced, and consumers were ready to pay more for wines that had received some sort of recognition from the state. A similar wine classification was adopted in Italy starting from 1963 with the introduction of the regulations establishing DOC (Controlled Denomination of Origin, or in Italian, *Denominazione d'Origine Controllata*) and DOCG (Denomination of Controlled and Guaranteed Origin, or in Italian, *Denominazione d'Origine Controllata e Garantita*). The system was brought to date in 1992 with the introduction of a new category, the IGT (Typical Geographic Indication, or in Italian, *Indicazione Geografica Tipica*).

Food manufactures were aware that a similar system, applied to their production, would increase the value of their goods, and protect them from those selling similar products of lesser quality under the same name and all kinds of fraud. Many member states had already created methods of registration, so when the European Union started issuing regulations on this matter, the existing quality denominations needed to be acknowledged and coordinated by the European authorities, and rules had to be set on how to establish new denominations. Every country rushed to have as many denomination products as possible, making negotiations difficult and long. Finally, in 1992, the European Union issued a regulation, the infamous 2081, that allowed the registration of more than 600 products in 10 years under two categories, the PDO (Protected Designation of Origin, or in Italian, DOP, *Designazione d'Origine Protetta*) and the PGI (Protected

Geographical Indication, or in Italian IGP, *Indicazione Geografica Protetta*).

The PDO refers to the name of a region, a specific place or a country describing a product originating in that same place, the quality or other characteristics of which are essentially or exclusively due to a specific geographical environment. This means that production and transformation must be carried out in the geographical area designated by the PDO regulations.

The PGI, however, indicates the name of a region, a specific place or a country describing a product originating in that same place and possessing a quality or reputation that can attributed to the geographical environment with its inherent natural and human components. The latter definition is clearly less strict than the former, allowing fame and traditional notoriety to play an important role. Furthermore, only one phase (production or transformation) must take place in the geographical area indicated by the PGI regulations.

Another less strict category was also established, the TSG (Traditional Specialty Guaranteed, or in Italian STG, *Specialità Tradizionale Garantita*), which does not refer to any specific area of origin, but to the traditional composition and production methods.

The objective of the regulations introduced in 1992 was to add value to specific high-quality products from a demarcated geographical area and to promote the diversification of agricultural production by acknowledging the value of rare or disappearing resources. To qualify for a PGI or a PDO designation, producers are required to specify the name of the product, the definition of the geographical area, the methods of preparation, the factors relating to the geographical environment, the details concerning the labeling, and the bodies charged with inspecting the application of the production rules. Of course, the registration can only be made by a group of producers, usually organized in a self-regulated consortium (a type of association), and addressed to the member state where the geographical area in which the product originates is located. The member states would then apply to the European Union to obtain the recognition.

The new regulation spelled danger for much of the food industry in the northern member states. Not many traditional products could comply with the new requirements. As of 2002, Denmark registered only 3 products, Finland 1, Sweden 2, and the Netherlands 5, out of 606. France, with 131, is the country that succeeded in registering more products. Furthermore, the northern countries produced local spin-offs more famed traditional gourmet products from the southern parts of the Union, especially in the field of cured meat and cheese. All these products had to be changed and adapted to the new regulations to avoid international law suits.

Italy managed to register 123 products, about 20 percent of the total. For instance, *parmigiano reggiano* producers could sue anybody who produces similar cheese under the same name anywhere else in the Union and could count on the Union's support in international litigation (i.e., against the Wisconsin parmesan producers that were using the name *parmigiano*). The new registrations, though, did not automatically mean protection of the products in their most traditional and so-called authentic version, if that ever existed. When in 1988 in the village of Genzano, a few miles from Rome, the local bread makers decided to found a consortium to define what their bread was supposed to be like and to boost their sales by adding value to its name, some of them decided not to join. The reason was that some of the producers, including three industrial ovens, were not willing to follow the old tradition according to which the bread is baked only in wood ovens, using chestnut-tree wood. When the consortium applied for registration following the European laws, it did not include the chestnut-wood oven baking in the requirements, and as a consequence, the PGI was issued accordingly. An old tradition was thus neglected by a regulation that was supposed to protect it.

Similar controversies took place all over Italy. For instance, in the case of the *lardo* from the village of Colonnata, in northwestern Tuscany, many enterprises outside the homonymous village are lobbying to change the PDO regulation so that they can use the prestigious name for the cured pork fat they produce.

The field is ever changing. In April 2003, the European Union issued a law that allows the registration of PDO products that were previously excluded from that denomination, such as bread and pasta, biscuits and pastries, beer, wine vinegar, essential oils, cork, flowers, and many others. Furthermore, stricter rules are applied to the packaging process, which has to be done in the production area. For instance, Prosciutto di Parma cannot be sliced and packaged anywhere else but in Parma and the surrounding area, in order to give better guarantees to consumers about the quality.

NOTES

1. Gianni Race, *La cucina del mondo classico* (Naples: Edizioni Scientifiche Italiane, 1999).

2. A. Dosi and F. Schnell, *Le abitudini alimentari dei Romani* (Rome: Edizioni Quasar, 1986).

3. Paola Galloni, *Storia e cultura della caccia* (Rome-Bari: Laterza, 2000).

4. Ariel Toaff, *Mangiare alla giudia* (Bologna: Il Mulino, 2000).

5. Federica Badiali, *Cucina medioevale italiana* (Bologna: Stupor Mundi, 1999).

6. Giovanni Rebora, *Culture of the Fork* (New York: Columbia University Press, 2001).

7. Lino Turrini, *La cucina ai tempi dei Gonzaga* (Milan: Rizzoli Libri Illustrati, 2002).

8. Maurizio Sentieri and Zazzu Guido, *I semi dell'Eldorado* (Bari: Dedalo, 1992).

9. Salvatore Marchese, *Benedetta patata: Una storia del '700, un trattato e 50 ricette* (Padova: Franco Muzzio Editore, 1999).

10. Giovanna Giusti Galardi, *Dolci a corte: dipinti ed altro* (Livorno: Sillabe, 2001).

11. S. Somogyi, "L'alimentazione nell'Italia unita," in *Storia d'Italia*, vol. 5, bk. 1: I documenti (Turin: Einaudi, 1973).

12. Piero Camporesi, "La cucina borghese dell'Ottocento fra tradizione e rinnovamento," in *La terra e la luna* (Milan: Garzanti, 1995).

13. G. F. Vené, *Mille lire al mese: vita quotidiana della famiglia nell'Italia Fascista* (Milan: Mondadori, 1988).

14. C. Pinna, "Le classi povere," in *Atti della commissione parlamentare di inchiesta sulla miseria in Italia e sui mezzi per combatterla*, vol II (Rome: Camera dei Deputati, 1954).

15. Viviana Lapertosa, *Dalla fame all'abbondanza: Gli italiani e il cibo nel cinema dal dopoguerra ad oggi* (Turin: Lindau, 2002).

16. Filippo Ceccarelli, *Lo stomaco della Repubblica* (Milan: Longanesi, 2000).

17. Rachel Laudan, "A World of Inauthentic Cuisine" (paper presented at the conference Cultural and Historical Aspects of Foods, Oregon State University, Portland, 1999), 136.

18. For the semiotic concept of myth, see Roland Barthes, *Mythologies* (New York: The Noonday Press, 1972), in particular the analyses of wine and milk and steak and chips. For the emerging of the utopian past as fantasmatic procedure, see also Yannis Stavrakakis, *Lacan and the Political* (New York: Routledge, 1999).

2

Major Foods and Ingredients

Because of its long history, the diverse and prolonged influences of neighboring populations, and local differences, Italian cuisine presents a stunning variety of products, food, and dishes. This inexhaustible bounty can be confusing to foreigners, and even Italians find it difficult to master. Italians are usually quite knowledgeable about foods and dishes that have nationwide diffusion and distribution. The contemporary food industry, increasingly important after World War II, makes sure that all Italians are familiar with mass-produced items such as pasta, canned vegetables, tuna fish, stock cubes, or coffee. These items are normally easy to find and affordable, which makes them particularly appealing. Companies are also trying to differentiate their offerings, creating high-end brands that give consumers the impression they are buying exclusive products. Many of these are marketed by employing images and concepts of a mythical, long-gone rural Arcadia that never actually existed but nevertheless is able to attract consumers who choose products to try to connect to their roots. In fact, internal migration and the subsequent urbanization of a large part of the population caused the abandonment of rural and small town lifestyles, which often provoked a crisis of local food productions. In recent years, though, local traditions, and, above all, artisanal food, have been rediscovered. Rare specialties produced in tiny quantities have become gourmet items, reaching high prices and enjoying new renown. The Italian government and local authorities are both creating rules and codes to regulate those products and ensure quality, while obtaining recognition from the European Union and protecting these specialties from counterfeits.

On the other hand, some of these products, which actually have acquired the status of cultural identity symbols, are defended against the European Union's attempts to implement regulations that would endanger them. This is the case with nonpasteurized cheese, or cheese matured in caves in the ground, which is considered unhealthy by some EU agencies.

Due to this complex and shifting situation, the best approach to Italian food is to describe the different products one by one, highlighting the traditions related to them, the local differences, and their use in the national and local cuisine.

WHEAT, BREAD, AND PIZZA

Grains, such as wheat, rice, and corn, constitute the main staple in Italian cuisine. Wheat, both in the hard and soft varieties, provides the bulk of dietary calories in the form of flour, bread, pasta, pizza, and such. The quantity of wheat actually harvested in Italy is now limited: although wheat is grown in Puglia, Sicily, and Sardinia, most of it is imported form other countries, such as Canada or Ukraine. Soft wheat is grown in the plain of the river Po. Flour is found in many types, but the basic distinction is between flours deriving from durum wheat, mainly used to produce dried pasta, and those from soft wheat, classified in many categories: O and OO types, the most refined ones, are used to make fresh pasta and pastry. Types 0, 1, and 2, which are less refined and hence tastier, are employed in the production of bread. Flours 1 and 2 are not easy to find for private customers and they are usually sold in bulk to bakeries. Gluten-rich flour coming from Canada, usually called American or Manitoba, is used to make cakes that require leavened dough.

The majority of the population consumes different types of breads, depending on personal taste and local habits, at every meal. Most breads are leavened, with the notable exception of *piadina*, a round and thin unleavened sheet of dough to which some fat—usually lard or oil—and baking soda are added to increase softness and lightness. *Piadinas*, a very popular fast food in Romagna, are usually cooked over a burning hot slab of stone, acquiring uneven color and crunchiness, and eaten warm together with *prosciutto* or some equivalent of cottage cheese. The same slab of stone, called *testo*, is also used to prepare *testaroli*, a local specialty in the northern tip of Tuscany. A fluffy, almost liquid dough made of flour and water is cooked in thin sheets over the stone, then broken into pieces, dropped in boiling water and, once strained, seasoned with *pesto*. Simple water and flour dough, with the occasional dash of olive oil but no leaven, is also used to make *cialde* or *ferratelle*. These are small pieces of the dough pressed between two flat metal slabs operated like a sort of heavy pliers with long arms, which are successively placed over the fire until the *cialda* is cooked.

Leavened dough, on the other hand, is employed to make all kinds of breads. It is virtually impossible to list all the different kinds of bread one can find in Italy. Breads can be broadly divided into salted and unsalted ones, the unsalted being more common in central Italy, especially Tuscany, Umbria, and Lazio. As to sizes, they vary enormously, but usually consumers can either buy single-portion breads, between 1 and 2 ounces each, or big loaves that can weigh up to 4 or 5 pounds. Breads are used during the meal to accompany any *secondo*, or main dish. For this reason everything that is not bread is called *companatico*, a word of Latin origin that literally means "with bread." Many people enjoy soaking pieces of bread in the sauce of their *secondo*, a practice frowned upon in formal meals. Slices of bread are often grilled and seasoned with all kinds of ingredients, including salt, olive oil, garlic, and tomato, to make *bruschetta*. Single-portion breads, or *panini*, cut in two and filled with all kinds of food, are also eaten outside the meal, often actually constituting a light meal by themselves. *Panini* are consumed as a form of lunch by those working far from home, traveling, or at picnics. As a matter of fact, most grocery shops are often willing to fix *panini*, which can also be bought already made at coffeehouses and gourmet shops.

Bread dough is traditionally used in Piedmont to make *grissini*, long, thin crunchy sticks with or without oil or butter. *Grissini* are now easy to find in the breadbaskets of most Italian restaurants, often eaten with *antipasti* or while waiting for the main dish.

A particular form of bread is the Sardinian *carta da musica*, or "music sheet," very thin, crunchy, round sheets of leavened dough that are passed several times in the oven with weights on top to keep them flat. They are used in many preparations, such as *pane fratau*: the sheets are soaked in hot water and covered with crushed tomatoes, grated *pecorino* cheese, and a poached egg.

Leavened dough is also the main ingredient of pizza, a dish so common all over the world that many people have forgotten its Italian origins. Pizza can be cooked in the oven without any toppings, simply seasoned with a dash of olive oil, salt, and some herbs. In this case it is usually called *focaccia*, but also *pizza bianca*, or "white pizza," is a common denomination. A famous kind of *pizza bianca* is the one originally made in Genoa, but now spread all over the country, which is very thick but at the same fluffy and delicate. More often, pizza is enriched by all kinds of toppings. The thickness of pizza varies depending on the local customs. For instance, in Naples it is thicker than in Rome, where it is extremely thin. The most traditional kinds of pizza are *margherita* (fresh tomato, buffalo mozzarella, and basil), and *napoletana*, with salted anchovies, but now all kinds of pizza are available, from the common mushroom, cheese, sausage, or *prosciutto* tops to the new creations with zucchini blossoms, salmon, or arugula. Nevertheless, Hawaiian pizza is unheard of, and the very idea of putting sweet ingredients on pizza sounds whimsical. The only exception is white pizza stuffed with Nutella, a hazelnut and chocolate spread, or with fresh figs. Pizza can be either eaten at the restaurant—in which case it is round and served on a dish—or in special pizza shops where pizzas are made in bigger rectangular pans and sold by the weight.

Calzone is an oven-cooked pizza folded in half and filled with ingredients that in Naples, its place of origin, are ricotta cheese, diced mozzarella, diced salami or *prosciutto*, and egg. Outside of Naples the filling varies, but it is usually without ricotta.

Besides bread and pizzas, wheat flour is also employed to make couscous in western Sicily, the only area of the country where this Middle Eastern dish can still be found. Sicilian couscous is usually served with vegetables or fish.

Flour is also used to make savory tarts or *torte rustiche*, using different sorts of dough depending on the area. In Liguria, tarts are made of the so-called crazy dough, or *pasta matta*, a simple and light mix of flour, water, and olive oil, usually quite thin and filled with fresh ingredients, mostly vegetables. In Abruzzo, on the other hand, a sort of phillo dough made with flour, eggs, and lard is filled with more substantial food, such as sausages, diced hard-boiled eggs, salami, and different kinds of vegetables. In most of the southern areas, people favor bread dough to prepare savory tarts, with fillings that vary even from village to village. In recent years, since frozen phillo dough has become largely available, savory tarts are easier to find everywhere in Italy and are also often homemade; a popular filling is ricotta and spinach.

PASTRIES AND CAKES

It would be impossible to make a complete list of all the traditional Italian pastry recipes based on wheat flour. Every area, if not every single town, is known for different cookies, tarts, and pies. Éclairs (called *bigné*, *paste*, or *pastarelle*) with all kinds of fillings are easy to find in any pastry

Locally made pastry in the shape of a snake, Perugia. © TRIP/L. Tribe

shop, often in two sizes: a larger one and a tiny one, called *mignon*. Fillings may include chocolate, egg custard, *zabaione* (made by cooking egg yolks in Bain Marie together with sugar and *marsala* sweet wine), hazelnut, coffee cream, and plain or sweetened whipped cream. The origin of the name *zabaione* is debated: Some think it comes from the Arabic root *zabada*, meaning "to churn milk or to foam"; others connect it with Saint Pasquale Baylon, protector of pastry chefs (San Baylon). Especially in the morning, pastry shops also display a choice of different croissants and other small pastries made of leavened dough enriched with butter. Croissants often have different fillings, such as chocolate, raisins, cream, or almonds. Other small pastries vary according to the different areas: In Naples, for instance, *babà* are made of very fluffy dough drenched in rum and sugar, while *sfogliatelle* present a layered and crunchy dough filled with cream and boiled wheat grain. Many pastries are made of fried dough with different fillings: If they are big, round, sprinkled in granulated sugar and filled with cream or chocolate, they are known as *bombe*. If they are smaller and filled with cream, they are called *bigné di San Giuseppe* (Saint Joseph's pastry) in Rome, or *zeppole* in Naples. Doughnut-shaped fried pastries are rather named *frittelle*. For Carnevale, the Italian equivalent of

Mardi Gras, long stripes of crunchy fried dough powdered with sugar, called *frappe*, *cenci*, or *chiacchiere*, and little fried balls covered in melted honey, or *castagnole*, are particularly popular. Tiny balls of fried dough, dipped in honey syrup, arranged in a wreath, and decorated with colored spangles, are called *struffoli*, and are a Christmas dessert in Naples. Also the dough for the renowned Sicilian *cannoli*, filled with a ricotta cheese-based cream, is actually fried. In Sardinia, *seadas*, shaped like ravioli and filled with fresh cheese, are fried and covered with honey.

Baked desserts and pies are also very common, both homemade and commercial. The word *biscotti* literally means "twice-cooked" and derives from the custom of baking the dough in slabs, cutting it into smaller pieces, and placing them in the oven again to dry, so that the lack of humidity allows them to stay fresh longer. The same method is used to make *fette biscottate*, very airy and crunchy slices of sweet leavened dough that are usually consumed for breakfast. There are many kinds of *biscotti*, often with other ingredients such as raisins, dried fruit, nuts, almonds, and pieces of chocolate. They vary according to the different areas and times of the year, particularly holidays. Although many still enjoy making their own cookies at home, above all on special occasions, most people buy them from bakeries and pastry shops. Commercial brands produced by food industries and sold in grocery shops and supermarkets are also extremely popular. A specific variety of cookies called *savoiardi* (which are similar to lady fingers), are used to make the popular *tiramisù*. The cookies, soaked in liquors and coffee, are placed in layers and covered with a cream made of *mascarpone* cheese (a sort of cream cheese), eggs, and coffee. The cake is then dusted with powdered cocoa.

Crostata is a thin layer of *pasta frolla* (quite similar to shortbread, made of flour and butter) spread over the bottom of a pan, topped with homemade jam or fruit preserves, and baked. The *crostata di frutta*, on the other hand, is covered by a thin layer of custard cream and decorated with thinly sliced fresh fruit. *Pastiera*, a typical pie from Naples, is also made with a sort of shortbread, filled with ricotta cheese, boiled wheat grains, diced candied citron, and scented with orange flower water. Shortbread pies, similar to *crostata* in that they have no dough top, are commonly served in restaurants like desserts. The fillings can be ricotta, often with the addition of small pieces of chocolate (*torta di ricotta*) or custard cream, with toasted pine nuts on top (*torta della nonna*).

Many desserts use a sort of sponge cake, or *pandispagna*, as a base. It can be used to make multilayered cakes with various cream fillings, usually called *torte*. When the cake is made with slices of sponge cake soaked in

Colomba and chocolate eggs.

liquors, layered in a mold, and filled with vanilla and chocolate cream, it is then known as *zuppa inglese*. Some prefer *pandispagna* to make *tiramisù*, instead of *savoiardi* The famous Sicilian *cassata* is also made with *pandispagna* filled with a cream made of ricotta cheese, sugar, candied fruits, and pieces of chocolate, covered with a thick frosting of white sugar and decorated with candied fruits.

The baked cakes that achieved the widest international recognition and popularity are *panettone* and *pandoro*, the Christmas cakes of Milan and Verona. It is possible to buy them in both artisanal and mass-produced styles, and the latter is also distributed in the United States. The artisanal ones are definitely better, but they are quite expensive and not as easy to find. The traditional *panettone* is light and airy, with raisins and candied fruit, and the top is often covered with an almond frosting. Now food industries flood the market with new types, with creative fillings, different fillings, or no candied fruits. Another baked dessert with dough reminiscent of *panettone* is the Easter *colomba* cake, which is shaped like a dove, as the name suggests. *Pandoro*, despite the great quantity of butter it contains, is lighter and puffier than *panettone*, usually baked in a high eight-pointed star-shaped pan and dusted with confectioner's sugar. Also *pandoro* is industrially produced in different and imaginative ways, but purists tend to prefer the classic, artisanal ones.

PASTA

The main Italian staple made of wheat flour is certainly pasta.[1] Kneading flour, often from soft wheat, with water or eggs makes fresh pasta. Homemade fresh pasta or *pasta fresca* has become increasingly rare, because it is now possible to buy it in specialized shops, which usually produce it with the help of machinery. To make pasta at home, flour is poured on a wooden plank in the shape of a volcano, often referred to as *fontana* or fountain. Water is poured in small quantities in the central hollow in the flour, allowing cooks to knead it into a dough starting from the center and adding water as they incorporate more flour in the dough. To give pasta different colors, sometimes tomato or spinach are added, but in that case less water or eggs are required, because the vegetables tend to increase the amount of humidity.

Once the dough is ready, it is kneaded in different ways. To make *fettuccine* or *tagliatelle*, for example, the dough would be flattened into a thin sheet or *sfoglia* with the aid of a wooden rolling pin and then cut into long ribbons with a knife. Obtaining an even, smooth *sfoglia* is no small deal: In Bologna the *sfogline*, or *sfoglia* women, who are in charge of this delicate operation, command high respect. Many cooks use a pasta rolling machine, operated by a manual or electric crank, composed of heavy metal cylinders between which the dough is rolled until it reaches the required thinness. Some of these cylinders also cut the pasta in the desired shapes. Once ready, the pasta must dry to lose excess humidity before it is dropped in boiling water to cook. Especially in the south, Italians like their pasta *al dente,* which means, literally, "hard to the tooth." Over-cooked pasta is often frowned upon.

To make *lasagne* or *cannelloni, sfoglia* is cut into squares or rectangles. For *cannelloni,* the squares are rolled and filled with meat, mozzarella, or vegetables, usually spinach. When making *lasagna,* the squares of pasta are placed in layers in a pan, with a filling in between layers that can contain meat, grated *parmigiano reggiano*, and béchamel sauce. *Lasagna* is then covered with sauce, diced mozzarella, and cheese and passed in the oven. Different versions of this dish are found in many regions of Italy. In Marche, for instance, butter and some drops of sweet wine like *Vin Santo* or *Marsala* are added to the dough, and the filling includes different kinds of offal. The resulting *lasagna* is called *vincisgrassi.* In many southern areas, a special pie called *timballo* is made: A pan is covered with *sfoglia* and then filled with cooked pasta such as *maccheroni* or *penne,* and then meat sauce, mozzarella, vegetables, mushrooms, and eggs are added. The pie is cooked in the oven and then cut in slices.

Pasta ripiena, or filled pasta, such as *ravioli, agnolotti,* and *tortelli,* are all square shaped, and *tortellini,* which is bite-sized rings, are conceptually similar to the above-mentioned *cannelloni* and *lasagna.* A small square of thin, fresh pasta is filled with various ingredients, usually meat, cheese,

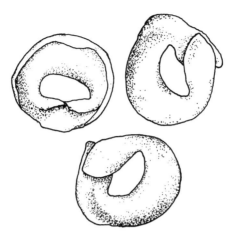

Tortellini.

and bread crumbs.[2] In the vegetarian versions, ricotta cheese and spinach are often used for the filling: These are called *ravioli di magro*, which means, literally, "lean," referring to the days when the religious calendar excluded the consumption of meat, which was considered fat. In Abruzzo, the ricotta-filled *ravioli* are sometimes sweetened with sugar, even if the light tomato sauce used to season them is savory. There are different theories about the origin of *pasta ripiena*: It could have been a method to recycle whatever was left over from a banquet, especially meat and the slices of bread that were used as dishes. This would explain the frequent presence of bread crumbs in the filling. Another theory considers this kind of pasta as a way to enjoy all the best the market and the pantry of a wealthy house could offer; hence the presence of *parmigiano*, *prosciutto*, and spices in the *tortellini* from Bologna and braised or roasted meat in the *agnolotti* from Piedmont. Others connect *pasta ripiena* with dumplings made of meat and other ingredients, not wrapped with dough, which are mentioned in recipe books from the Middle Ages and which still exist in Trentino, like *canederli*, big round balls made of bread, smoked ham, and liver that are cooked in boiling water. Whatever the origin, *pasta ripiena* is an all-time favorite in all its versions. It is usually consumed in meat broth or seasoned with melted butter, more rarely with heavy cream or sauce. An unusual type of *tortelli* is made in the city of Mantova, in Emilia, with a filling composed of pumpkin, *amaretto* cookies, and *mostarda*, candied fruits in syrup spiced by mustard seeds. The sweetness of the filling is balanced by melted butter and sage used to season the ravioli. In recent years, new *pasta ripiena* has been created to boost sales and give consumers a wider choice of unusual treats. Filling can vary from all kind of vegetables to fish and lobster, but the concept remains the same.

Besides *pasta ripiena*, shapes of homemade fresh pasta vary according to local traditions. In Piedmont, thinly cut and thick *fettuccine* with some grated *parmigiano reggiano* in the dough are called *tajarin*, usually cooked in a soup together with beans, *lardo* (cured pork fat), onion, potatoes, and other ingredients.[3] The *garganelli* from Romagna are made with a dough with grated *parmigiano reggiano* and nutmeg; the *sfoglia* is cut in squares that are then wrapped around a thin stick and rubbed against a sort of comb that gives them an uneven surface. In Puglia, people are particularly fond of *orecchiette*. The dough is kneaded into long, thin cylinders and then cut in small pieces that are shaped to suggest an ear (hence the name, which means "small ears"). The process is carried out by hand, with swift finger movements that are mastered only with practice. In Abruzzo, *spaghetti alla chitarra* are very popular: large and long rectangles of pasta are placed on top of a special tool, called a *chitarra* or "guitar," made of thin metal strings pulled over a wooden frame. With the help of a rolling pin, the pasta is pressed and cut through the strings in the shape of thick spaghetti with a square section. In the Veneto region, *bigoli* are made by pressing dough through a little extruder and by cooking it without drying it for very long.

A peculiar type of dough that cannot actually be considered pasta is the *passatelli* from Romagna. A liquid mixture of bread crumbs, beef marrow, eggs, and nutmeg is passed through a skimmer directly into boiling broth.

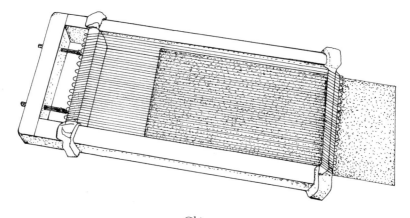

Chitarra.

While in the past fresh pasta was more common in the northern and central part of the peninsula, until the late nineteenth century *pasta secca*, or "dried pasta," was mainly limited to southern Italy. The reason for this geographical difference is probably that dried pasta is made with durum wheat, mainly grown in the south, and it also requires a less humid climate to dry more quickly and uniformly. These conditions were clearly absent in most of northern regions, with the exception of Liguria, which, for its mild climate, has been an important pasta-producing region since the thirteenth century.

In recent years pasta industrial producers have been trying to introduce new shapes, but usually with little success. To widen consumers' choices, they now prefer to rediscover old or almost forgotten traditional or local shapes and mass-produce them. Nevertheless, numerous small companies still make dried pasta in a more traditional way, defined as *artigianale*. The difference lies in the material of the dies in the pasta-extruding machinery. While big producers employ plastic or aluminum alloy dies, which allows faster production and shorter drying periods, the makers of pasta *artigianale* stick to the more traditional bronze dies, the surfaces of which make machines work slower, but at the same time ensure a rougher surface to the final product. Because of this, sauce adheres better to the pasta.

Different pasta shapes tend to be used with different sauces and condiments according to local tradition or nationwide habits. New combinations are acceptable and are actually implemented, but some long-lasting pairings are maintained, and in this case variations are frowned upon. For instance, the Italian-American dish spaghetti bolognese is virtually unheard of in Italy. In Bologna, spaghetti would never be seasoned with the minced meat and tomato sauce that gets its name from the city, used only for *tagliatelle* or *fettuccine*. *Linguine* (a kind of slightly flatter spaghetti) would normally be used with *pesto* or fish and seafood-based sauces, but seldom with meat. Spaghetti are probably the most versatile kind of pasta: They can be served *carbonara* style (with onions, bacon, and eggs), *aglio e olio* (just garlic sautéed in olive oil with some red chili pepper), or with a simple tomato and basil sauce. *Bucatini* (thick spaghetti in the shape of a thin pipe) are popular with *amatriciana* sauce (pork cured cheek or *guanciale*, onions, crushed fresh tomatoes).

Pasta is not only seasoned with sauces. In recent years it has not been rare to see it used as the main ingredient in cold salads that are particularly popular in summer, especially with young people who do not particularly like to cook. Tossing a few ingredients together with boiled pasta can make a quick dish for dinner or a party.

SOUPS

Pasta is also a very common ingredient in vegetable soups or *minestre*, also called *minestroni*: Vegetables and herbs are cooked together with different kinds of pasta, sometimes with potatoes or beans added to increase the thickness. Although regional and local habits determine which vegetables, herbs, and pasta go together, this kind of dish is widely popular all over the peninsula. When pasta is absent, this dish is called *zuppa*. In Liguria and Tuscany, olive oil is the main fat ingredient in the *minestrone*, while in other parts of the country is not unusual to find minced lard, pork rinds, or *prosciutto* in these dishes. The most common *minestra* is probably the ubiquitous and simple *pasta e fagioli* (pasta and bean soup), particularly popular in Veneto but otherwise appreciated all over Italy. Carrots, celery, cabbage, squash, chickpeas, peas, fava beans, and artichokes are some of the vegetables used in *minestre*, which were perceived in the years of industrialization as a legacy of poverty and backward life, or at least exclusively considered as comfort food. Starting from the 1980s, these dishes have been rediscovered as elements of a cultural identity that risked disappearing, while their health value is now highly appreciated, constituting an important element of what nowadays is called a Mediterranean diet.

The richest *minestra* is probably the *virtù* (virtues), a traditional dish prepared at the beginning of spring in Abruzzo, with at least seven kinds of dried pulse, seven fresh vegetables, seven kinds of pasta, cheese, lard, prosciutto, and pork rinds. In the local rural culture, whatever was left in the cupboard after the cold and dreary days of winter ended up in the boiling pot, so that the *virtù* symbolized the passage to the new season.[4]

Tuscan Tomato and Bread Soup (*Pappa al Pomodoro*)

- 1/3 cup extra-virgin olive oil
- 1 medium onion, finely minced
- 1 stalk celery, finely minced
- 1 medium carrot, finely minced
- 1 clove garlic, finely minced
- 1 tablespoon finely minced parsley
- 3 cups stale Italian bread, crust removed, cut into 1 inch cubes
- 1 1/2 pound red tomatoes, peeled, seeded, and chopped
- 3 cups chicken broth
- 4 basil leaves, minced

- salt

- pepper

Heat the olive oil in a soup pot over medium heat. Add the onion, celery, carrot, garlic, and parsley, and sauté until the vegetables are soft. Add the bread and stir for a couple of minutes. Add the tomatoes, let cook for 5 minutes, and then add the warm broth. Season with salt and pepper. Reduce the heat and let simmer, uncovered, till the bread dissolves into a thick, creamy soup. Remove from the heat and allow the soup to rest for 20 minutes. Serve at room temperature, garnishing each portion with a drizzle of extra-virgin olive oil and a sprinkling of basil.

RICE

Rice is widely used in *minestre* instead of pasta. In Veneto, dense and thick vegetable and rice soups are very popular, the most renowned being *riso e bisi,* rice and peas. The grains are poured into the boiling broth, in such quantities that at the end of the preparation they absorb most of the liquid. Peas and other ingredients are added at the end, so that they do not melt in the soup. Another traditional way of cooking rice is *risotto.* The grains are first sautéed in butter and onion until they become translucent, and then hot meat broth is added slowly, ladle after ladle, while stirring and waiting for each ladle of broth to be absorbed before adding another.

This process is carried out in a pot without a lid. This is the main difference with the Turkish style *pilaff* rice, in which the pot is filled with broth, covered, and put into the oven till the liquid is absorbed. Nevertheless, the cooking process is quite similar, giving good reasons for scholars to consider an Oriental origin for the diffusion of rice in Italy. It is not certain how rice become a staple in Italy, since until the Middle Ages it was mainly used as a thickening agent or an ingredient in medicine. It is certain that Muslim peoples grew rice in Sicily during their domination there and that the Crusaders brought the cereal back from the Holy Land, but rice never became popular in the south.

At the end of the Renaissance, we already find it as a staple in northern Italy, in the plains along the Po River, especially in the Piedmont areas of Vercelli and Novara, and around the cities of Mantova and Pavia in Lombardy. Innumerable rice recipes are available in these regions. The most famous one is probably the *risotto alla milanese,* cooked with saffron. In Piedmont we find the *risotto all'albese,* named after the city of Alba, with shaved truffle and roasted meat gravy; the *risotto* with frog meat (before the use of chemicals in agriculture, the rice pads in the area provided plenty of fresh frogs); and the *paniscia,* where the rice is sautéed in onion, *lardo*, and a special salami called *d' la duja*, before adding broth and other ingredients. In Lombardy, besides the already mentioned rice with frog meat and *risotto alla milanese*, people are fond of *risotto* made with different kinds of freshwater fish, depending on the area (crawfish, perch, pike, or tench). Around Mantova *riso alla pilotta* is particularly popular: The grains are boiled and then seasoned with grated *parmigiano reggiano* and ground-up salami and meat previously sautéed in butter.

In recent years, fish-based *risotto* (*risotto alla pescatora*) has become very popular in all its possible versions, often with the addition of fresh tomatoes to give it more color. These dishes seem to have conquered the southern regions, where rice, though well known, was never considered a staple.

In the south, rice was mainly used for special dishes, often boiled and then fried in small balls, filled with different ingredients and powdered with bread crumbs. In this category, we can list *supplì* in Rome, where the rice is seasoned with tomato sauce and filled with diced mozzarella before frying, and *arancini* in Sicily, containing usually peas or ham. Rice would also be the main ingredient for special festive dishes. We can mention the Sicilian *tummala*, a gratin made of *risotto* and different kinds of boiled and roasted meat, the *tiella di riso, cozze e patate* (a casserole of rice, mussels, and potatoes) in Puglia, cooked in a ceramic crock pot in the oven, and the Neapolitan *sartù*, a semispherical pie filled with *prosciutto*, tiny meatballs, mozzarella, and provolone cheese.[5] Southern populations got acquainted with rice as an everyday staple only after the unification of Italy, when they were required to join the Army and were often served overcooked rice soups that at first did not help making the cereal more palatable.

Italian rice grains tend to be more rounded than varieties from other countries. From the commercial point of view, rice is classified in four categories that show different degrees of resistance to heat: *comune* or *originario* types (including varieties such as Balilla or Raffaello); *semifino* (the most renowned variety is Vialone Nano); and *fino* and *superfino*, among which are the most famous Arborio, Carnaroli, and Baldo varieties. When they cook, Italian rice varieties tend to release starch and thus are particularly good for creamy *risotto* or thick soups.

In the past 20 years, rice salads have become common dishes. Just like pasta salads, they constitute a practical way to assemble a fast meal without too much work. Rice salads are usually consumed in summer. Boiled cold rice is mixed with all kinds of ingredients, according to the cook's taste. These dishes require different kinds of rice than the ones traditionally grown in Italy: The results are best when the grains stay separated, yet fully cooked. Precisely for this reason, long-grain rice, such as the U.S. Carolina rice, have become popular, together with parboiled rice.

Mussel and Potato Rice Casserole from Puglia

- 3 pounds fresh mussels
- 1 1/2 pounds starchy potatoes, such as Yukon Gold
- 1 pound fresh zucchini
- 1 pound white onions
- 1 pound short-grain rice, such as *arborio*
- 5 ounces grated Romano cheese
- 2 tablespoons chopped fresh parsley
- 4 tablespoons extra-virgin olive oil
- 1 medium ripe tomato, sliced
- salt
- pepper

Clean the mussels with a stiff brush and place them in a large pan with some water. Cover the pan and put it over medium heat, until the mussels open. Discard any unopened mussels. Remove the mussels and filter the liquid left in the pan through a fine sieve to eliminate all traces of sand. When cool, remove the top shell of each mussel, leaving the mussels attached on the half shell.

Peel the potatoes and cut them in 1/8-inch slices. Wash and thoroughly dry the zucchini. Trim the ends and cut into 1/8-inch slices. Peel and slice the onions. Mix the raw rice with the grated cheese and the parsley. Season it with salt and pepper.

Lightly oil the bottom of a large baking dish or, better, a glazed earthenware pot, with 2 tablespoons of olive oil. Cover the bottom with half of the sliced onions and layer some mussels over the onions very close to each other. Cover with a layer of potatoes, then a layer of zucchini, and finally a layer of rice. Repeat the layering, starting with the onions. Remember that the last layer must be potatoes and that the dish must not be full to the brim, because the rice tends to expand when cooked. Arrange the tomato slices on top for decoration, and pour the reserved mussel juice over all the ingredients. Add enough warm water to reach the last layer. Pour the remaining 2 tablespoons of olive oil on top of the casserole. Cover with foil and bake at 350°F for 45 minutes, until the liquid is completely absorbed and the potatoes are tender. Let sit for 15 minutes before serving.

MAIZE

While wheat and rice have been grown in Italy for centuries, maize (called *mais* or *granturco*, Turkish grain, to express its exotic origins) was introduced only in the sixteenth century, enjoying an almost immediate popularity, especially in the northern regions of Italy. Its popularity spread so far that in certain areas of Veneto and Friuli Venezia Giulia, it almost replaced any other grains. These Italian populations had not learned to treat maize with alkaline substances to avoid a lack of vitamins such as B12. Because in times of scarcity maize constituted most of their daily carbohydrate intake, they commonly suffered from a disease derived from insufficient vitamin intake called *pellagra*, which caused skin eruptions. Although corn on the cob is appreciated both grilled and boiled, and corn grains have found their way into cold and warm salads, maize is mainly consumed in the form of *polenta*. Kernels are ground into flour similar to American grits, with the difference that the kernel germ is not eliminated by a soaking in wood ash, lye, or baking soda as in the case of grits. The flour is then slowly simmered in boiling water to various degrees of thickness, according to different recipes and local traditions.

In some areas other ingredients are added during the cooking process. In Piacenza and Reggio, in the Emilia Romagna region, beans or fava beans, together with *lardo* or *pancetta*, are used to flavor *polenta*. In Piedmont, *polenta* is called *cunsa* with the addition of small dices of *toma*, *fontina*, and *parmigiano* cheeses. In Lombardy a mix of ground lard, garlic, and parsley is spread on top (*gras pistà*), while in Veneto various condiments with a dried cod base are preferred. *Polenta* is often simply used as an accompaniment for all kinds of dishes. In this case it is cooked very thick, cut in slices, and then sautéed in a pan or grilled. Slices of *polenta* can be arranged on a low, flat pan, covered with all kinds of seasoning (for example, gorgonzola cheese, *porcini* mushrooms. or bacon) and then cooked in the oven to a crisp. Another common way to use *polenta* is to cook it until it is liquid, pour it onto a dish, and cover it with different kinds of tomato sauce, usually with beef meat or sausages. In Veneto, one of the regions where *polenta* is particularly popular, the sauce sometimes is made with horsemeat or even larks in the *polenta con gli osei* (literally, "polenta with birds").

Polenta with *Porcini* Mushrooms

- 2 quarts (8 cups) water
- salt
- 3/4 pound *polenta* (coarsely ground cornmeal)
- 7 ounces dried *porcini* mushrooms
- 1 clove garlic
- 1 teaspoon fresh parsley, chopped
- 2 tablespoon olive oil
- 3/4 cup whole milk

- 5 ounces imported *fontina* cheese, diced
- 1 tablespoon flour
- 2 tablespoons butter

In a heavy-bottomed pot, bring the 2 quarts of water to a boil. Add salt. Slowly whisk in the *polenta* in a steady stream, stirring continuously so that the *polenta* does not form lumps. After all of the cornmeal is added, let simmer over medium heat for about 40 minutes, stirring with a wooden spoon, until the *polenta* is thick, soft, and smooth. It the *polenta* thickens too quickly, add some hot water.

Meanwhile, soak the dried mushroom in warm water. Drain them and filter the soaking liquid through a very fine sieve to remove any sand. Roughly chop the mushrooms. In a pan, sauté the garlic and the parsley in the olive oil, and then add the mushrooms. Add 2 tablespoons or so of the mushroom water and let simmer for about 10 minutes. Bring the milk to a boil in a pot. Whisk in the cheese, the flour and the butter. Stir until the cheese melts into a smooth fondue.

Divide the *polenta* among the serving dishes. Place the mushroom sauce on top of the *polenta* in the middle and pour the fondue around. Serve hot.

OTHER GRAINS

In Valtellina, a valley near Sondrio, corn flour is often found mixed with another grain, buckwheat, and the result is called *polenta taragna*. In Italian, buckwheat is called *grano saraceno* (Saracen wheat), or grain from the Muslim world. It is unclear if the name derives from its dark color or from the fact that it was believed to be introduced to Italy by the Muslims. In the same Valtellina Valley, buckwheat is used to make a special kind of pasta, *pizzocheri*, cooked together with *verza* cabbage and diced potatoes, and then seasoned with garlic and onion sautéed in butter, grated *parmigiano reggiano*, and diced *bitto* (a local cheese). In Valtellina, buckwheat is also the main ingredient for *sciatt*, a sort of pancake fried in lard and flavored with cheese and *grappa*.

Barley and *farro* have also made a comeback in the past few years, appreciated for their high-fiber content and health benefits. Barley, especially the so-called pearled variety, is sometimes ground to a flour, but more often it is used whole in soups. *Farro*, a very ancient cereal native to Italy, is mainly grown in Garfagnana near the town of Lucca, an area in the Northwestern corner of Tuscany, Umbria, and Lazio. Favored for soup, *farro* is also versatile in cold summer salads. Millet, oat, and rye are much less common, used at times to make different kinds of brown breads that in the past decades have become very popular because of their high-fiber content and nutritional value.

Farro Soup *(Zuppa di Farro)*

- 1/2 cup extra-virgin olive oil
- 2 ounces *pancetta,* diced
- 1 medium onion, minced
- 1 medium carrot, diced
- 1 medium stalk celery, diced
- 1/2 cup *farro,* soaked for 2 hours and drained
- 1 1/2 tomatoes, peeled, seeded, and diced
- 2 quarts (8 cups) warm chicken broth
- salt
- pepper

Heat 4 tablespoons of the olive oil in a large soup pot over medium-low heat and add the *pancetta* together with the onion, carrot, and celery. Sauté until the *pancetta* is translucent and the diced vegetables are soft. Add the *farro* and the tomatoes, stir, and add the broth. Cover and bring it to simmer. Cook for 45 minutes, until the *farro* is tender. Remove from the heat and season with the remaining olive oil, salt, and pepper. The soup should be served thick.

PULSES

Pulses, together with grains, were always especially important in the dietary pattern of Italian populations. Some Roman family names originated from the names of pulses: Cicero from *cicer* (chickpeas), Fabius from *faba* (fava bean). Etruscans and Romans ate them in the form of porridge. In some areas, fava beans and chickpeas are still consumed in this traditional form. In Puglia, Calabria, and Sicily, dried and peeled fava beans are slowly cooked in hot water until they become a purée, seasoned with salt and fresh olive oil. This dish is accompanied in Puglia with boiled wild chicory, while in Sicily, where it is called *maccu,* a potato or some pasta is added to it. On the northwestern coast of Italy, chickpeas are often ground to a sort of flour. In Liguria, *panissa* is made by mixing chickpea flour in water and then slowly bringing the batter to a boil until it acquires the texture of porridge. It is then consumed in three different ways: cold, cut into small pieces, in salads or with some olive oil or lemon juice sprinkled on it; sautéed in a small pan with olive oil and sliced onion; or cut into pieces and fried in olive oil.[6] The latter preparation is very popular in Palermo and western Sicily, where these pieces of fried chickpea porridge are called *panelle* and are often served in *panini (pane e panelle).*

On the coast of Liguria and Tuscany, chickpea flour is also mixed into a thin batter with water and olive oil and then spread on large, flat copper pans to be baked in the oven. The result, called *farinata*, is a sort of flat *focaccia*, not thicker than a fifth of an inch, which is usually cut into pieces, seasoned with olive oil, and consumed warm.

Chickpeas and fava, as well as beans and peas, are also consumed whole, often boiled and seasoned with oil, pepper, salt, and other herbs, or with fresh chopped onions in a salad. In Lazio, in spring, fava beans are consumed raw together with pecorino cheese: This is still considered the typical picnic meal for the traditional May Day outing. In some areas, fava beans are braised with small pieces of *lardo* or *pancetta* or *guanciale*. Fava and peas are cooked together with artichokes in a traditional Sicilian ragout called *frittedda*, used to season pasta. On the coast of Tuscany and Liguria chickpeas are prepared as *cacciucco*, with chard, or prepared with salted cry cod (*baccalà*). In Tuscany, beans are stewed *all'uccelletto*, with tomato and sage, or sometimes cooked with water, olive oil, garlic, and sage, inside a glass flask (*fiasco*) laying on the embers inside the hearth. The recipe is thus called "beans in the flask" or *fagioli al fiasco*. In Lazio, beans are often cooked in tomato sauce with the skin of *prosciutto*, called *cotica*. As has been mentioned, pulses are also used for soups (*minestre*), with or without pasta. Pasta with beans (*pasta e fagioli*) and rice with peas (*riso e bisi*) are some of the most common soups based on the pairing of pulses and cereals.[7]

Some pulses are also consumed dried, between 6 and 12 months from the harvest. Before cooking, they have to be soaked in water for a few hours, sometimes with the addition of some baking soda to make them softer. Lentils are peculiar in that they are only used dry. The most famous ones are grown on hills and in volcanic soil, such as the ones from Castelluccio in Umbria, Altamura in Puglia, and the Vesuvius near Naples. Some think it is necessary to soak them before cooking, while others believe that boiling them for a period between 30 to 90 minutes is sufficient. Lentils are usually boiled with onion, garlic, grains of pepper, bay leaves, and other herbs and then cooked either with pasta, and often tomatoes, in a soup or stewed with tomatoes and served as a side dish. Lentils are also cooked with *cotechino* (see the meat section later in this chapter) and tomato for a popular New Year's Eve dish.

Most pulses are now sold already cooked for all kind of dishes. Easy to find in any grocery or supermarkets, they are usually packaged either in tin cans or in glass jars. Peas and fava beans are also available frozen.

Besides the most common ones, it is still possible to find some pulses that were popular in ancient times but have almost disappeared, such as *cicerchia* (with a taste in between peas and chickpeas, and a particularly tough skin); black-eyed peas, which originated in North Africa and then were almost completely replaced by the beans coming from the Americas; and lupines, are still sold on the street like a snack, boiled and salted.

Chestnuts, although a fruit, were in the past used like pulses, that is to say they were boiled in soups or ground into flour. They played a fundamental role for the poor populations of the Appennine Mountains, who could rely on these fruits to survive in times of scarcity. Due to the low content in gluten, chestnut flour, as well as fava bean or chickpea flour, is not particularly apt to make bread or pasta, but can be made into a thick and nourishing porridge. Chestnut flour is also mixed with sugar, pine nuts and raisins to make *castagnaccio*, a dessert that can be baked or fried, which used to be very popular in Tuscany and Rome. Nowadays, chestnuts have become quite expensive because of their high gathering costs, and they are rarely consumed in these traditional forms. Rather, they are roasted and eaten peeled like a snack, especially in winter.

POTATOES

Just like chestnuts, potatoes ensured the survival of many populations during hard times and long winters. Introduced in the sixteenth century, they were not widely adopted until the eighteenth century, despite efforts from local authorities and scientists who pointed out the popularity of the tubers in other parts of Europe. During the wars that led to the unification of Italy, the Austrian enemies were often contemptuously labeled as potato eaters, *mangiapatate*. Potatoes can be gathered between April and November. When they are pulled out in spring, they are smaller and softer, with a higher content in water and a thinner skin. They are called new or *novelle*, usually roasted or sautéed without peeling but not very versatile for other purposes. Older potatoes, with less water and a higher starch content, are used in innumerable ways. The ones with a white pulp are particularly apt to be mashed and used in purées, croquettes, and similar dishes. The yellow pulped ones are better for frying, for cooking in pieces, and for salads. Dried and ground, potato flour is particularly useful when making cookies or when it is necessary to lighten any dough too rich in fat and eggs. Many potato-based preparations are similar all over the world. Also in Italy, potatoes can be mashed into a purée with butter and milk, fried, sautéed, boiled for a salad, roasted with grilled meat or fish, baked under wood-fire ashes, and sliced and baked in a terrine with different ingredients such as mushrooms or cheese. Some recipes, on the other hand, are typically Italian, such as the above-mentioned *tiella di riso, cozze e patate*. Potatoes are diced and cooked in a soup with other vegetables to which small-sized pasta is added to make *pasta e patate*. They are mashed and mixed with eggs, small pieces of salami and ham, pepper, and chopped parsley into a mozzarella-filled pie that is cooked in a frying pan; hence the name *frittata di patata* (potato omelet). In Tuscany and Romagna, potatoes mixed with eggs and cheese are used to fill ravioli-shaped fresh pasta, called *tortelli di patate*. Moreover, potatoes are often consumed with other vegetables, such as artichokes or string beans, in warm or cold salads.

Probably the most renowned Italian dish made of potatoes is *gnocchi*, which is easy to find all over the world. The word *gnocchi* refers to any little dumpling made of flour and water (or egg). For instance, *gnocchi alla romana*, which are flat and round shaped, are made with semolina flour and baked in the oven with butter and cheese; the already mentioned *canederli* are made with bread and small pieces of *salumi* or liver. In Tuscany *gnocchi* are made with maize flour, while in Friuli a sweet version of gnocchi is made with plums, flour, and potatoes. Even pumpkin pulp is at times used to make small dumplings. Potato *gnocchi* are usually made with white pulped tubers, considered more floury, boiled, passed in a strainer, and kneaded with wheat flour. Some add eggs to make the dough more solid. The dough is then shaped in long, thin rolls that are cut in small pieces and dropped in boiling water till they float again. Sometimes spinach is boiled, wrought out, thinly chopped, and added to the dough to give it a green color and a delicate flavor. Potato gnocchi can be seasoned in many ways; the simplest is just pouring melted butter and cheese on them. In some areas of Lombardy, melted butter is mixed with garlic, sage, and grated *parmigiano reggiano* to make the condiment tastier. Elsewhere a light tomato sauce is preferred, while some would rather use a thick meat and tomato sauce. In Liguria basil *pesto* is one of the favorite condiments. Other root vegetables, like beets or radishes, do not have a large diffusion. The only exception is carrots, which are eaten raw in salads, boiled with other vegetables to make soups, braised, or steamed as a side dish.

Potato Frittata (*Frittata di Patate*)

- 2 pounds starchy potatoes, such as Yukon Gold
- 1 cup grated *parmigiano reggiano*
- 3 large eggs
- 3 ounces fresh mozzarella, diced

- 3 ounces *speck* (smoked ham) or *prosciutto crudo* (cured ham), sliced 1/8 inch thick
- 3 ounces salami, sliced 1/8 inch thick
- 1 tablespoon chopped fresh parsley
- 2 tablespoons extra-virgin olive oil

Boil the potatoes in salted water until tender. Peel and, while still warm, crush them or pass them through a sieve into a large bowl; let cool. Mix in the eggs and the grated Parmigiano Reggiano. Dice the *speck* (or *prosciutto crudo*) and the salami, and add it along with the chopped parsley to the potato mixture. Heat the olive oil in a large, deep nonstick sauté pan, and when the oil is hot, pour in half of the potato mixture to form an even layer. Scatter the diced mozzarella evenly on top and cover with the rest of the potato mixture. Cook until the pie forms a golden crust. Using a large plate or pot lid, flip the *frittata* and cook the second side until golden. Serve hot, cut in slices.

VEGETABLES

Besides pulses and potatoes, many vegetables have traditionally played a very important role in the Italian dietary patterns, due to frequent lack of meat, which has been too expensive and hard to find in many rural areas. Nevertheless, in the sixteenth century, vegetables began to appear frequently on the tables of the wealthy. Rich, fresh salads have always been served as side dishes, and in summer they often become whole meals, especially when it gets particularly hot. They allow displays of creativity both in the ingredients and in the condiments, usually based on olive oil. Besides, many also opt for salad meals for health or diet reasons. In Italy, despite the growing supermarket and frozen-food culture that makes vegetables available year round, people still have a strong sense of the season in which each of the different vegetables is freshest.[8] Older generations knew very well that, besides being cheaper, vegetables are at their best in their growing season. Younger generations, after a few decades of confusion due to the social and economic changes, are now rediscovering this traditional wisdom, and most quality restaurants are very careful to change their menus according to the season. Nevertheless, many vegetables are pickled and conserved either in olive oil (*verdure sottolio*) or in vinegar (*verdure sottaceto*). These can be easily bought in any grocery shop or supermarket, but many Italians still prefer to make their own vegetables. Some other vegetables, like capers (*capperi*), are cured in salt.

In the past, onions were a very important food for peasants all over the country, often eaten on bread. In time, they have become the main ingredient for the cooking base in many dishes and sauces, called *soffritto*: garlic, onion, and celery, thinly chopped (and sometimes with *lardo* added) and slowly browned in either olive oil or butter. Onions are eaten raw in salads, either chopped or thinly sliced. They can be baked in the oven or stuffed with meat. They can be cut in rings and fried or mixed with eggs in an omelet (*frittata di cipolle*). They are used as the main ingredient for soups or as a side dish. Small, fresh onions (*cipolline*) can be pickled with vinegar and served as snacks with drinks or as a side dish with boiled meat. *Cipolline* can also be braised with butter and stock (*glassate*), sometimes with the addition of sugar and vinegar (*in agrodolce*). Similar to onions, scallions (*scalogno*) were traditionally eaten raw with bread by the peasants in Emilia Romagna. They are now cooked, used as the basis for many dishes (the already-mentioned *soffritto*) instead of onions. *Lampascione*, a slightly bitter vegetable similar to a small onion with a red, hard skin, is found only in the south. They are boiled and seasoned with olive oil and vinegar, baked with olive oil, salt, and pepper, or first boiled and then covered in flour and fried. In Puglia they are also thinly sliced, boiled, and sautéed with tomato sauce and beaten eggs. Leeks, which belong to the same family as onions and garlic, are mostly used to make soups, as in Lombardy where they are cooked with rice and chard and baked in the oven in a gratin, with béchamel sauce or cheese.

Garlic, because of its more intense and persistent flavor, is rarely eaten alone, as with the sauce called *agliata* from Liguria, in which it is mashed with olive oil and bread crumbs. Besides being chopped in *soffritto*, garlic is also used in whole cloves, peeled and sautéed in olive oil as a base for many meat, fish, or vegetable dishes. Crushed, it is inserted in small holes pierced in meat before roasting, together with herbs and spices. It is also rubbed on grilled bread to add taste to *bruschetta*.

Although introduced in relatively recent times, other vegetables, such as eggplants, sweet peppers, hot red chili peppers, and tomatoes, play very important roles. Eggplants were actually introduced by the Muslims in Sicily, but it took centuries before they were widely accepted. It seems that the first community to fully adopt them was the Jews, who all along kept closer contact with the Middle East. The very Italian name, *melanzane*, probably derives from the expression *mele insane*, poisonous apples. To this day, their use is mostly limited to the center and the south of the country, although they are also popular along the western coast all the way to the French border. Eggplants deploy all their versatility in southern cuisines. The most common dish is probably *parmigiana*, an eggplant pie that has nothing to do with the city of Parma in Emilia Romagna but gets its name from one of the ingredients, *parmigiano reggiano*. In fact, the dish is likely to have originated in Campania. Slices of eggplant, fried in abundant oil, are laid in layers in a baking pan, with tomato sauce, grated *parmigiano reggiano*, and diced mozzarella in between layers. The pie is then covered with a top layer of tomato sauce and grated *parmigiano* and successively put in the oven till the mozzarella melts and a crust forms on the surface. In other areas, diced, hard-boiled eggs are added, as well as diced *salame* and *prosciutto*. Another pie is the Tuscan *tortino*, in which the eggplants, sliced, covered in flour, and deep fried, are set in a baking pan, covered with beaten eggs and chopped marjoram and parsley, and baked. Stuffed eggplants (*melanzane ripiene*) are also cooked in the oven. The vegetables are cut in half lengthwise, and then the pulp is removed and mixed together with various ingredients, such as olive oil, bread crumbs, milk, garlic, mushrooms, eggs, and grated *parmigiano reggiano*, depending on the area. The hollow halved eggplants are then filled with this stuffing and baked. A very popular Sicilian dish is *caponata*, whose name may derive from *caupona*, the Latin word for tavern. Eggplants and other vegetables (celery and sweet peppers for instance) are diced and deep fried, sautéed in a frying pan with fresh capers, olives, basil, pine nuts, and raisins, and finally savored with vinegar and sugar. The dish is commonly served cold as an appetizer. A similar dish is the Neapolitan *cianfotta*: diced eggplants, tomatoes, potatoes, zucchini, and sweet peppers are sautéed in olive oil with celery and onions. These recipes show a certain similarity to the southern French *ratatouille* and other Middle Eastern dishes, revealing the culinary connections between different areas along the Mediterranean shores. Eggplants can also be simply diced and sautéed, with other ingredients such as chopped parsley and vinegar (*melanzane al funghetto*); they can be sliced, rolled, filled with mozzarella and tomato, and then baked (*involtini di melanzane*); they can be pickled and canned in olive oil. The list is almost endless.

Tomato (*pomodoro*) is another vegetable that has become extremely important, especially in southern Italy, where various methods were created to keep tomatoes in winter. They were sliced and dried under the sun or puréed and boiled in bottles to sterilize them (*passata*). At times, the strained purée was dried in the heat until it became a paste (*concentrato*) that could be added to all kind of dishes for color and flavor. Now tomatoes are available all year long in cans and bottles. They are available peeled (*pelati*) and crushed (*polpa*), as well as in the forms of *passata* and *concentrato*. Ready-made sauces are sold in cans, and fresh tomatoes are available even in winter, imported or grown in greenhouses.

Besides being used to make sauces for pasta, tomatoes can be sliced in salads, such as the summery *insalata caprese* (slices of tomato and buffalo mozzarella seasoned with olive oil, salt, and basil). Green tomatoes are often used in salads, while riper tomatoes are used for cooking. Tomatoes can also be grilled or filled with rice and baked in the oven. Some varieties are particularly good for sauces, like the famous San Marzano from Campania. In recent years, small cherry tomatoes from Pachino, in southern Sicily, have become the rage, not only in Italy but all over the world. This variety remained quite obscure until foreign markets started demanding it because of its shape and its versatility in salads and on pizzas.

Sweet peppers (*peperoni*) can be consumed fresh, sliced in salads, pickled, sautéed, fried, grilled, of baked. Because of their shape, they are often stuffed. The spicy hot variety (*peperoncino*), both green and red, is added to many dishes, mainly in the south (especially in Abruzzo and Calabria). It is used either fresh or dried, both whole and crushed. It is also soaked in olive oil to make the oil spicy.[9]

Other vegetables from the Americas, such as pumpkins (*zucca*), have a more limited diffusion. They are served as a side dish, baked, or made into a purée, or they are put together with pasta or rice, as in the pumpkin *risotto*. The famous *tortelli di zucca* from Mantova, in Lombardy, are stuffed with pumpkin, crushed *amaretto* cookies, and mustard-flavored candied fruit (*mostarda*).[10] In Sicily, pumpkins are diced, fried, and then sautéed with sugar and vinegar. A close relative of the pumpkin is the cucumber (*cetriolo*), originating from East Asia. In Italy cucumbers are mostly used fresh, sliced in salads. Zucchini are largely consumed all over the country, especially in summer when they are in season, due to their delicate taste and their low caloric content. They can be fried, braised as a seasoning for pasta, baked (in this case they are halved, emptied of their content and stuffed with various ingredients, often meat), grilled with a sprinkle of olive oil, or just diced and sautéed with fresh herbs.

Asparagus (*asparagi*) is very popular, both in its cultivated and wild varieties. In spring, when it is in season, it is possible to find thin, dark green, very tasty wild asparagus in fields, which is best in omelets or for *risotto*. Asparagus must be prepared carefully, first peeling the stems, then tying them together and placing them standing in boiling water, leaving the tips out of the water for a couple of inches so that they get steamed and they do not directly touch the boiling water. Once ready, they can be baked au gratin, served with melted butter and fried eggs in the *asparagi alla Milanese*, or stewed in tomato sauce with other vegetables, such as peas and artichokes. Other wild field greens are actually still used for cooking, such as nettle *(ortiche)*, wild fennel, watercress, and Roman chicory *(puntarelle)*, which in Rome are cut in four along the length, soaked in water till they curl, and seasoned with a sauce made of oil, vinegar, anchovies, and garlic.

Artichokes (in Italian, *carciofi*), with their characteristic iron taste that makes them quite difficult to pair with wine, also require special preparation. After cutting the tip, the external and harder leaves are discarded, and the fluffy material at their core is eliminated. Once cleaned, artichokes must be soaked in water and lemon, to avoid a change of color, and then dried before cooking. Innumerable preparations list artichokes as the main ingredient. Besides being eaten raw, or sliced in salads, they are cut in eighths, battered or floured, and then deep fried. In Sicily, they are stuffed with sausage, grated *parmigiano reggiano*, eggs, pine nuts, and raisins, and then covered in beaten eggs, fried, and successively braised in a tomato sauce. In Rome, two recipes are particularly popular. One, called *alla giudia* ("the Jewish way"), is a traditional Jewish dish: Artichokes are deep fried in abundant olive oil, but pressure is applied on them so that they open up against the bottom of the frying pan, allowing every leaf to become crunchy. The other recipe is called *alla romana* ("the Roman way"): Artichokes are quickly sautéed and then stuffed with chopped garlic, parsley, and marjoram, laid upside-down in a baking pan, and covered for half their height with water and olive oil. They are then cooked in the oven till soft. A close relative to the artichoke is cardoon *(cardo)*, a harder, thorny white plant the only edible part of which are the ribs, which require a long cooking time to become soft.

Fennel *(finocchio)*, a typical Mediterranean vegetable, can be boiled, braised, or baked au gratin. It is also often eaten raw, in salads or by itself, usually dipped in the condiment called *pinzimonio* or *cazzimperio*, made of olive oil, salt, and pepper, mostly as an appetizer. This simple condiment is used with many other fresh vegetables, such as sweet peppers, endives or celery. The latter is also added to salads, and it often becomes an ingredient for *soffritto* and soups. It is more rarely boiled or braised.

Leaf vegetables can be divided between those that are consumed raw in salads, and those that need cooking (although some of them are used raw at times). In the first category we find lettuce, escarole, cress, the increasingly popular arugula, and *radicchio*, a particular type of chicory, the most valued varieties of which are grown in Veneto, in the towns of Treviso and Chioggia. *Radicchio* is also often cooked, either grilled and seasoned with olive oil and salt, or used for more complex preparations, such as *risotto with radicchio*. The most common leaf vegetables that need cooking are chard *(bieta)*, spinach *(spinaci)*, wild chicory *(cicoria)*, cabbage *(cavolo)*, cauliflower *(cavolfiori)*, broccoli, and broccoli rabe *(broccoletti)*. They can be added to soups, boiled and seasoned with olive oil, or sautéed in the frying pan with olive oil, garlic, and other herbs. Spinach, boiled and minced, is also added to pasta dough to give it a green color, or mixed with fresh ricotta cheese to make a very popular stuffing for *ravioli*. Vegetables with harder leaves, such as cabbage, are also stewed or braised. Boiled and sautéed broccoli rabe, very typical in Puglia, is a classic accompaniment for *orecchiette* pasta.

Eggplant Relish *(Caponata)*

- 2 cups extra-virgin olive oil
- 2 medium onions, chopped
- 1 medium red bell pepper, cored, seeded, and diced into 1/4-inch pieces
- 1 teaspoon oregano
- 3 large stalks celery, diced into 1/4-inch pieces
- 1/4 cup black olives, pitted and chopped
- 2 tablespoons small capers, drained and rinsed
- 1/3 cup red wine vinegar
- 1 tablespoon sugar
- 1/2 tablespoon crushed red chili pepper (optional)
- salt

Heat a half cup of the olive oil in a large sauté pan. Add the onions and sauté until translucent. Add the bell pepper and a pinch of salt, and cover the pan. Stir occasionally until the peppers begin to soften. Add the oregano. Remove from the heat and set aside.

In another pan, pour another half cup of olive oil, add the diced celery and sauté until it starts to soften. Drain from the oil and set aside. Discard the oil. Pour the remaining cup of olive oil into the pan. When it is hot, add the diced eggplants and cook, stirring frequently, until golden brown. Remove from the oil and place on paper towel to drain.

Add the celery and the eggplants to the pan with the pepper mixture. Place the pan on medium-low heat, cover, and simmer, stirring occasionally, for about 15 minutes, until the different flavors blend. Be careful not to overcook the vegetables.

Before removing from the heat, add the capers, the chopped olives, the vinegar, and the sugar, and stir for a couple of minutes. Adjust the seasoning. For a spicy relish, add the crushed red chili pepper. Serve at room temperature. You can keep the relish refrigerated in an airtight container for 4 or 5 days. Serve as an appetizer, with crackers or leaves of fresh endive.

MUSHROOMS AND TRUFFLES

Mushrooms (*funghi*) and their close underground relatives, truffles (*tartufi*), have been appreciated in Italy since Roman times. The emperor Claudius loved *ovoli* mushrooms so much that its scientific name (*amanita caesarea*) derives from him. *Ovoli* mushrooms are still the most expensive: They are very rare, mostly consumed thinly sliced with a little olive oil. In some areas they are accompanied with slivered *parmigiano reggiano*, or with an anchovy-based sauce. Second only to *ovoli*, *porcini* mushrooms enjoy vast appreciation all over Italy. Both species can only be gathered, which makes them particularly expensive. Other species, such as white champignons and the so-called portobello—the same ones that are usually found in U.S. grocery shops—are commonly grown, but they lack the flavor intensity of wild mushrooms. Of course, it is dangerous to consume gathered wild mushrooms without having them checked by some experts or by the local health offices. Some species are highly poisonous, and they are similar enough to the edible species to constitute a real threat. Among the most common edible species, we can mention chanterelle (*galletti* or *finferli*), honey mushrooms (*chiodini*), oyster mushrooms (*gelone*), and morels (*spugnole* or *morchelle*). Mushrooms can be dried (usually sliced), pickled, and canned in olive oil, vinegar, or salted water, or consumed fresh. Dried *porcini* mushrooms, with their particularly intense flavor, need to be soaked in warm water before use, often in sauces or to make *risotto*. Fresh mushrooms can be grilled (usually the larger and meatier ones), sautéed in a frying pan with a little olive oil, garlic, and fresh parsley (*trifolati*), or also battered and deep fried.

Truffles, which are gathered wild with the help of specially trained dogs or sows, are probably among the most expensive foods in Italy. White truffles, particularly rare, are found near Alba, in Piedmont, and in smaller quantities in Emilia Romagna, Tuscany, and Umbria; they are best when consumed raw, thinly sliced over egg with butter, pasta, *risotto*, or meats. On the other hand, black truffles, which are less rare and usually found in Umbria and Tuscany, can be cooked. In Umbria, they are traditionally grated in warm olive oil and garlic to season fresh pasta; elsewhere, they are sliced and placed under the skin of roasted poultry, especially capon and pheasant, or ground and mixed in pâtés or terrines. Cheaper truffles, such as the white *bianchetto* and the black *scorzone* or summer truffle, have a much less deep flavor and are often sold at exorbitant prices to non-experts.

HERBS AND SPICES

Despite the craze for spices in the Middle Ages and in the early Renaissance, these exotic ingredients no longer play a very important role in Italian cuisine, with the exception of pepper *(pepe)*, both black and white. This has become a very common ingredient, and it is often ground fresh on many dishes and salads. Saffron, which gives a nice golden hue and a unique flavor to dishes like *risotto alla Milanese* and fish soups, is grown in Abruzzo, in the province of Aquila. The production is limited and extremely expensive. As a consequence, shops sell the somewhat cheaper saffron from Spain or the ersatz spice curcuma, from the Middle East.

The only areas where spices are still widely used in the kitchen are Lombardy and Emilia in the northeast, probably under the influence of Venice, which for centuries was a key trade center for spices. Later, the Austro-Hungarian Empire, which dominated the area, introduced dishes and habits from central and eastern Europe. In these areas, nutmeg *(noce moscata)* is often added to meat fillings in stuffed pasta and sometimes gives its flavor to braised meat; cloves *(chiodi di garofano)*, paprika *(paprica)*, and cumin *(cumino)* appear both in savory and sweet dishes. Cinnamon *(cannella)* is used all over the country, mostly for pastry.

Herbs, on the other hand, enjoy a much wider use. While in the past higher classes tended to prefer spices to herbs, which were considered less refined and fashionable, in the seventeenth century the use of herbs expanded from the kitchens of the poor and the bourgeois to rich tables. Herbs are still widely used in *haute cuisine*, especially by creative chefs who are finding interesting and stimulating ways to mix local traditions with the flavors of more exotic ingredients. Some chefs, experimenting in fusion cuisine, at times try to make their cuisine more original and interesting by an inordinate use of foreign spices in their dishes.

Basil *(basilico)* is one of the more versatile herbs in Italian cuisine. It is used fresh in salads, added to more elaborated dishes, or just chopped together with *parmigiano reggiano*, *pecorino* cheese, garlic, pine nuts, and olive oil to make the famous *pesto*, an extremely popular condiment for pasta originally from Liguria, probably the most renowned area for basil. Other typical Mediterranean herbs are oregano *(origano)*, particularly in the south, and rosemary (*rosmarino*), the latter often used in soups and to flavor roast meat. Bay leaves (*alloro*) and juniper berries (*ginepro*) are also used with roast meat. Parsley (*prezzemolo*) is mostly used chopped and sprinkled fresh on dishes, while salvia is particularly tasty with melted butter to season stuffed pasta or fish. Thyme (*timo*) and myrtle (*mirto*) are not very common, with the exception of Sardinia, where these herbs grow in greater quantities (myrtle is also used to make liquors). On the other hand, herbs like dill (*aneto*) and tarragon (*dragoncello*) are almost considered foreign and their use is quite limited.

FRUITS AND NUTS

Together with herbs, fruits and nuts of all kinds are grown all over Italy. Although now all kinds of fruit are available year round, most consumers are still very keen on buying only what is in season, not only because it is less expensive to buy then, but above all because the produce is at its best, even if at times it does not look that great. Imperfect-looking seasonal fruit is often much tastier than the beautiful, shiny, impeccable fruit that many outdoor markets and supermarkets offer. In the past decades, many tropical fruits have made their ways to the Italian table, such as bananas, pineapples, grapefruit, and coconuts. In recent years, also mangoes, papayas, and avocados have become more usual. Kiwi, originally from New Zealand, is now widely grown all over the country, to the point that Italy has become one of the most important producers in the world. The most common fruits are oranges, tangerines, pears, and apples in winter; strawberries and cherries in spring; peaches, plums, medlars, apricots, figs, melons, and watermelons in summer; persimmons, grapes and chestnuts in the fall. Fruits play a very important role in the Italian diet. A bowl full of fruit is often on the table all day long for quick snacks. Fresh fruit is consumed regularly at the end of every meal, before, after, or instead of dessert; fruit is more rarely eaten for breakfast. It also can be used as an appetizer; in summer, figs and melons are served together with cured raw ham (*prosciutto crudo*). Fruit is also cooked as dessert, diced and sliced into fruit salads, or used as an ingredient for savory recipes. For instance, it is not unusual to find cooked plums or apples as accompaniment for a pork roast.

Fruit is also dried and consumed during the winter, especially plums, figs, dates, and apricots. Some fruit is candied and used in pastry making. The most traditional are orange and citron, together with pumpkin, although now candied exotic fruit like papaya and guava are not rare.

Raisins are also very common; the most common varieties produced in Italy are the small and golden *sultanina* and the bigger and darker *Malaga*. Other varieties are imported from the Middle East.

Although they can be used fresh, nuts are mostly consumed dried or toasted. Walnuts, pine nuts, hazelnuts, almonds, pistachios, and peanuts can be bought as snacks, usually with added sugar or salt, or mostly as ingredients for all kind of desserts. In northern Italy, they are mixed with raisins and apples and wrapped in sweet dough to make *strudel*. In Tuscany, whole almonds are added to small cookies called *cantucci*, often dipped in sweet dessert wines. In central Italy, whole hazelnuts are kneaded with flour, honey, pepper, and other ingredients to make *pan pepato* (pepper bread). In Rome, a typical Christmas dish is *pan giallo* (yellow bread), made of flour, cocoa, raisins, dates, almonds, walnuts, and hazelnuts.

Almonds constitute a fundamental ingredient in pastry traditions. They can be used to make cookies like *amaretto* and specialties such as *panforte* from Siena, a sort of fruitcake with candied fruit and honey. Grounded and mixed with maize flour, almonds are one of the main elements of the *torta sbrisolona* from Mantova, a hard, flat, thin cake that cannot be cut but only broken in pieces. *Torrone* is a kind of nougat with toasted almonds (sometimes substituted by hazelnuts), honey, and sugar; it comes in different kinds: hard, soft, and chocolate covered. In Abruzzo, almonds are crushed in small pieces and mixed with egg whites and sugar to make hard cookies called *spumantini*. In Tuscany, thin diamond-shaped soft cookies made of almond dough are called *ricciarelli*. In many areas of the south, almonds are ground to a fine paste and, with the addition of sugar, made into marzipan (*marzapane*), which is used in many desserts. In Sicily, marzipan is often called *martorana*, from the name of a convent in Palermo famous in the past for its production, and it is actually shaped and painted with edible colors to look like peaches, apples, or figs. For Easter, marzipan is shaped like a lamb and given to the children as a symbol of the holiday.

OLIVES AND OLIVE OIL

Olives are a particular kind of fruit. Olive trees are traditionally part of the landscapes of many areas of Italy, from north to south. Sun and wind are very important elements for their growth. The light favors the formations of the nutrients and the flavor elements that characterize the fruits; and breezes facilitate the pollination of the hermaphrodite flowers and

Olives.

hence guarantee production output. Since ancient times, numerous varieties of olives (usually called *cultivar*) have appeared in Italy. Today there are more or less 500 varieties, with 50 being the most common.

In northern Italy, olive trees are found around lake Garda, the northernmost growing area for the olive. Further south, we find olives in Liguria, on the hills northwest of Venice, in Cividale del Friuli, and in Brisighella in Emilia Romagna. Central Italy is one of the main growing territories; oils from Tuscany, Umbria, and the Sabina area in Lazio are especially appreciated. Olive trees can also grow in relatively arid soils, if sufficient watering is provided, and that makes them particularly apt to thrive in the south. The most renowned production areas in the south are Campania, where the Greeks first planted olive trees, and Puglia, with a quite impressive output especially from the dry plains. Good crops can also be found in the southern and western parts of Sicily and in Sardinia (near the cities of Cagliari in the south and Alghero in the north of the island).

To guarantee high quality, olives must be whole and intact, not frozen or affected by any pest, insect, or mold. Especially in the south, when olive trees are vast and tall, farmers place nets under the branches and wait for the fruits to fall when they are ripe, or else beat the branches with long sticks to make the fruits fall. These methods, though, very often tend to bruise the olives, with the result that oils are more acid because the microscopic cavities containing oil in the pulp cells are broken. Gathering by hand (*brucatura a mano*), although slow and very expensive, is the best method to ensure the fruits are not spoiled. Moreover, once gathered, the olives must be brought to the mill (*frantoio*) and processed as soon as possible. In most areas the harvest takes place between November and December, cold months that favor a good extraction. Only in the south are olives gathered in spring.

There are two main milling systems: the traditional method with its three separate steps—grinding, pressing, and separating—and the continuous cycle, in which all the phases are unified. The traditional method starts by crushing the olives with massive circular stones *(macine)* and mashing them into a paste with the addition of water to lower the temperature. The paste, made by oily, watery, and solid components (the latter are called *sansa*) is then kept for 15 to 60 minutes in a state of slow movement *(gramolazione)* that facilitates the aggregation of oil in larger drops, which is easier to extract. The paste is successively spread on large disks called *fiscoli* (traditionally made of woven hemp, now plastic or stainless steel), piled on top of each other and squeezed under a hydraulic press. In this phase the solid part or *sansa* is removed from the oily and watery mixture *(olio mosto)*, which is then either centrifuged to separate the

Traditional olive press.

oil from the water or treated with a process called *sinolea*. In this case, *olio mosto* is passed through multiple stainless steel blades to which oil drops stick, allowing the extraction. Before bottling, oil needs to be filtered to remove dregs and sediments, usually sieved through cotton, although some producers skip this step in order to obtain a more opaque, rustic product, which nevertheless has a shorter shelf life.

In the continuous cycle method, on the other hand, olives enter the machinery at one end, and oil comes out at the other. Metal hammers crush the olives, which are then kneaded and passed into a decanter that extracts the oil by centrifugation. This method ensures a better handling of olives, a higher level of hygiene, and less contact with water, which avoids oxidation. Nevertheless, since the crushing by stone wheels usually ensures better-tasting oil, many producers have adopted a combined method, mixing traditional-style grinding and modern systems.

Each variety of olive, or *cultivar*, differs in size, taste, and growing periods, making the oils deriving from them different. Mixture of olive varieties (*olivaggio*) and *terroir* (depending on character of the soil, weather, exposure to the sun and wind, and cultivation methods) determine the character of the final product. Only in recent years has the profession of olive oil taster been publicly recognized, and also more refined consumers are now aware of the impact of elements such as growing areas, *cultivar*, and harvesting times. Small productions, difficult to purchase and quite expensive, enjoy growing success. Nevertheless, for everyday use, most consumers still buy mass-produced olive oils, displaying a sensitivity to prices as well as quality.

Oils are classified according to extraction methods, taste, and content in oleic acid. Extra-virgin olive oil must have an acidity lower than 0.8 percent, with an absolutely perfect taste; if the acidity is between 1 percent and 2 percent, but the taste is still good, then the oil is called virgin. It is simply labeled as olive oil when virgin oil also contains some chemically refined oil and its acidity is lower than 1 percent. *Olio di sansa d'oliva*, on the other hand, is obtained by extracting oil chemically from the *sansa* and mixing it with virgin olive oil, with a final acidity not higher than 1 percent. To be called refined, *olio di sansa d'oliva* must present an acidity lower than 0.3 percent.

Despite widespread prejudice, olive oil is very good for frying, because it is more stable than other oils at high temperatures. Of course, oil must be changed often, because if it is exposed to high heat for too long it develops peroxides that can be toxic. Besides, fried food should be consumed immediately, as soon as it is drained from the oil, before it undergoes oxidation. It is also a good rule never to warm up previously fried food. It is advisable to choose olive oils with a light taste, so that their aroma does not cover the food flavor. Despite the relevance of olive oil in the Italian diet, other vegetable oils are used for cooking and frying. The most common are those made from peanuts (*arachidi*), corn (*mais*), sunflower (*girasole*), and the so-called mixed seeds (*semi vari*). Lard was also formerly used for frying, but health concerns have now basically banned it from kitchens.

Food can be fried by itself, like potatoes, or covered with various elements: egg, bread crumbs, or batter, for example. Dollops of flour and water-based batters, enriched with different ingredients, can be dropped into frying oil to make all kinds of so-called *frittelle*. *Misto fritto* (mixed fried food) can be found on restaurant menus all over Italy. In Rome, for instance, many pizza places serve fried food as an appetizer, usually battered cod, rice *supplì* (rice balls seasoned with tomato sauce and diced mozzarella), potato croquettes, and zucchini flowers filled with mozzarella cheese and anchovies. Fried fish is also extremely popular all along the coast, especially in summer. Small fish, squid, and shrimp are usually just covered in egg or bread crumbs and fried. All over the country, meat (lamb chops and pieces of chicken and rabbit) and all kinds of vegetables are consumed fried.

Besides being used to make oil, olives are commonly pickled and cured: 35 percent of all Italian varieties are grown only for the table, with Sicily and Puglia having the largest production. These olives are either black or green. They are processed with various methods in order to free them of any bitter taste and make them last longer. Olives are commonly served as appetizers, as side dishes, as salads, and also as ingredients in many dishes. A flavorful way of serving black olives, for instance, is with diced blood oranges, olive oil, and oregano. In the town of Ascoli, in the Marche region, big green olives are pitted, stuffed with meat, covered in bread crumbs, and fried.

WINE AND VINEGAR

Vines have always been an important element in the landscape of many areas. Wine is a basic component in everyday meals. Nobody would renounce it; consumers would rather limit themselves to lesser-quality products.

The long tradition of vine growing means there are hundreds and hundreds of local varieties of grapes, called *vitigni autoctoni*, many of which

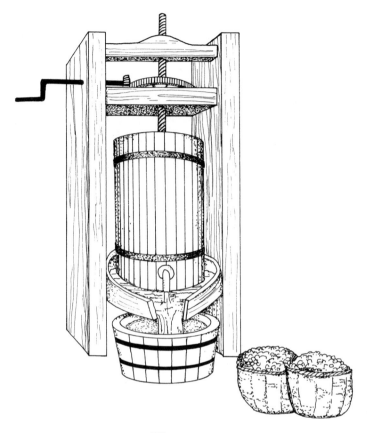

Wine press.

risked disappearing in the past.[11] Nowadays the production is limited to
vitis vinifera grapes, while fermented drinks from other grapes such as *uva
fragolina* cannot be called wine. The *phyllossera* disease that heavily hit all
of Europe, and Italy at the end of the nineteenth century, almost destroyed wine production and local grapes. It was necessary to import
plants from the Americas, which were resistant to the disease, and graft
the indigenous varieties on them to ensure the survival of the European
wine industry. After decades of oblivion, some producers rediscovered
many local grapes and applied new wine-making methods to them,
achieving standards of quality that have positively influenced the Italian
market at all levels. It is more difficult to export these wines abroad,
because their unfamiliar names and the sheer variety of these grapes in-
timidate many foreign consumers, used to Merlots or Chardonnays. Nev-

ertheless, these products are gaining more and more exposure, conquering an audience ranging from connoisseurs to amateurs.[12]

The three northeastern regions—Veneto, Trentino-Alto Adige, and Friuli—play a important role in the Italian wine market. More than one-third of the DOCs are produced in this area, even if it accounts for less than a sixth of the nation's total production. One of the most important wine fairs in the world, Vinitaly, is held every year in Verona, Veneto, while two very renowned oenology schools are located in Conegliano, in Veneto, and in San Michele all'Adige, in Trentino. Famous wines from this area are Tocai, Prosecco, Verduzzo, Refosco and Raboso, Teroldego, Recioto, Amarone, Lagrein, Marzemino, and Collio.

Piedmont is traditionally one of the most famous regions for red wines such as Barolo and Barbaresco—made from the local grape Nebbiolo—Barbera, and Dolcetto; among white grapes, Moscato, Arneis, and Cortese are particularly interesting. Oltrepò Pavese near the town of Pavia, the Valtellina Valley not far from Switzerland, and Franciacorta around Brescia constitute the main wine areas in Lombardy, with Franciacorta producing internationally renowned sparkling wines based on Merlot, Cabernet, Pinot Noir, or Chardonnay grapes.

Going further south, Emilia-Romagna is one of regions with the widest extension of plains in Italy. Lambrusco, often used to make sparkling red wines, is the typical grape variety in the northern part of the area, while in the southern part the white Albana and the red Sangiovese are dominant.

Two native varieties stand out along the Adriatic coast, the white Verdicchio in the Marche region and red Montepulciano, which originated in the Abruzzo and is now extensively planted also in other areas. In the Marche we can also find such fine reds as the Marches' Rosso Piceno and Rosso Conero.

The core of Sangiovese growing territory is Tuscany, where it prevails in Chianti—the nation's archetypal wine—as well as in Brunello di Montalcino, Vino Nobile di Montepulciano, and many other reds. Among the other red Tuscan wines, we can mention Morellino di Scansano, while for the whites, Vernaccia di San Gimignano is surely the most famous. In Umbria, besides the popular whites Grechetto and, above all, Orvieto, mostly made of Trebbiano, the reds Sagrantino di Montefalco and Torgiano have gained a deserved fame. White Malvasia reigns in Rome's region, especially in Frascati and the wines of the surrounding hills, also combined with the ubiquitous Trebbiano in Est Est Est wine.

In Campania varieties dating back to the Roman times, such as the white Greco di Tufo, Falanghina, and Fiano d'Avellino, have undergone a process of modernization that put them back on the map, with a vengeance. The red Aglianico, also grown in the neighboring Puglia and Basilicata, is producing great results.

Puglia and Sicily vie for leadership in volume produced, much of it in the blending wines shipped to northern places or in bulk wines distilled into industrial alcohol. Yet producers in these regions have become increasingly aware that the future lies in quality, as the volume steadily decreases. A wide variety of reds dominate Puglia and provide a delight to the wine lover's palate: Salice Salentino, Copertino, Squinzano, Aglianico, and Carignano. Sicily boasts famous wines such as Marsala, Moscato di Pantelleria, and Malvasia di Lipari. Besides these, many estates are working on white Inzolia and red Nero d'Avola to create high-quality wines. Calabria, a mostly mountainous region, produces interesting Cirò reds, whites, and rosés. On the other big Italian island, Sardinia, only a few wines have reached national fame: the whites Vernaccia di Oristano, Vermentino di Sardegna, and the red Cannonau grape.

Italian wine covers large portions of the world market, with France, Argentina, Chile, and Australia as the main competitors. This is a new phenomenon, after many years of low-quality production almost entirely absorbed by local consumption. After World War II, rural reform marked the virtual death of the huge underdeveloped estates that—especially in

Vino.

the south—had been a common form of ownership. Sharecropping was abandoned, and many farmers were able to decide about their own production. Italy, especially its southern regions, had become famous for dark bulk wines with high alcohol levels that were often used for blends with other wines. In 1956 the winter was particularly fierce, freezing vineyards in many wine-producing areas. At the same time, massive internal migration to the industrial cities resulted in a lack of labor. Landowners responded by adopting modern techniques and mechanical tools. As a consequence, in the 1960s and 1970s wine cultivation went from mixed cultures with vines planted together with other trees or vegetables to specialized vineyards, but at the same time producers became more concerned about the output quantity than anything else.

In the same years, following the French example, a classification system was adopted in other European countries, including Italy, which in 1963 introduced the DOC regulations. However, the first DOC zone, Vernaccia di San Gimignano in Tuscany, was only declared in 1966. Rules were established to determine who had the power to create new DOCs and how. Production regulations (called *disciplinare*) delimit the zones in which the wines originate and specify type (or types, since a denomination may include a range of versions), color, grape varieties, minimum alcohol levels, maximum yields in grapes per hectare and wine from grapes, basic sensory characteristics, fermentation (in wood or otherwise and possibly in sealed tanks), required minimum aging periods, and special designations identifying particular subzones, such as *classico* or *superiore*. The same 1963 law created the DOCG (Denomination of Controlled and Guaranteed Origin, or in Italian *Denominazione d'Origine Controllata e Garantita*). The first DOCG, Brunello di Montalcino in Tuscany, was actually established in 1980. A DOCG wine must meet standards that are stricter than those stipulated in DOC regulations. One of the main differences is the lower yields imposed by the DOCG rules. The limitations in output have probably done more to boost the quality of the wines than any other provision in the regulations, which also require in-depth chemical analyses for all DOCG wines. To this day, there are only 27 of them: Asti Spumante-Moscato d'Asti, Barbaresco, Barolo, Brachetto d'Aqui, Gattinara, Gavi, Ghemme in Piedmont; Franciacorta sparkling wine, Valtellina Sfurzat, and Valtellina superiore in Lombardy; Bardolino, Recioto di Soave, Soave Superiore in Veneto; Ramandolo in Friuli; Albana di Romagna, Brunello di Montalcino, Carmignano, Vernaccia di San Gimignano, Vino Nobile di Montepulciano, Chianti and Chianti Classico in Tuscany; Vernaccia di Serrapetrona in Marche; Sagrantino di

Montefalco and Torgiano Rosso Riserva in Umbria; Montepulciano d'Abruzzo in Abruzzo; Fiano d'Avellino, Greco di Tufo, Taurasi in Campania; and Vermentino di Gallura in Sardinia

Very soon, nevertheless, producers felt that this definition was at times both too restrictive and too inclusive. As a consequence, a new category was created in 1992, in compliance with the European Union regulations: the IGT (Typical Geographic Indication, or in Italian, *Indicazione Geografica Tipica*). The IGT regulations require use of authorized varieties, most of them establishing the use of one type only or in a ratio of at least 85 percent to other approved grapes. The IGT wines are identified with specific territories, most of which are larger than the zones specified in the regulations for DOCGs and DOCs. Some are region-wide, as in the case of Toscano in Tuscany and Sicilia in Sicily, while others are limited to a valley or a range of hills. For consumers, the IGT denomination primarily indicates a wide range of wines of acceptable quality available at highly competitive prices. It also allowed many local wines to acquire a higher status than the regular Table Wine (Vdt or *Vino da tavola*), that can come from anywhere in Italy and can be bottled anywhere or even sold in bulk *(sfuso)*. Italy is still one of the most important producers of bulk wine in the world.

Just as the government started implementing the new classifications, some innovative wine producers, who were particularly interested in experimenting, found the DOC regulations too restrictive. Back in 1968, in Tuscany, Count Incisa della Rocchetta, with the help of the oenologist Giacomo Tachis, created Sassicaia, still considered by many one of the best Italian wines. In 1971, again in Tuscany, Antinori started producing Tignanello. These producers substituted the white grapes that at the time were part of the DOC Chianti wines and introduced new varieties in the blend, such as Cabernet. Though officially classified as *Vini da tavola* since the beginning, these wines, known in the United States as Supertuscans, boasted an extremely high quality, which allowed them to be sold at high prices. In time, together with others such as Ornellaia or Guado al Tasso, they were able to compete with the great Bordeaux on the international market.

Italy was ready for a huge leap in quality. Many producers decided to change their production methods, renouncing large outputs to achieve a better quality: fewer plants per acre, intense pruning, and hiring oenologists with international experience. One of the first experts that tried to explain these changes to the general public, making wine popular and more accessible, was Luigi Veronelli, who in 1976 published the monumental *Catalogo Bolaffi dei Vini d'Italia*, the first serious guide to Italian wines.

While the innovative trends in wine production were receiving recognition, Italy was struck by a scandal that had deep consequences for many years. Methanol, a poisonous substance, was found in some wines from the regions of Lombardy, Liguria, and Piedmont, killing 14 people and causing intoxication and a few cases of blindness. Some producers had used methanol to cut wine in order to raise the alcohol content of their products. Although the Italian government issued many emergency regulations, the general perception about wine was profoundly tainted. Consumption fell to a historical low, while many Italians adopted, at least for a while, beer. On the international market Italian wines were considered with growing suspicion. The economic damage was incalculable.

It was only in the 1990s that wine reached a new popularity. Young people, who had for many years been attracted to soft drinks and, above all, beer, began drinking wine. It is now common for many Italians to buy good bottles on special occasions, and a few enthusiasts have nice collections, often stored in special cellars. Most families still have a bottle of wine on their table for every meal but breakfast, even if in some areas of the northeast, in winter, it is not unusual to see older people drinking wine in the morning. Wine is still bought in bulk for everyday consumption, but the general appreciation for high-quality wines is growing. At a restaurant, or when inviting friends over, hosts are careful when choosing wines to offer with every course. For this reason, wine-tasting classes and courses for professional sommeliers are now extremely popular.

Nevertheless, not all the wine is consumed as such. Some of it is traditionally fermented into vinegar, one of the most common condiments in Italian cuisine since ancient times. Although sometimes it is still produced at home, adding some vinegar or some "mother of vinegar" (*madre dell'aceto*, a colony of bacteria taken from another vinegar maker) to red or white wine, nowadays vinegar is mostly industrially produced and bought ready-made. Vinegar is used to season salads, to cook, and to cure vegetables. A special kind of vinegar, exclusively produced in the area of Modena in Emilia, is balsamic vinegar (*aceto balsamico*). Although many ersatz versions of it are now available all over the world, and sprinkling some of it on any dish seems to have become a fad, the real traditional balsamic vinegar is difficult to find, and extremely expensive. Grape must is cooked and allowed to slowly ferment in order to let it naturally turn into vinegar. The vinegar is then poured into small wood barrels, successively moved to increasingly smaller ones as the vinegar evaporates. Each barrel is made of a different kind of wood (oak, chestnut, and cherry, among others) so that the vinegar acquires different aromas in a process that lasts at least five years. The final result is a thick syrup, both sharp and sweet, which is perfect both on a salad and on ice cream or strawberries.

SPIRITS AND BEER

Italian spirits are traditionally made either by the distillation of the by-products deriving from the wine-making process or by macerating herbs and fruit in different types of alcohol. The most famous distilled spirit is *grappa*, obtained from pomace of grapes previously crushed for wine. Mostly produced in the northern regions of the country, it is usually clear but sometimes it shows amber hues because of the aging process in wood. Grape skins, drenched in must and freed from seeds to obtain the best products, are poured in an alembic placed on a heat source. The vapors are cooled into a liquid that is rich in alcohol (86 percent) and aromatic substances, which is often mixed with distilled water to lower its alcohol content. Usually the liquid obtained at the beginning and at the end or the process (called head, *testa*, and tail, *coda*) is discarded, and only the heart *(cuore)* is successively bottled or aged in small wood barrels. In the past, *grappa* was often considered a plebeian drink for mountain people. Only in the past couple of decades has this spirit enjoyed growing success, which in turn pushed the producers to improve the quality. It is now possible to buy *grappa* obtained from a single kind of grape *(monovitigno)* or from blends of different grapes *(polivitigno)*. Some producers flavor their *grappa* with fruit or herbs, a practice often scorned by purists. A less popular but related spirit is grape aqua vitae *(acquavite d'uva)* distilled not from skins, but directly from the wine must.

A whole category of spirits that enjoys widespread favor is called *amaro* (bitter) or *digestivo* (digestive), usually obtained by the maceration of herbs in alcohol and water. As the name suggests, these products have a low sugar content and a very peculiar, bitter flavor, which make them difficult to export abroad. Mostly consumed at the end of meals, *amaro* is often mentioned as a typical example of acquired taste. Other spirits obtained from the maceration of *sambuca* (elder) or *anisetta* (anise) are also consumed mostly within the country. On the other end, sweet liquor like *limoncello*, obtained through the maceration of lemon grinds in alcohol and sugar, is reaping the benefits of a growing popularity in Italy and abroad, also promoted by effective marketing campaigns.

The modern history of industrially produced beer dates back to the beginning of the nineteenth century. Consumption grew drastically in the second half of the century, when new techniques for refrigeration were developed. The first meeting of Italian beer producers took place in 1872, with around 150 companies. With the new century, the number of producers shrunk, while the output increased enormously with the rise of fascism and World War II. The industry, which is particularly strong in the sector of low-fermentation lagers, grew again starting from the 1950s, introducing big bottles that made beer available also for family use. Consumption is growing steadily, especially among young people who are more used to travel and are also exposed to foreign beers. Pubs have become popular, with many beers on tap, which unfortunately are not poured and served correctly. Bottled beer is sometimes a better option. Among the most important Italian producers are Moretti and Dreher (now both acquired by Heineken), Peroni (which also owns Wührer), Forst (based in Merano, in the Alto Adige), and Splügen and Poretti (both owned by Carlberg). A few small producers are limiting their activities to higher-quality, more expensive beers, such as Menabrea in Biella (Piedmont) or Castello near Udine (Friuli).

MEATS

While pulses traditionally constituted the main source of protein for most Italian populations and meat was limited to festive or special occasions, in the past 50 years the per capita consumption of meat has dramatically increased. In the past, the so-called Mediterranean diet, mainly based on carbohydrates and vegetables, was probably a forced choice for many farmers or less-affluent people in the country. When the economic development allowed them to afford more meat, they bought it. The trend is now reversed. In the past few years, also as a consequence of the mad-cow-disease scare, Italians are consuming less meat, especially less beef.

From the culinary point of view, there are various traditional ways to cook meat besides the most common methods of frying it in some kind of fat, roasting it in the oven, and grilling it. Boiled in water, it can be made either into *lesso* or *bollito*. *Lesso* means that the meat is placed in a pot with cold water, usually together with vegetables such as potatoes or carrots and herbs, and brought to a boil in order to obtain a rich broth. In this case, the meat ends up being quite bland to the taste, and it is customarily used to make meatballs, which are made richer in flavor with various ingredients and cooking methods (stewing, frying, or braising). In the case of *bollito*, meat is dropped in boiling water. The sudden contact seals the surface of the meat, keeping all its juices inside. If the resulting broth is less tasty and rich, the meat, on the other hand, is scrumptious and succulent. Various cuts of meat (beef, poultry, and pork cured cuts) are cooked together to prepare *bollito* in the northern areas of Italy, especially all along the river Po plain, where meat production is more diffused. The richer the *bollito*, the more cuts are added. This dish is traditional served with boiled potatoes, carrots, and onions, but a few sauces are also popular in some specific areas. In Piedmont, *bagnet verd* is made with parsley, garlic, egg yolks, bread crumbs, anchovies, and capers; *sausa d'avìe* has honey, walnuts, stock, and mustard as its main ingredients, while *cognà* is based on grapes, apples or pears, figs, cinnamon, and cloves. In Veneto, the most common sauce for *bollito* is *pearà*, made with bread crumbs, stock, beef marrow, butter, salt, and pepper.

Brasato (braising) is a cooking method particularly useful for bigger cuts of meat. The piece, first seared in butter, lard, or olive oil, is covered with liquid (wine, water, a marinade, milk, or broth) and left to simmer slowly with spices and herbs. *Stufato* is a method similar to braising, but the meat is simmered in liquid since the beginning, with no initial searing. When the meat is cooked to the point that it breaks down, the dish is then called *stracotto*. The most common stewed dish is *spezzatino*, made of small pieces of meat often cooked with legumes or vegetable. In Venezia Giulia, a particular kind of *spezzatino* is *gulash*, also common to many areas of central Europe, made of chunks of beef cooked with tomato, paprika, and potatoes. When meat is cooked with tomatoes, the resulting sauce is called *ragù*, and it is mostly used to season pasta. Sometimes this preparation is also known as *Bolognese* sauce. In the north, ground meat is mostly used, while in the south, especially in Naples, there is a preference for larger chunks. The meats of choice for *ragù* are usually beef and pork, although some people like to add some *pancetta* to it.

BEEF

While in the past poultry and pigs were the most important source of meat because they could be raised easily, in more recent years the consumption of beef and veal has increased enormously. Both are used for different purposes and dishes. The various cuts have different denominations according to the age and the area where the meat is sold. At times, even Italians do not have an easy time understanding what they are buying, especially if they are in a region other than home. *Vitellone* is male (castrated or not) or female (before giving birth) between 18 and 24 months. *Manzo* is a castrated male under 4 years of age or a female that has never given birth under 3 years. When the castrated male is older than 4 years, it is called *bue*, while the noncastrated male older than 2 is called *toro*, or bull. A female older than 3 or a younger one that has given birth is called *vacca*. Any animal younger than 18 months that weighs less than 300 kilograms and that has only sucked milk is called *vitello*. Veal meat is paler, its smell is vaguely milkier, and its fat is totally white, with no rose or red stripes. Sometimes hormones are used to raise the calves and make them bigger, although these procedures are outlawed in Italy. In this case the flesh has a higher content of water. Even at its best, *vitello* meat is not as tasty as the adult meat; nevertheless, it is more tender and more versatile for all kinds of preparations. It is especially popular in northern Italy. For instance, it is consumed in a light milk sauce, called *guazzetto*, or with a tuna fish-based sauce (*vitello tonnato*). A famous dish made of veal rib roast is the so-called Milanese cutlet (*cotoletta alla Milanese*): The rib is covered first in egg and then in bread crumbs before being fried in butter till its turns golden. Another recipe from Milan is *ossobuco*, slices of cross-cut shank (including the bone and the marrow) quickly passed in flour, slowly braised with onion, stock, and white wine, and then seasoned with chopped rind of lemon, parsley, and garlic. A veal cut that is quite appreciated all over the northern part of Italy is the lower part of the shank (*stinco*), either braised or roasted, while *scaloppina*, a thin, round slice from the rump, is popular all over the country. Veal is considered particularly good for small children, since it is supposedly softer, easier to digest, and less fatty.

Some cuts of beef are even eaten raw, as in Piedmont, where the best meat is roughly chopped and seasoned with olive oil and pepper (sometimes lemon is added to it). Beef is also thinly sliced and seasoned with lemon juice and salt to make *carpaccio*, which is often served with fresh arugula and tiny bits of *parmigiano reggiano*. In Lombardy, on the other hand, parts of the thigh are cured with pepper and salt and then aged. This *salume* is called *bresaola*, and it is usually consumed thinly sliced and seasoned with olive oil or lemon. Many also like to eat the bitter vegetable *arugula* with it.

Although beef and veal are now available all over the country, it was not so in the past. Cows were much more prevalent in the north, especially around the big Po River plain, where they were used to plow fields and had enough space to graze. The widespread presence of cows also made butter the most common cooking fat. In the rest of the peninsula, especially in the mountain areas in the south, cows were more infrequent and considered prized items. The consumption of their meat was uncommon and limited to the highest strata of the population.

Beef Stew with Peppers (*Spezzatino ai Peperoni*)

- 2 yellow peppers
- 1 1/2 pounds lean beef
- 2 tablespoons extra-virgin olive oil
- 1 large onion, thinly sliced
- 1/2 cup dry white wine
- 1 pound ripe tomatoes, diced
- fresh sage
- fresh rosemary
- salt
- pepper

Wash the peppers and cut them into thin slices, discarding the seeds and the white parts in the interior. Cut the beef in 1 1/2-inch-thick dices. Pour the olive oil into a large, heavy-bottomed pot. Heat the oil over a medium-high flame and add the diced meet, stirring until it is nicely browned all over, for about 10 minutes. Remove the meat from the pot and keep it warm between two plates. Add the sliced onion to the pot together with a few leaves of sage and a small twig of rosemary. Sauté until the onion softens. Add the meat and stir. Season with salt and pepper. Pour in the wine and cook until it evaporates. Add the diced tomato, cover with a lid, lower the heat, and let simmer for an hour, adding water if necessary. Add the sliced peppers and simmer for about an hour, until the meat is soft.

HORSE

In some areas, such as Veneto and Puglia, horses provided nutritious and tasty red meat, although it was constantly considered with suspicion, because only the older animals that had worked for years in the fields or for transportation were butchered, and the slaughtering conditions were not the best. It is still required that horse meat be sold in specialized shops with a specific seal (a letter E, like *equino*, another word for *horse*) so that it can not be passed for beef. Special breeds have been selected to obtain better meat, and nowadays its quality is quite high. High in protein and low in fat, horse meat, which has a sort of sweet taste due to the presence of the sugar glycogen, is considered particularly good for children and the sick. Horse meat is consumed as steak. It is usually grilled; braised for a very long time till the meat breaks down, as in the case of *pastissada de caval* from Verona; or, in southern Italy, rolled and used to make a tomato-based sauce for pasta. Horse meat was also eaten in Lazio as *coppiette*, thin salted and dried strips. Traditionally consumed when drinking wine, *coppiette* have almost disappeared.

PORK AND *SALUMI*

Well into the twentieth century, the small amounts of meat most people were able to obtain were not beef or horse, but rather pork, mutton, and poultry. Small animals were easy to keep in the villages or on the farms and did not require significant investments of money.

Pigs have always been popular in Italy, and it is well known that almost every part of the animal can be used one way or another, including inedible elements such as bristles and bones. The intestines and the skin (*cotenna*) are used to encase the ground pork meat that is cured, seasoned, and aged to become an *insaccato*, such as *salami*. Parts that in the United States would not be considered suitable for eating, like the tail, the whole head, the snout, the ears, and the feet, are delicacies in many parts of Italy. For instance, in central Italy, cheeks, ears, snout, and tongue are cut into pieces, boiled in water, aromatized with herbs and spices, wrapped in a cloth, and left to cool under a weight till it takes a solid form. This specialty, called *coppa* in Rome, is served sliced, often as a cold appetizer. In Naples, street stands sell pieces of snout and feet boiled in water with bay leaves and with lemon juice squeezed on them (*o pere e o musso*, literally "the snout and the feet" in Neapolitan dialect). When pork fat is rendered, the tiny bits of meat that are left from the preparation, called *ciccioli* or *sfrizzoli*, are used in several recipes. When the pig is killed, even the blood is gathered and used to make sausages or desserts (*sanguinaccio*), with the addition of ingredients such as sugar or chocolate, especially in the south.

Not much of the pig is actually consumed as fresh meat. The parts commonly used this way are those around the ribs and the vertebrae, the back, and the loin, in cuts such as pork chops, spare ribs, center rib roast, more rarely loin, tenderloin, and shoulder. These cuts are usually roasted or grilled, and more rarely, stewed. In central Italy, whole pigs are roasted with various spices, including garlic, pepper, and rosemary, till the skin is golden and crunchy. This preparation, called *porchetta*, is sold by the weight, with the tasty skin being extremely in demand. Sliced, it is often eaten in a *panino*. *Porchetta* is often sold on the street in specialized vans or in huts in the countryside that also sell wine and bread.

Nevertheless, most of the noblest parts of the pig are used for curing. Since pre-Roman times, pork meat has been cured and conserved all over

Italy. Most techniques to preserve meat were developed by Celtic cultures first, and then by Germanic cultures later. The Celts discovered ways to extract salt from the soil (as in the area of Salsomaggiore near Parma, in Emilia Romagna) and to use it to make pork meat, one of their favorites, last longer. When different waves of German populations migrated to northern and central Italy, they revived the strong interest in pork and wild bore, an element that had never subsided during Roman times. Furthermore, the vast extensions of wood and uncultivated land favored the expansion of pig herding, which did not require much care and organization. Since then, cured pork has always been a very popular ingredient all over Italy and on all kinds of tables, from noble banquets to farmers' pantries. Its success was due to the long duration and the culinary versatility of these kinds of products, which ensured cheap animal proteins when fresh meat was difficult to find or simply too expensive. If nomadic populations tended to consume very lean and almost wild pigs, which lost most of their fat during their outdoor life, the Romans began keeping pigs in smaller spaces in the proximity of homes and farms. The animals got less exercise, so their meat became fatter. Anyone who could afford it would raise their own pigs to slaughter them in the fall, usually October or November, when the cold climate would make the curing easier and the meat last longer. Sausages and other cuts would then be hung in cellars, in kitchens, or any place that the specific aging process for each product required. Pigs were raised all over Italy, with the notable exceptions of the coasts of Liguria, Tuscany, Lazio, and Puglia, which traditionally cannot boast any cured products derived from pig. The reason might be the abundance of olive trees in these areas, which enhanced the consumption of olive oil.

These traditional procedures and habits survived without much change until a few decades ago, when a new consciousness about healthy eating started favoring the leanest varieties of pigs again. At the same time, it became more unusual for families to raise and kill their own pigs; the animals are now raised, slaughtered, and cured in specialized plants varying in scale from small local producers to huge industries.

Cured pork meat can be generally called a *salume*, which indicates that salt has been used to preserve it. *Salume* need to be distinguished from *salame*, a particular category of *salume* made of ground pork meat and spices. When the cured meat is wrapped in a piece of pig intestine, skin, or other kinds of artificial wrappers and then aged, *salume* is usually called *insaccato*. We can distinguish two main types of cured pork meat—those that are made of whole parts of the animal, either with or without wrapping, and those made of ground meat, which necessarily require some sort of wrapping, usually a piece of intestine.

The most famous whole-cut *salume* is definitely *prosciutto crudo,* cured raw ham from the rear thigh of the pig. *Prosciutti* are produced in many areas, but the most appreciated are those from San Daniele, in the Friuli province of Udine, and those from the province of Parma, in particular around the town of Langhirano. The San Daniele *prosciutto* also includes the lower leg and the foot of the animal, while the Parma variety is only made with the thigh. The first phase of the aging process for the San Daniele requires the use of a press so that the *prosciutto* ends up looking thinner, while the Parma definitely look fatter. Other renowned areas for the production of *prosciutto crudo* are Valdossola in Piedmont; the Colli Euganei area in Veneto, including parts of the provinces of Padova, Vicenza, and Verona; Carpegna and Montefeltro in the province of Pesaro, in the Marche region; Norcia in the Umbria region, near the town of Perugia; and the Nebrodi mountains in Sicily. Each area developed its own techniques to cure and age the *prosciutto crudo,* according to the local climate conditions (including winds, humidity, precipitation, and altitude) and the cultural traditions. For instance, in the case of *prosciutto di Parma*—probably the most world famous because it is produced in larger quantities than any other—only salt is used in the first phases of the aging process, which takes place in a very cold environment. Only the upper thigh, still covered in its skin, is used. After a few weeks, all excess parts of the *prosciutto* (protruding bone, extra meat) are cut away to give it its usual look, and the meat parts are covered in a paste made of rice flour, pork fat, salt and pepper. The second and longer aging phase takes place in warmer temperatures. The whole process lasts between 12 and 30 months. At the end of the minimum age, inspectors from the consortium (the association of producers that certifies the quality) test the *prosciutto.* By inserting a needle made of horse bone in five specific places and by smelling the odors that stick on the bone, they can determine whether the *prosciutto* is fit for packaging and consumption.

Other *prosciutti,* similar in terms of curing and aging techniques, are made from leaner pigs, probably a result of the older custom of letting the animals roam free. These are called mountain *prosciutti (prosciutti di montagna),* which are usually lower in fat content but higher in salt. Besides, they tend to be slightly less tender, but nevertheless rich in flavor and texture. Sometimes *prosciutto* is cooked, and in that case it is called *prosciutto cotto,* produced both at the artisanal and at the industrial level. The same cooking process is applied to the so-called shoulder (*spalla*), the front thigh.

A very particular kind of *prosciutto* is *speck* from Alto Adige, an area close to Austria. The thigh, deboned and cleaned, is left for a couple of weeks in vats with water, salt, juniper, garlic, and sugar. The cured meat is then dried and exposed to the smoke of aromatic wood for about three weeks. Successively, *speck* is aged for six months in cool cellars.

Procedures similar to those for pork *prosciutto* are used to cure and age thighs of other animals such as goose in Mortara, Lombardy, and in Palmanova, in the province of Udine of Friuli; goat in Lombardy (the so-called violin); wild board in Tuscany, in the province of Siena.

Among the cured pork products that do not require any kind of wrapping or protection, *lardo* and *pancetta* are particularly important because of their extensive use in cooking. Although the word *lardo* can be used to refer to the fat under the skin of the animal (often ground and rendered to make *strutto*), it more specifically refers to the fat on the rear part of the pig's back. *Lardo*, which contains almost no lean meat, can be cured in different ways: in wood containers, as in the case of the *lardo* from Arnad, in Val d'Aosta region, or in marble vats, as for the *lardo* from Colonnata, in northwestern Tuscany. Different aging periods and the spices used to cure the meat together with salt give to each kind of *lardo* its specific flavor and texture. *Lardo* can be made into a paste used as a cooking base for sauces or soups. The same paste can be used to make roasts more tender and tasty. In this case small holes are made in the meat and then filled with *lardo* (or *strutto*) mixed with salt and herbs. When *lardo* is particularly tasty, as in the case of *lardo di Colonnata*, it can be eaten raw in thin slices, especially on top of freshly grilled bread, or *bruschetta*. *Pancetta*, on the other hand, is obtained by curing the ventral region of the animal. It usually contains more lean meat, and it is cured either with salt and spices or through a smoking process following the spicing phase. *Pancetta* can be bought either flat (*tesa*) or rolled up (*arrotolata*). Unlike bacon, it is seldom eaten by itself, although it is widely used in many local cuisines as a cooking base, thinly sliced or diced, sautéed in a pan and then added to specific dishes. A very special kind of *pancetta* is *guanciale*, obtained from the fatty meat right under the neck and the jaw of the pig (*guancia* actually means "cheek"). It is very popular in central Italy, especially in Lazio, where it is used to make a typical pasta dish, *pasta all'amatriciana*, together with fresh peeled tomatoes and onions. *Lardo*, *pancetta*, and *guanciale* were commonly used for cooking, together with *strutto* (also called *sugna*), made by boiling the fattest parts of the animal and then filtering it and letting it cool down to a paste. In the past few decades the culinary use of these products is less and less popular because of their impact on cholesterol levels.

The most renowned whole-cut meat in a wrapping is *culatello*, probably the most expensive *salume* in Italy, which is produced in the villages of Zibello and Soragna near Parma, in the Emilia Romagna region. From the name, it is clear that *culatello* is made from the buttocks of the animal (*culo* is the Italian word for "buttocks"). The buttock is separated from the rest of the thigh, and when the meat is still warm after the slaughtering, it is massaged in salt, pepper, spices, and wine and then aged for a couple of weeks. Then the meat is placed inside the pig's bladder and tied up in a peculiar fashion that gives it its characteristic drop shape. *Culatello* then needs an aging period of at least 11 months, favored by the humid climate of the Po River plain, where the towns of Zibello and Soragna are located. In this area, the anterior part of the pork's thigh is not discarded but used to make the so-called *fiocco*, processed as a *prosciutto*. The rest of the leg is deboned and sowed, after a treatment with salt and spices, in a triangular form. It is called "priest's hat" (*cappello da prete*, which used to be triangular) and usually served with a vegetable sauce.

Another cured pork cut aged in a wrapping is *capocollo* or *coppa*, obtained from the meat between the neck and the sixth rib, which is salted and often massaged with wine and spices (the recipes differ according to the production area). It is then placed inside a piece of intestine that protects the meat during its slow aging process. A similar *salume* is *lonza*, made from the middle back of the animal, which is slightly fatter than the *capocollo*.

Ground meat *salumi* are even more diffused than the whole-cut ones, especially because of their lower prices and the richer taste provided by the presence of fat and spices in the meat mix. *Salumi* can be distinguished in two main categories: those that can be consumed raw, and hence require a longer aging process, and those that need to be cooked. Between the latter, the most common are surely sausages *(salsicce)*, ground pork

Prosciutto and *culatello*.

meat seasoned with salt, pepper, and spices that are pressed into the pig intestine and then divided in smaller portions by twine knots, with the exception of *luganega*, a very long sausage that is cut according to different needs. Sausages, which are more or less spicy, are usually consumed within a few days after production. Otherwise they can be conserved in olive oil or *strutto* (rendered fat), which avoid the contact between the sausages and the atmosphere. In this case the sausages are usually eaten raw, spread on slices of bread. *Cotechino* is a special kind of sausage, made with meat, lard, and skin, all ground quite roughly and put into the pig's intestine, usually consumed after a long boiling and accompanied by various sauces. When the same mix is put inside the skin of the pig's leg, with the foot still attached, it is called *zampone* (big leg), which also needs to be boiled for a long time before eating. *Zampone* is very popular especially at Christmas and New Year's Eve, when it is consumed with mashed potatoes, vegetables, or lentils. A very particular kind of ground meat *salume* that needs cooking is *salama da sugo* (salami for sauce) from Ferrara, in the Emilia Romagna region. The mix, containing liver, tongue, and noble parts of the animal such as the sirloin, is mixed with red wine and other spices and then put inside the pig's bladder. The sausage is hung in a cool place for at least one year, until it dehydrates and hardens. When it is time to eat it, the *salama da sugo* is left soaking in a big pot of cold water, hanging from strings so that it does not touch the metal, and then brought to a slow boil for a few hours. The hardened meat then becomes moist and tasty again, and it is usually consumed with mashed potatoes or pumpkins.

The aged *salumi*, usually harder and eaten raw in slices, are called *salami*. They are innumerable all over Italy, and making a list would be impossible. Among the most renowned ones, we can mention the medium-grained *cacciatorino* and the fine-grained *salame Milano* from Lombardy; the *felino* from the area in Parma, in the Emilia Romagna region, which contains 15 percent of ground *pancetta*; the *salame Fabriano*, made near Ancona, in the Marche region, where *ciauscolo* is also made, a very soft *salame* that is usually spread on bread; *finocchiona* in Tuscany, with its characteristic flavor given by the presence of fennel seeds and of ground *guanciale* fat; the spicy *ventricina* from Abruzzo; the hard and spicy *salsiccia di Napoli*, quite similar to Spanish chorizo; and the soft and extremely spicy *soppressata* in Puglia, Calabria, and Sicily.

The same system is used to make similar products from other kind of meats, such as cow *salami* in the Val d'Aosta region, donkey and horse *salami* in Piedmont and Alto Adige, the goose *salami* in the Jewish tradition, the wild boar *salami* in Tuscany.

Another very famous ground-meat pork product is *mortadella*, commonly known in the United States as *bologna*, taking its name from the city where it originated. For many years, *mortadella* from Italy had been banned, because of epidemics that struck the pigs in Italy many decades ago; in the meanwhile Americans got used to ersatz products that rarely taste anything like the real thing. First-rate pork cuts are finely ground and mixed with cubes of fat, salt, spices, and whole grains of pepper. Sometimes pistachios are added. Then the mix is cooked in special dry-air ovens for a period of a few hours to a whole day, depending on the meat. After that, the fresh *mortadella* is run through cold water, dried, and left to cool.

Salumi play an important role in the dietary customs of Italians. Their use in cooked dishes is limited, with the exception of sausages, which are always very popular, and other fatty cuts such as *pancetta* or *lardo*. *Salumi* are also used to make various fillings: *prosciutto* for *tortellini* and *salami*, and sausages for many savory tarts and puffy pastry delicacies. *Salumi* are mostly consumed as cold cuts, either in panini or as an appetizer. It is common to find on restaurant menus a selection of local cold cuts, often served together with cheese, olives, or other vegetables conserved with oil or vinegar. At home, a choice of cold cuts is always a good option when people do not feel like cooking. Is it not unusual to keep some *salumi* in the pantry or in the fridge for any emergency. Most groceries sell them by the pound and slice them on demand, while supermarkets tend to sell them already cut in vacuum packages to maintain the flavor and the aroma.

MUTTON AND GOAT

Together with pork, mutton was the most common meat in central and southern Italy, especially on the mountain areas. Chapter 1 mentioned *transumanza*, a tradition dating back to the pre-Roman populations of Italy who in winter used to lead their flocks from the northern part of the Apennines to the southern plains of Puglia and in summer would make their way back north. Things have not changed much since then, and most sheep are still free ranging. The traditional Italian breeds (from Sardinia, Puglia, and Abruzzo) are becoming rarer, because of their low yield in terms of milk and meat, while foreign ones are taking over. From the commercial point of view, mutton is sold in various categories, classified according to the animal's age: suckling lamb (*agnello da latte o abbacchio*, butchered at three or four weeks); lamb up to 16 pounds that has followed a mixed milk and grass diet; lamb more than 16 pounds nourished with grass only; and adult sheep, some of which are castrated to get a softer meat and a less pungent flavor. Suckling lamb is usually roasted or grilled. Older lambs can be prepared in other ways, such as *in fricassea* (an egg, parsley, and lemon-based sauce cooked in the lamb juice, and in some areas with artichokes) or *alla cacciatora* (sautéed with oil, garlic, rosemary, and white wine). In Abruzzo, one of the regions with the highest consumption of this kind of meat, lamb is typically prepared in a cheese and egg sauce (*cacio e uova*), or with bell peppers and tomato. In Campania, a traditional recipe is lamb with sweet peas and eggs. In Puglia and Basilicata, the meat is stewed with onions, celery, small tomatoes, spicy chili pepper, thyme, and bay leaves to make *cutturiddi*. Older mutton is either roasted or stewed or, more rarely, used to make soups or pasta sauces because of the intense flavor. Goats, which are definitely less common than sheep, are mostly butchered when they are still kids, because the meat tends to become tougher with age. In the best butcher's shops, the animals are sold with the head and the tail on to differentiate them from lambs. The smell is different, and the meat is almost totally devoid of fat. Also baby goats are mostly consumed grilled or roasted either in a pan or on the skewer, although in the south other more complex preparations are quite popular.

COURTYARD ANIMALS

Together with pork and mutton, poultry and rabbit were the most common kind of meat for the lower classes all over Italy. Almost everybody was able to raise a couple of hens and some rabbits near the house, to the point that these two very different animals are often classified under the general denomination of so-called courtyard animals. Nowadays, chicken (*pollo*) is certainly the most-consumed kind of poultry (also in the form of capon or *cappone*, a castrated and fattened male chicken), followed by turkey (*tacchino*), duck (*anatra*), goose (*oca*), Cornish hen (*polletto*), guinea fowl (*faraona*), pigeon (*piccione*), and quail (*quaglia*). In the past, especially in Roman times, peacocks and cranes were also highly appreciated, but they are no longer consumed. As in the United States, free-ranging chickens are harder to find and more expensive, but are of definitely better quality. The meat is more compact, does not fall off the bones when cooked, and is also usually tastier, especially if the animal has been fed with grains and natural fodder. There is less fat and it is evenly distributed all over the body. Chicken is prepared in various ways: cut in pieces or whole, boiled, stewed, roasted, grilled, or sautéed, with all kinds of sauces and accompaniments. In central Italy, for instance, chicken is often served *alla cacciatora* (cut in pieces sautéed with oil, white wine, garlic, and rosemary, sometimes with the addition of capers and black olives) or *alla diavola* (sautéed with red bell peppers and hot chili pepper). In Tuscany it is possible to find recipes of fried chicken similar to those in the United States. In Trentino, chicken is stuffed with beef marrow, walnuts, pine nuts, liver, and eggs and then boiled. In Umbria, it is prepared *in porchetta;* that is to say, it is roasted in a pot with the same condiments used to make pork *porchetta*—wild fennel, rosemary, garlic, and *pancetta.* In many areas, pieces of chicken are boiled inside the animal skin together with various ingredients and eaten cold in a jelly made from chicken stock. This dish, usually served sliced, is called *galantina.* Older chickens are commonly boiled to obtain broth, while the long cooking process allows the meat to become softer. Capon, usually fatter and more tender than chicken, is mostly boiled. At Christmas, capon broth is very popular with stuffed fresh pasta like *tortelli* or *agnoli* in Piedmont, Lombardy, and Emilia Romagna. It is also served roasted or stuffed. Until a few years ago, guinea fowls were considered semiwild animals; the meat, darker and firmer, tended to be tastier, and required longer cooking times. Nowadays they are raised like free-ranging chickens, and their meat is similar to other poultry while maintaining a certain gamy flavor.

Turkey has been popular since its arrival from the Americas, due to its similarity to chicken and its ability to be kept in courtyards. In Italy, turkey is usually preferred roasted, and it is often stuffed on festive occasions (that is the case of the Christmas turkey in Lombardy, where the fowl is stuffed with sausage, ground veal meat, apples, chestnuts, and other ingredients). In the village of Canzano, in Abruzzo, it is deboned, boiled with abundant pepper, and left to cool in its own stock till this becomes a jelly. In the past few years turkey consumption has definitely increased, often used as a lean substitute for red meat.

Ducks are also often considered red meat, and hence they eaten rare or medium rare, especially in the case of lean breasts. Thighs require longer cooking. Domestic ducks tend to be quite fatty, so it is advisable to drain the extra melted fat during the cooking process. Wild ducks, increasingly rare in Italy, have a gamier flavor and firmer meat. Younger ducks are preferred roasted, while older animals are rather braised with different sauces. In many areas, ducks are stuffed before braising. In Italy duck *foie gras* is virtually absent in the traditional cuisine, although it is now possible to buy it in most gourmet shops and to consume it according to the French tradition.

Goose *foie gras*, a preparation created by the Romans, survived in certain areas and in Jewish communities all over the country. As a matter of fact, for centuries Italian Jews used geese instead of pigs, making *salumi* and even rendered fat. Due to their large size and their scarcity, geese are now mostly prepared for festive or special occasions. Goose meat, more tender than duck, is preferred roasted or braised.

Pigeon has seen a certain revival in factory farms, raised industrially with the exception of the Torresano variety in Veneto, where the birds live in structures similar to actual towers, hence the name (*torre* means "tower"). Pigeons are at their best before they start flying and their meat becomes tougher. For this reason each pigeon is usually good for a single portion, although foreign varieties tend to be bigger, ensuring two portions per bird. Pigeons are usually sold without feathers but with their livers, which do not contain gall. Pigeons are cooked in the oven, often stuffed, or braised with various sauces that change according to the local tradition.

Rabbits are usually regarded as courtyard animals, with their white meat that is similar to poultry and that is now particularly appreciated for its leanness and its high protein content. In the past, rabbit was considered a second-rate meat because often the animals were fed the wrong kind of grass, and the taste was unpleasant. Today greater care is dedicated to choose the right fodder, and the results are definitely more enticing. Young rabbits, between two- and five-months-old, are the more versatile in the kitchen, while older ones are better when braised with sauces like *salmì*, made with red wine in which the meat is marinated together with spices, different herbs, and sometimes stock. Rabbit meat is also often sautéed in small pieces, with peppers or olives and other herbs.

GAME

If rabbits are traditionally raised on farms and in courtyards, their wild counterparts, hares, are still among the most praised catches for hunters. Despite a growing sense of unease toward this activity, which is often considered a cruel and pointless sport, hunting still plays an important role in rural environments, although it is now strictly controlled. It is not possible to hunt year round, but it is necessary to wait for the legal season, determined by local governments according to the geographical character of the different areas and the animals that inhabit them. Many species are protected, although poachers are still a problem all over the country. At any rate, getting a gun permit is not as easy as it is in the United States.

The protection regulations, which are usually quite effective, have been able to prevent the extinction of certain endangered species, although at times the opposite result has occurred: Some previously endangered animals that were once protected have overpopulated certain areas. This is the case with wild boars, which literally invaded some hill areas where they constituted a threat to the local agriculture, to the point that now it is much easier to legally hunt them. It is not by chance that in some areas of Abruzzo or Tuscany it has become common to find boar sausages, *salame*, or *prosciutto*. Besides wild boar, many birds are still hunted, such as pheasants, woodcocks, and partridges. Roe deer, although rare and very protected, are very appreciated in the north. Most game meat needs to ripen for a couple of days or more in order to lose the peculiar gamy flavor. While the smaller birds and the tenderest cuts of bigger animals are usually grilled or roasted, the tougher pieces are braised or stewed.

INNARDS

In the past, hunting and poaching were effective ways for farmers and the poor to obtain the animal protein they usually lacked. For city dwellers, it was not so easy to obtain wild animals that could not be purchased. Many had to resort to innards and low-quality cuts. In Rome, for instance, a whole cuisine developed around the so-called fifth quarter, or *quinto quarto*. Many workers in the local slaughterhouses were paid with whatever was left from the butchering process, hence the name *quinto quarto*, in which *quarti* were the noble quarters of meat that those people could not afford.[13] Brain, sweetbreads, liver, kidneys, testicles, spleen, hearts, and lungs are still popular, even if the youngest generations consume increasingly less of them. Also, pig feet, heads, tongue, and oxtail are often part of scrumptious recipes that can be found all over Italy. Innards are called *frattaglie* when they derive from beef, mutton, or pork; they are called *rigaglie* if they come from poultry. Spleen, for instance, is the main stuffing for *guastedde* in Palermo, a kind of leavened bread with sesame seeds and cheese. In Tuscany, it is sautéed and ground together with onions, anchovies, and stock to make a sort of spread that is used with *crostini*, small pieces of sliced bread. Beef tongue is either braised or *salmistrata*—that is to say, cured with salt and saltpeter, which gives it a particular red color. Brains, on the other hand, are often cut in small pieces, battered, and fried. Chicken livers, called *fegatini*, can be cooked with butter and sage, with artichokes, or diced in small pieces and added to soups or pasta. Beef liver is prepared with onions in Venice (*fegato alla veneziana)*, sautéed in a pan, or cooked with figs. This is a very ancient recipe, dating back to the Romans. As a matter of fact, the Italian word for liver, *fegato*, derives from the Latin expression *ficatum*, or "cooked with figs."

Stewed Oxtail (*Coda alla Vaccinara*)

- 4 1/2 pounds oxtail
- 2 ounces pork fat, finely ground, or lard
- 3 tablespoons extra-virgin olive oil
- 1 medium onion, chopped
- 2 cloves garlic
- 2 cloves
- 1 cup white wine
- 2 (28-ounce) cans peeled, whole tomatoes
- 2 medium stalks celery, cut into long slivers
- 1 tablespoon pine nuts
- 1 tablespoon raisins
- 1 teaspoon cocoa powder
- salt
- pepper

Cut the oxtail into pieces. Wash the meat thoroughly. Heat the pork fat and olive oil in a large, heavy pan. Brown the meat and add onion, garlic, cloves, salt, and pepper. Cook for 5 minutes, add the white wine, cover the pan with a lid and cook for 15 minutes. Add the tomatoes and cook for one hour. Add enough water so the meat is covered with the sauce, cover the pan again, and cook very slowly for 5 or 6 hours, until the meat falls off the bone. Remove the oxtails from the cooking liquid and set aside. Boil the celery stalks in salted water until tender. Simmer the oxtail juices with the cooked celery, the pine nuts, the raisins, and the cocoa powder for 5 minutes. Pour the sauce over the meat when ready to serve.

EGGS

Hen eggs constitute a very important element in the everyday diet, just like anywhere else in the world where hens are readily available. Other kinds of eggs, like the small ones from quail or the larger ones from ducks and geese, are difficult to find and rarely used. Eggs are prepared in uncountable ways: scrambled, poached, hard boiled, or fried in oil or butter. Omelets, called *frittata* from the verb *friggere*, "to fry," are often made tastier by adding various ingredients: milk and grated cheese; vegetables such as mushrooms, onions, artichokes, or zucchini; all kinds of herbs; and sausages and *prosciutto*. Eggs used to be baked under the ashes when hearths were common, but now those have become quite an unusual delicacy. Among the most interesting local recipes with eggs, we can mention the Roman *stracciatella* (eggs beaten in boiling broth), the Sicilian "black eggs" (*uova nere*, hard-boiled eggs cured in vinegar and fennel seeds), and the hard-boiled-egg soup from Padova (*sopa de vovi duri*, diced hard-boiled eggs with diced fried bread in broth).

MILK AND ITS DERIVATIVES

Milk is not as popular a drink in Italy as it is in the United States. Italians might have it in the morning in *cappuccino* or *caffellatte*, but during the day its use is limited to the kitchen for some specific preparations. It is used to soften gratins, to prepare purées, or in pastry making.

Butter is often used as cooking fat, especially in the north. In other areas, olive oil and pork fat were traditionally more available and, in the case of pork fat, also more affordable. Butter is used to sauté specific dishes, like *scaloppine*, thin slices of veal meat covered in flour. It is also melted and poured over pasta, sometimes with grated cheese or together with herbs such as sage. Butter is widely used in pastry making but seldom used as an ingredient in sauces, with the exception of *béchamel*, the only classic French sauce that is commonly used in Italian cuisine.

Sour cream and buttermilk are virtually unknown. Plain cream is sometimes used in pastry or specific recipes. Starting from the 1970s, maybe under the influence of French *nouvelle cuisine*, it became fashionable to season pasta or *tortellini* with fresh cream together with other ingredients such as salmon or peas and ham. Nowadays, this custom is frowned upon as unhealthy and passé. Cream is often whipped with sugar and used in pastry or added to espresso.

Yogurt was not very common in the past. It became popular in the 1960s, when it started being mass-produced. It is not often used for cooking, with the exceptions of a few Greek or Middle Eastern recipes. It is instead consumed as a snack. Plain yogurt is considered too tart and acidic. It is often mixed with fruit, cereals, coffee, or even chocolate. Very few Italians have the patience to make it at home; most people prefer to buy the industrial brands, most often the low-fat varieties. Interestingly enough, the single-portion pots of yogurt are much smaller than in the United States, as is the case with much prepackaged food.

Cheese is by far the most important derivative of milk.[14] Italians consume it alone or in *panini*, but they also use it as an ingredient in many recipes. Mozzarella and *fontina*, which melt in long strings when cooked, are diced to make *lasagna* and other dishes. On the other hand, dry, hard cheeses such as *parmigiano reggiano*, *pecorino romano*, or *grana padano*, which melt without making strings, are grated and added to *risotto* or to the stuffing of *tortellini* and savory tarts. Grated cheese is also often sprinkled on top of pasta and soups.

Hundreds of cheeses are available in Italy. Their flavors, textures, and aromas differ, depending on the areas of production, available herbs, habits of the shepherds and herdmen, traditions, and technical know-how, among other things. There are myriad factors that make each cheese unique. Of course, this is only the case for traditionally produced cheese, which nowadays constitutes a tiny portion of all of the cheese sold and consumed in Italy. They are often limited in availability and distribution, being produced in small quantities and not all year round; they are also more expensive, because the production process is slow and often totally artisanal. It is important to point out that some of the most interesting, rarer cheeses are not necessarily protected by any DOP (or PDO, Protected Designation of Origin) and IGP (PGI, Protected Geographical Indication) regulations, which cover only 30 types of cheese. Some of these are actually produced in quite large amounts, even if under very strict quality control. Nevertheless, starting in the 1960s, growing levels of consumption developed a strong demand for cheeses that would be cheaper and available all over the country, maybe with less character but for this very reason more acceptable to some palates that were not accustomed to intense, sometimes almost offensive flavors. Responding to these needs, modern dairy industries created products and found ways to make them popular. Today shelves are full of heavily advertised products that are often soft, like cottages cheese or processed melted cheese, wrapped in aluminum foils in small triangles or circles, that do not require a long aging process. This does not account for the growing low-fat cheese market. Some industrial brands, such as Bel Paese Galbani, have acquired a certain respect because they have been around for a few decades and many people grew up eating them.

Going back to traditional cheeses, they can be classified in several ways. From the texture point of view, there are hard, semihard, soft, and fresh ones. If we consider the ingredients, cheese is mainly made with three kinds of milk: cow, water buffalo, and sheep. Goat milk is definitely rarer, often mixed with other kinds of milk. Geographically, cow milk is prevalent in the north, on the Alps, and in the Po River plain. In the peninsula and on the islands, sheep are the most common dairy animals; water buffaloes are raised only in southern Lazio and northern Campania to make mozzarella.

It would be impossible to give a complete list of Italian cheeses; we will limit ourselves to the most renowned. Starting from the northwest, the Val d'Aosta region is known for *fontina*, a quite fatty (45 percent) semi-hard cow-milk cheese that is very popular for gratin dishes. In Piedmont, *castelmagno* is one of the highest-priced and sought-after products of the region, from the homonymous village in the province of Cuneo. It belongs to the category defined in Italy as *erborinato*, showing greenish-blue veins that give a peculiar flavor. The wheels, exclusively made of cow cheese, are quite large, weighing around 8 pounds. Always in Piedmont, *bross* is made of leftover pieces matured in aqua vitae till the mixture acquires a very pungent flavor and smell. *Toma* is made with either whole or skim cow milk in the shape of a round dish, two- to four-inches thick, with a soft texture. At the border of the region of Lombardy, *gorgonzola* is probably the most famous *erborinato* cheese from Italy; its creamy texture and its ivory color are now appreciated all over the world, even if recently it has become difficult to find the strong kind that was popular decades ago. In the Valsassina Valley, *robiola* is a square-shaped, fresh or semihard cheese, usually aged in caves. In another Lombardy valley, Valtellina, *bitto* is made between June and September by cooking whole cow milk, to which up to 10 percent of goat milk can be added. The summer mountain herbs eaten by the cows give it its typical flavor. Also the PDO *taleggio* is produced in Lombardy, using uncooked whole cow milk. It is square-shaped, soft, and quite fatty (at least 48 percent). *Grana padano* and *parmigiano reggiano* are probably the most renowned Italian cheeses, exported all over the world. The former is produced in a very large area stretching into Piedmont, Lombardy, Veneto, Trentino, and Emilia Romagna. It is a hard cheese, made once a day by mixing the cow milk obtained in the evening with the fresh milk of the morning and adding veal whey. The curd is then cooked and shaped into big wheels weighing 12 to 20 pounds. The wheels are left to age in a temperature between 15 and 22°C for at least 9 months. *Parmigiano reggiano* is similar to *grana*, but the wheels are kept floating in salted water between 20 and 30 days, and the aging process lasts at least 12 months. The longer preparation makes this cheese more expensive than *grana*, also because the production area is limited to a few provinces of Emilia Romagna and the province of Mantova in Lombardy. In the Po River plain and in the neighboring areas, *provolone valpadana* is a very common cheese. Although at first it was probably produced in the south, now it is made in the north, with whole cow milk brought to a temperature of 37°C. Rennet is introduced, forming curds that cheese makers break into small pieces and then cook at a temperature around 45°C. The paste that is obtained, freed from all traces of whey, is worked by hand, left in salted water for some days, and then aged for at least 30 days. Provolone is found in a sweet version (*provolone dolce*) and in a harder, stronger one (*provolone piccante*).

Moving east toward the Veneto region, we find *asiago* cheese, which is actually produced around Trento by mixing the morning's fresh cow milk with the skim milk from the previous evening, salting the wheels, and then aging them for at least 6 months. This cheese is semihard, with a fat content ranging from 34 percent for the so-called *d'allevo* variety to 44 percent for the pressed type (*pressato*). Further east, *montasio* is a hard cow-milk cheese produced in Friuli and part of Veneto, ready to be consumed 2 months after being salted; it can also be grated after 12 months. Going south, past the Po River, sheep-milk cheese becomes the rule. The most common name for it is *pecorino* (from *pecora*, sheep). There are four different PDO *pecorino*. While *pecorino toscano* (from Tuscany) is soft or semihard, aged between 20 days and 4 months (for the hardest version), *pecorino romano* is hard, weighing 40 to 70 pounds, aged for at least 5 months and perfect to grate. Although the name would suggest this cheese comes from Rome, it is actually produced in Lazio, southern Tuscany, and Sardinia. In the late nineteenth century, when *pecorino romano* became very popular all over the world and the demand outgrew the actual output, cheese makers found that milk from Sardinian sheep gave very similar results, and part of the production was moved to the island. The actual *pecorino sardo* (from Sardinia) is slightly softer, aged for 20 to 60 days, made into small wheels (2 to 5 pounds), and not covered in the black rind that is typical of the *romano* variety. The Sicilian variety (*pecorino siciliano*) is made into wheels weighing 20 to 35 pounds, aged in baskets for at least 4 months and with a white-yellow rind that shows the traces of the basket.

Common sheep cheeses are *caciotta* or *casciotta*, usually quite soft but firm, with a 45 percent fat content and a delicate taste; *fiore sardo*, produced in Sardinia, with less fat but harder and with a more pungent flavor; and *ricotta*, which literally means "re-cooked." This popular cheese, which can also be made of cow milk, gets its name from the process of reheating leftover whey from the cheese-making process and then adding a little fresh milk. The resulting soft, relatively low-fat cheese (less than 20 percent fat content) is eaten fresh and used to season pasta, prepare savory tart fillings (often mixed with spinach), and make pastries such as the Sicilian *cannoli* and *cassata* cake. *Ricotta* can be pressed and dried and then left to age; it thus acquires a slightly spongy texture and a salty, milky flavor. This type, called salted ricotta (*ricotta salata*) is usually eaten on bread or crumbled over pasta or in salads. Sometimes it is baked in the oven (*ricotta al forno*).

In the south sheep-milk cheese is not an absolute rule; in fact, some interesting cow-milk cheese is made there. The most common are probably *scamorza* and *caciocavallo*, both semihard and similar in shape to a truncated cone, sometimes with a small knob at the top, depending on local customs. These kinds of cheeses are produced in many areas, such as Campania, Molise, Basilicata, Puglia, and Calabria.

The most famous southern cheese is definitely *mozzarella*, traditionally made with milk from the water buffaloes that are still living in the marshy areas in southern Lazio and the coasts of Campania. It is a fresh cheese— usually shaped as a round lump—that should be consumed when it is still drenched in whey. Many similar cheeses are also inappropriately called *mozzarella*, even if they are not made with buffalo milk and they are produced in other areas of Italy. The correct names for those products are *fior di latte, ovolo, ovolina,* and *treccia,* shaped like braids. Similar to *mozzarella* is *burrata di Andria,* from Puglia, which is stuffed with pieces of the same cheese mixed with thick cream.

ICE CREAM, SORBET, AND GRANITA

Ice cream is the final result of technical developments dealing with the problem of refrigeration and preservation of food. As early as the eighth century B.C.E., the Chinese were able to store mountain ice all summer in underground caves or pits kept cool by evaporation. They might have invented the first device to freeze flavored syrup into sorbet, placing jars containing the liquid mixture in a combination of snow and saltpeter, or potassium nitrate, a kind of salt they also used to make explosive powders. Nevertheless, it is unlikely that these contraptions were brought to Europe by the merchants traveling to China during the Middle Ages, such as Marco Polo. The Italian habit of making sorbets was absorbed from the Muslims, who ruled Sicily for almost three centuries. Since the beginning of the caliphate, in the seventh century C.E., snow and ice, wrapped in straw, were carried to the courts of Damascus and then Baghdad from the surrounding mountains. The word *sorbet* derives from a Turkish word, *chorbêt*, which in turn comes from the Arab word *charâb*, indicating a sweet fruit drink. The same word *charâb* is the origin of syrup. It is interesting how terms connected with confectionery and ice-related techniques are borrowed from the Muslims, who excelled in those culinary arts and had learned how to produce sugar from India. The Sicilians improved the methodology, and the new desserts conquered other Italian courts and soon the rest of Europe. In the seventeenth century, ice creams had already become the rage in the fashionable coffeehouses in all the capital cities.

By the 1870s, ice-making machines had been invented. These were often of industrial size, employing the expansion of compressed air or evaporation to volatile substances like ether and, successively, ammonia. These new techniques allowed a worldwide diffusion of sorbets and ice creams and industrial-level production. In Italy, people enjoy both mass-produced brands (*gelato confezionato*), which are available in groceries, supermarkets, and bars, and artisanal ice creams (*gelato artigianale*) sold in special shops (*gelaterie*), which are often open year round and often show the sign *Produzione Propria* (produced by the owner).

A simple frozen dessert is *granita*, a granular-textured, soupy ice flavored with lemon, orange, coffee, or other extracts. Since it is quite liquid, *granita* has to be consumed in a glass. Sicilians love to have it for breakfast together with a brioche (*brioscia*), a delicacy that is also often served with *gelato*. Its even simpler version is known in Rome as *grattachecca*, shaved ice with syrups and pieces of fresh or candied fruits on top, sold from street stalls that in summer are literally swamped by crowds, especially at night. Sorbet (*sorbetto*), made of water, syrups, or puréed fruit, and sometimes some milk or egg whites, is churned smooth while freezing. It has a creamier and more compact texture, which allows it to be eaten on cone-shaped wafers (*coni*) on the go. Very popular sorbet flavors are blackberry, raspberry, strawberry, lemon, orange, peach, apricot, and many other summer fruits. *Gelato*, on the other hand, is made with egg custard, sugar, and various flavorings, the most common flavors being vanilla, milk, chocolate, hazelnut, pistachio, coffee, and *zabaione*. Some gelato makers (*gelatai*) add milk or cream to achieve a denser texture. In Sicily, the base is often a sort of milk pudding thickened with corn starch, called *crema rinforzata* or strengthened cream, which is similar to blancmange (*biancomangiare*). This dessert, probably of Arabic origin, was extremely popular in the Middle Ages and the Renaissance all over Europe, and it is still found in Sicily, at times prepared with crushed almond milk (*latte di mandorla*). In the past few years, frozen yogurt has become a popular alternative. In this case the base is yogurt, which makes the result lighter and less fatty. For the lactose intolerant and the fat-free aficionados, it is now possible to find soymilk-based ice creams.

When *gelato* is blended with crushed ice and milk, it is called *frappé*, often with the addition of fresh fruit. A soft pie or a tart, filled with gelato and served semifrozen, is known as a *semifreddo*. *Semifreddo* is usually served in a cup or in slices on a saucer, and it is always eaten with a spoon.

FISH AND SEAFOOD

Strangely enough, despite its geographical position and the extension of its coasts, Italy has never enjoyed an abundance of fish and seafood, which are rare and expensive. This is because the Mediterranean is much less rich in fish than the Atlantic and the Pacific. Marine biologists explain this phenomenon by its higher salt content, its lack in nutritive elements such as plankton, and the level of exploitation, which is historically very intense. After World War II, while the countries around the Mediterranean underwent a process of fast industrialization, pollution became an urgent problem that has been tackled only in the past few years. Filtration plants near the coasts and greater attention from the industries are rapidly improving the state of the sea.

The fish industry was paramount during the Roman Empire. Romans developed amazing techniques to raise fish and seafood in artificial basins, and fishermen were able to send their catch all over the country. Of course, this kind of consumption was mostly limited to richer citizens. With the arrival of the Germanic populations, these seashore fishing traditions virtually disappeared. When the expansion of Christianity increased the demand for fish due to its dietary norms (meat could not be consumed during many days of the year), the attention of farmers turned to freshwater sources—lakes, brooks, and marshes. The area around the northern lakes and the plain along the Po River, with its wide and intricate delta, became the center for this kind of production. Trout (*trota*), pike (*luccio*), and, above all, sturgeon (*storione*) acquired great prestige, reaching the tables of nobles and churchmen. In many areas around the Po, this fish is still added to *risotto*. Local lords would reserve the biggest fish for themselves and, in case of sturgeon, also its caviar. Farmers would be left with less refined fish, such as perch (*pesce persico*), tench (*tinca*), and carp (*carpa*), whose muddy taste often revealed their provenance from marshes and still waters. In some areas in northern Italy, these fish are still forced to swallow vinegar before being killed to avoid that unpleasant flavor. Eels (*anguilla*) also reached a certain status, appreciated for their delicate and fat meat. Eel, especially the larger and meatier female known in southern Italy as *capitone*, is still very popular on Christmas Eve; they are consumed grilled, stewed, or fried. River shrimp were extremely abundant in the past but were shunned by the higher strata of society, as in the case of crawfish in the southern United States. Nowadays they have virtually disappeared, destroyed by an epidemic at the end of the nineteenth century and by growing river pollution due to massive industrialization. Also frogs were caught and eaten, especially the legs. Along the shores, most of the fish was still gathered to reach the market and ended up on rich tables. Fishermen were left with the smallest fish and less valuable seafood, often using them to make soups. This explains the presence of many recipes for fish soups all along the coast of Italy, each with different ingredients (tomato, wine, vinegar, saffron, sweet pepper).

Nowadays, sea fish is widely available both fresh and frozen. The most prized species are surely the sea bass (*spigola*) and the gilthead bream (*orata*), for which rich recipes can be found all over the country. Sea bass is served with a thick parsley-based sauce in Tuscany (*al verde*), stuffed with seafood near Naples, or grilled with lemon over olive wood in Sicily. Gilthead bream is roasted in the oven with pomegranate juice near Venice, served with chopped herbs and *prosciutto* in the Marche, or filleted and sprinkled with orange juice in Sicily. Flat fish such as sole (*sogliola*) and turbot (*rombo*) are usually roasted in a pan, although sole is often filleted, floured, and fried. Skate (*razza*) is one of the main ingredients for a famous Roman dish, *minestra d'arzilla*, together with broccoli. Among the most appreciated fish we can name wreckfish (*cernia*), dentex (*dentice*), John Dory (*pesce San Pietro*), red mullet (*triglia*), and scorpionfish (*scorfano*). Salmon is also quite common and eaten both fresh and smoked.

A special category—in a classification that can absolutely not be considered scientific—is the so-called blue fish (*pesce azzurro*), which includes fish that live far from the coasts, with a steel-blue color on the back and a white-silver color on the belly. Small fish such as herring (*aringa*), anchovies (*alice*), sardines (*sardina*), mackerels (*sgombro*), and big ones like tuna (*tonno*) and swordfish (*pesce spada*) fall into this category. Small *pesce azzurro* is quite cheap on the market, despite its high nutritional value. The most popular, anchovies, can be consumed fried, baked in the oven (covered with bread crumbs, parsley, garlic, and lemon), and raw, simply marinated in vinegar or lemon. Anchovies are also cured in salt and olive oil, and they appear as ingredients in many recipes, especially in southern Italy. Tuna is eaten fresh, mostly grilled, but it is also conserved in water or olive oil. Canned tuna fish is extremely popular, added to salads, eaten with beans or potatoes, or used to enrich tomato sauces.

Fish is usually served whole and not filleted as in the United States. Most consumers would buy frozen filleted fish, while they would be extremely suspicious about fresh filleted fish, since it would be almost impossible to assess its actual freshness. Buyers like to personally check the state of the eyes and the gills, the color, the shine, and the smell; all of these elements cannot be controlled when the fish is filleted. Furthermore, Italians are not disgusted when served a whole fish, something that is often perceived as repulsive in the United States. Not everybody is actually able and willing to debone the fish; in restaurants, waiters usually do it for the patrons. In some areas, fish roe is eaten. The most famous is dried mullet roe, or *bottarga*, from Sardinia, often grated on pasta.

Cooking methods are similar to the rest of the Mediterranean: Fish can be grilled, roasted in the oven (often with herbs, lemon, and potatoes), boiled, stewed, sautéed, fried, steamed, or cooked in aluminum foil (this method is called *al cartoccio*). A more unusual method is called *carpionatura* or *saor*: The fish is covered in flour and fried, and then it is left to marinate in vinegar and various herbs for at least one day.

Different cooking methods have been elaborated to prepare stockfish (*stoccafisso*, codfish dried by hanging in the cold air) and salted dried codfish (*baccalà*), extremely popular although not a Mediterranean fish. Both require soaking in water to lose all of the extra salt. When fresh fish was hard to get, these dried products offered a convenient and relatively cheap solution, especially in times when the liturgical calendar required one to avoid meat. They were also extremely important as food for sailors, during long journeys; ironically, many recipes originated in seaports, where one would expect that the sailors, back from a long trip, would hate to see on their table the same cod they ate for long months out at sea. In Liguria, stockfish is stewed with olive oil, garlic, onions, anchovies, diced tomatoes, diced potatoes, olives, and pine nuts (*stocche accumudou*); it is also boiled in small pieces and then beaten into a smooth paste together with potatoes, tomatoes, onions, lemon juice, and spices (*stoccafisso mantecato*). A similar recipe is found in Venice, where *baccalà* can also be boiled and beaten, with the addition of olive oil, till it has the same texture as whipped cream (*baccalà mantecato*); in Trieste milk and fresh chopped parley are added to this recipe. Another famous *baccalà* recipe is found in another Veneto city, Vicenza: It is *baccalà alla vicentina*, in which the fish is stuffed with chopped parley, anchovies, and garlic and then cut into pieces, covered in flour mixed with grated cheese, and sautéed in a pan with milk and olive oil. Further south, in Florence, we find *baccalà alla fiorentina*: Pieces of the fish are cut, covered in flour, and sautéed with tomato sauce. In Livorno, on the coast of Tuscany, stockfish is used instead of *baccalà*, and celery, basil, and parsley are added to the tomato sauce. A similar recipe is found in Calabria, where it is called *piscistoccu a ghiotta*.

Crustaceans, shellfish, and all kinds of mollusks are appreciated all over Italy. Along the southern coasts, many of them, such as mussels *(cozza)* and sea urchins *(riccio di mare)*, are eaten raw, with a little lemon freshly squeezed on them, just as in the rest of Europe, where consumers prefer oysters. Besides mussels, the most common shellfish are clams *(vongole)*, cockles *(tartufo)*, telleens *(telline)*, scallops *(capesante)*, and razor clams *(cannolicchi)*.

Sea and land snails are appreciated all over the country. Land snails need to be fed wheat bran and vegetables for a few days before cooking to clean their innards. They can be prepared in many different ways: stewed in tomato sauce with the shell, shelled and sautéed, or shelled and fried.

Sea shellfish are usually sautéed with garlic, olive oil, and fresh chopped parsley, stewed with tomato or wine, or more often just baked in the oven with bread crumbs, garlic, and other herbs. They are also a popular condiment for pasta, especially spaghetti. Spaghetti with clams or mussels are an absolute classic, flavorful and easy to make, but quite different from the heavily creamed versions that are served in many Italian restaurants in the United States. Cooks add shrimp, squid, and sometimes octopus to make the pasta even tastier. This recipe is called *spaghetti allo scoglio*, or *al cartoccio* when pasta is cooked in aluminum foil together with the seafood.

Clam and mussel shells.

The same mollusks are simply boiled and then served cold in salads (sea salads, *insalata di mare*), with fresh parsley, back olives, and sometimes fresh tomato.

Squid and calamari are often added to soups, but they are well loved when covered in egg and bread crumbs and fried. Squid can also be stewed, together with peas, and stuffed (in this case it is usually sautéed or grilled). In Florence, it is served with chard in the famous *inzimino*. The ink is used to make pasta, *risotto*, or to cook the squid itself. Less common and more expensive, octopus is grilled or boiled and served in cold salads.

Shrimp are probably the most popular of all crustaceans, also due to their reasonable price. Prawns, lobsters, and crabs are definitely more expensive and found mainly in restaurants. These crustaceans are usually served simply boiled, whole (with fresh lemon or a light mayonnaise) or cut in pieces in a salad. More rarely, they are cut along the length and grilled or cooked with tomato sauce to season pasta. A curiosity from Venice are *moleche*, tiny soft-shell crabs, that are left to soak in beaten eggs—still alive—for a few hours and then covered in flour and fried.[15]

Frogs used to be popular in areas with lakes or marshes. Thighs were especially considered a delicacy. Nowadays they are much harder to find because of the pollution of freshwater sources all over the country.

Swordfish with Capers, Black Olives, and Tomatoes

- 1 1/2 tablespoons extra-virgin olive oil
- 4 swordfish steaks, 1/2 inch thick
- 1/2 cup dry white wine
- 3 tomatoes, peeled, seeded, and chopped
- 1 tablespoon capers, rinsed and drained
- 2 tablespoons black olives, chopped
- 2 tablespoon sun-dried tomatoes, soaked and chopped
- 1 tablespoon minced parsley
- salt
- pepper

Heat the olive oil in a skillet over medium-high heat. Place the swordfish steaks in the skillet and season with salt and pepper. Cook the steaks for 3 minutes on each side. Add the white wine. When it has evaporated, reduce the heat and top each steak with a mix of fresh tomatoes, sun-dried tomatoes, capers, and black olives. Cook over low heat for 2 minutes longer. Place the steaks on a serving platter and sprinkle with the chopped parsley. Serve warm.

COFFEE, TEA, AND TISANES

Several drinks made by infusion or decoction of leaves, grains, or roots in boiling water are commonly enjoyed in Italy. Beyond any doubt, the most common is coffee. The most appreciated kind is the *arabica*, with a rich aroma and a low caffeine content (1.1 to 1.7 percent), more expensive than the variety *robusta*, which is less aromatic and has a higher caffeine content (2 to 4.5 percent). Despite its density, Italian coffee often contains less caffeine than American coffee. Besides being drunk in much smaller quantities, the roasting process is longer than in other parts of the world, lowering the caffeine content but increasing the bitterness. In southern Italy, coffee is usually roasted longer than in the north. See chapter 4, "Typical Meals," for more information about the use of coffee.

Tea is a recent addition to the Italian diet, adopted at the end of the nineteenth century following the example of Great Britain. Most people use ready-made blended ground tea in bags. Only connoisseurs are familiar with different kinds of tea, their provenance, and their aroma and use a teapot to prepare the beverage. Tea is usually consumed with sugar and a slice of lemon in it. Very few enjoy it with sugar and milk, as the British do. Even fewer use the whole leaves in infusion, as the Chinese do. Other

Stove-top coffeemaker.

infusions, such as chamomile tea, linden, mint, and verbena, which are appreciated for their calming effect, are also popular.

CHOCOLATE

Chocolate is very popular in Italy.[16] In pastry making, cocoa powder is added to dough in many preparations for cakes and cookies. It is also used to prepare fillings, creams, and custards. It is commonly served mixed with hot milk, often topped with sweetened whipped cream (*cioccolata calda*). Chocolate is often consumed in the form of small, flat slabs (*tavoletta di cioccolato*) and as *cioccolatini*, small candies often filled with creams or liquors. *Cioccolatini* can be both artisanal and mass-produced. Various ingredients can be added to cocoa. For instance, in Piedmont, hazelnuts, the most common nuts in the area, are finely ground in the *cioccolatini* called *giandujotti* or added whole to chocolate bars (*cioccolato alle nocciole*).

In the past few years, a growing interest in rare cocoa beans has become a fashion. Some small semi-artisanal companies make chocolate by grinding selected beans from a single, high-quality variety, with concentrations varying from 50 to 70 percent. These products are usually labeled as bitter chocolate (*cioccolato amaro*) and contain little milk, as opposed to other chocolates with higher milk content (*cioccolato al latte*). Purists condemn the replacement of cocoa butter with other cheaper ingredients, often used by large food industries. It is now mandatory for producers to indicate the fat substances used to make chocolate.

NOTES

1. Franco La Cecla, *La pasta e la pizza* (Bologna: Il Mulino, 1998); Françoise Sabban and Serventi Silvano, *La pasta* (Rome-Bari: Laterza, 2000).

2. Slow Food, *Ricette di sua maestà il raviolo* (Bra: Slow Food Editore, 1993).

3. Giovanni Goria, *La cucina del Piemonte* (Padova: Franco Muzzio, 1990).

4. Slow Food, *Ricette di osterie dell'Abruzzo: panarde, guazzetti e virtù* (Bra: Slow Food Editore, 1997).

5. Jeanne Carola Francescani, *La cucina Napoletana* (Rome: Newton Compton, 1992).

6. Paolo Lingua, *La cucina dei genovesi* (Padova: Franco Muzzio, 1989).

7. Flavio Birri and Coco Carla, *Cade a Fagiolo* (Venice: Marsilio, 2000).

8. Riccardo Di Corato, *838 frutti e verdure d'Italia* (Milan: Sonzogno, 1984).

9. Vito Teti, *Il peperoncino: Un americano nel Mediterraneo* (Vibo Valentia: Monteleone, 1995).

10. Salvatore Gelsi, *Zucca e tortelli* (Mantova: Edizioni Tre Lune, 1998).

11. Mario da Passano, Antonello Mattone, Franca Mele, and Pinuccia Simbula, *La vite e il vino: storia e diritto, secoli 11–19* (Rome: Carocci, 2000).

12. Zeffiro Bocci, *L'evoluzione del settore vitivinicolo negli ultimi trent'anni* (Verona: Gruppo Italiano Vini, 1997).

13. Livio Jannattoni, *La cucina romana e del Lazio* (Rome: Newton Compton, 1998).

14. Piero Camporesi, *Le vie del latte, dalla Padania alla steppa* (Milan: Garzanti, 1993).

15. Giuseppe Maffioli, *La cucina veneziana* (Padova: Franco Muzzio, 1982).

16. Tiziana Plebani, *Cioccolata: la bevanda degli dei forestieri* (Venice: Centro Internazionale della Grafica, 1991).

3

Cooking

For centuries, women were, and in some ways still are, in charge of food at home. When Italy was a predominantly rural society, both men and women would work in the fields or tend the animals, especially in times of intense activities like sowing or harvesting. However, women usually took care of the space closer to the home, like courtyards, orchards, and kitchen gardens. Chickens, turkeys, and rabbits were kept in small pens right outside the house and women fed them, as well as bigger animals like pigs, sheep, and cows, which lived in enclosures or stables also quite close to the living quarters of the farmers. Women also milked them and prepared the butter, if necessary. While men plowed and toiled in the outer fields to produce the crops for sale and took care of the fruit trees, women cultivated vegetables for the family consumption in small patches near the house. When cities were not so densely populated as they are now, it was fairly common to find small vegetable gardens in the courtyards or between buildings, especially in the expanding outskirts. When in the 1960s many farmers from the south abandoned their land and moved into the cities to work in the growing industrial sector, they brought with them many culinary habits that required fresh vegetables. If no patch of cultivable land was available near the home, they even tried to grow tomatoes and other plants in bathtubs or tended vases on the balcony where basil, rosemary, marjoram, and other basic herbs could grow. Needless to say, these habits provoked sarcasm from the already citified neighbors who had already given up the old ways and were proud of their urban manners.

Not many families in the country were lucky enough to own their own farm and some land. Many of them rented the land from the landowners, often under the form of *mezzadria,* in which the owner gave seeds and tools to the farmers, who paid him back with half of the crop output. The vegetables produced in the kitchen gardens were usually excluded from the computation. In the south, where *latifondi*—large properties belonging to a single landowner—were common, the poorest peasants would be hired and paid by the day both by richer farmers and landowners. On special occasions, when wheat was reaped, grapes were harvested, or olives were picked, laborers received frequent meals throughout the day, cooked by the women of the family for whom they were working. These meals were often traditionally codified and ensured not only that the workers had enough energy to finish their job, but also took deeper meanings, related to the rhythm of growth and the seasons.[1]

On normal days, laborers, including masons, cabinetmakers, and other specialized workers, brought their own lunch from home. It mostly consisted of some bread with a few vegetables or some cured meat and a little wine. If they worked close enough to home, the young women in the family or the wife herself brought warm food from the kitchen.

In humble families living in the cities, women were in charge of the home while the men worked outside, unless the husband's wages were so low that his wife and at times even his daughters had to work, usually as cooks, maids, or cleaning staff in private homes or restaurants. All through the nineteenth century, most Italians did not go to school past elementary school, where they learned to read, write, and to do some calculations. Illiteracy was rampant, because teenagers were supposed to help the family with their work. It was considered even less useful for girls and young women to go to school, with the exceptions of the bourgeois and noble families, who took care of their daughters' instruction. This included singing, playing an instrument, sewing, embroidery, cooking, and good manners. Even a well-off woman was supposed to know how to cook and run a kitchen, in order to be able to keep cooks and maids, usually from the countryside and often ignorant, under control. It was not uncommon for bourgeois women to take care of shopping, even if staff actually carried the groceries. If they did not do the cooking themselves, they decided the menu with the cook, especially for Sunday or special dinners and when guests were invited. On those occasions, menus had to reconcile the family budget and the desire to impress (*fare bella figura*).

Early in the twentieth century it became important for women to get a more complete education. At the same time new appliances made their work in the kitchen much easier, starting with first coal and then gas stoves. Another important change came with the diffusion of iceboxes and refrigerators. Canned and dehydrated food had become available, especially in cities, making cooking even less time consuming. In the 1920s urban women started taking clerical jobs, such as secretary or typist. Electric appliances made cooking faster, together with a general push to introduce rational methods, inspired by science, into the kitchen with scales, clocks, and aluminum pots.

Only after World War II, with the massive immigration toward the industrial north, the growing urbanization, the abandonment of the countryside, and the economic boom, did it become normal for women to work full time outside the house. However, jobs that left time for cooking and housekeeping were still preferred. Only since the 1980s has it become socially acceptable for women to dedicate themselves to their careers, worrying less about family and children.

MEN IN THE KITCHEN

In the past, with the notable exception of professional chefs, only shepherds, soldiers, and sailors, who were forced to spend long periods far from home, were in charge of daily cooking, due to the absence of women. At times, hunters also roasted the game they caught, if the outings lasted more than one day; otherwise they brought their quarry home for more labor intensive or complicated preparations that were the province of the women.

Most of the time, both urban workers and farmers were excluded from the life of the kitchen, except to express preferences or vent dissatisfaction with the menu. Most Italian men did, and still do, move directly from their mothers' homes to living with their wives, from one doting woman to another. As a consequence, there was no need for them to learn how to cook, or how to clean, or to wash and iron clothes. Husbands were supposed to work and bring home the so-called bread for the family, while their wives were in charge of the home. When women started to join the workforce, this whole social system developed wider and wider cracks. Especially in cities, men had to accept that their women held jobs outside the house, because one salary was often not enough to maintain the family. Women's emancipation (*emancipazione femminile*) was a matter of fact from the economic and practical point of view, but many men could not picture themselves in a new role in which they were not the only bread-winners in the family. Men from older generations still expect their women to do the shopping, the cooking, and the cleaning even when they have their own jobs. Younger couples usually find different balances, and chores tend to be shared, especially when it comes to grocery shopping and the kitchen. However, the charge that Italian men remain childish even when they grow up, with a tight connection to the maternal figure, is partly true. A special expression has been created to indicate a man psychologically and materially dependent on his mother: *mammone*. The high unemployment rates, the fact that apartments are very expensive both to rent and buy, and the habit of staying with one's parents until marriage still allow many young men to enjoy their mother's attentions and their family's social protection. Besides, young people, both men and women, do not leave home while they attend college, unless there is no university in the area where they live. In general, they are not required to work and contribute to the family budget because they are supposed to concentrate all their energy and attention on their studies. It is still relatively uncommon, especially in the countryside and among the lower classes, to find young men living by themselves. Nevertheless, it is becoming customary for young men to learn how to make at least some simple dishes.

FAST COOKING

Since many women now have full-time jobs, various dishes and culinary traditions that require intensive and lengthy preparations are slowly disappearing. Neapolitan-style *ragù* that needs to simmer for hours, *timballo* and *sartù* with myriad ingredients, and desserts that require long leavening and frequent kneading are among the victims of the busier and faster lifestyle many families have embraced. To respond to these changes, food industries are investing in creating and mass-producing ready-made alternatives that still maintain some connection with the dishes of the past. Ragù sauces are available by the jar, fish soups are sold frozen, and so are many other specialties. Most desserts can be bought either at the grocery shop or from artisanal pastry shops. These foods tend to be expensive, but their quality is usually acceptable, even if it is not comparable to the freshly made equivalent.

Curing and pickling vegetables in one's kitchen and making jams and preserves at home made sense when fruits and vegetables came from one's gardens or orchards, and they needed to be stored for the winter when less fresh food was available. Until a few years ago, in summer most southern families bought tomatoes in bulk at the peak of their season, when they were less expensive, and spent the whole day peeling, crushing, bottling, and boiling them to prepare their winter provisions. Tomato sauce was also left to dry until it become a paste that could be added to soups and other dishes, while others preferred to just cut the vegetables in two and let them dry under the sun. Now summer has become the time of the year when most Italians take their vacations, so very few are ready to spend time and energy preparing food for the winter. Besides, the same products can be bought from shops and supermarkets. For instance, tomatoes are available in cans, already peeled and seeded. Only food enthusiasts still dedicate part of their leisure time to prepare their own winter provisions, but it is definitely more a hobby than a necessity.

Beef Rolls (*Involtini di Manzo*)

- 12 thin slices beef top round
- 12 slices *prosciutto crudo* (cured ham)
- 2 small stalks celery, cut into strips
- 2 small carrots, cut into strips
- 1 ounce *prosciutto crudo* fat
- 1 clove garlic
- 1/2 medium onion, sliced
- 1 tablespoon extra-virgin olive oil
- 1 to 2 tablespoons flour
- 1 bay leaf
- 1/2 cup dry white wine
- 1 1/2 pounds ripe tomatoes, peeled, seeded, and cut into strips
- nutmeg
- salt
- pepper

Pound the slices of beef with a meat mallet to flatten them. Place a slice of *prosciutto* on top of each, and then place some strips of celery and carrot on top of the *prosciutto*. Roll up tight. You can use toothpicks to make sure the rolls do not open up while cooking, or you can sew them close with cooking thread. Finely chop the *prosciutto* fat to make a soft paste. Chop the remaining celery and carrot. Heat the fat in a sauté pan with the olive oil. Add the remaining celery and carrot, the garlic, and the onion, and finely mince everything together. Heat the olive oil in a pot and add the chopped fat and vegetable mixture. While it is slowly cooking, dip the meat rolls in the flour, shake off any excess, and put them in the pan to brown on low heat. Turn them gently from time to time. Add the bay leaf and pour in the wine. When the wine has evaporated, add the tomatoes and season with salt, pepper, and nutmeg. Cover and let simmer for about 1 hour, always on low heat. When they are ready, remove the rolls and place them on a serving dish. Blend the pan juices in a food processor and pour over the rolls. Serve warm.

COOKING TECHNOLOGY: TOOLS, METHODS, AND PROCEDURE

Italian domestic kitchens, in both rural homes and urban apartments, tend to be quite large, as these are also areas for families to gather and relax. In the older countryside homes, the kitchen (la cucina) used to be the largest room, and also the warmest one in winter, heated by the fireplace or the stove. In some small city apartments the kitchen is now reduced to a cooking area (angolo cottura) in the dining space, but there is a clear preference for larger rooms, because most food, especially for dinner and during the weekend, is prepared at home. Little food is sold already cooked, to buy as so-called take-out, and home deliveries are still quite rare.

Despite the reduction of the space dedicated to cooking, it has never been easier to cook at home. The times when food was prepared in pots hanging over the hearth or placed over wood or coal stoves are long gone. Now most kitchen stoves are operated with gas, either through a connection with the city gas-pipe network or with small gas tanks that can be bought where there is no gas piping, which is actually still the case in some villages. Electric stoves are also widely available, but many people prefer the gas-operated ones because the burners are easier to regulate. Most stoves have four burners, but some have a fifth, usually an elongated one, in the center, where it is possible to place long pots like those used to prepare fish.

Home ovens are either electric or gas. Many are now equipped with special turning gears to which a spit can be applied, so that chickens and sausages can be roasted on the revolving spit. Usually a pan with potatoes or other vegetables is placed underneath to gather the drippings.

Apartments do not usually come with stoves, refrigerators, or most appliances, including dishwashers and washing machines. Each family has to purchase its own kitchen appliances and take them away when they move. That is why they are pretty common wedding gifts, or, in the case of a single person, housewarming gifts. The kitchen always comes with a sink, quite often composed of one or preferably two basins, and a slightly inclined surface used to dry dishes and pots. Above the sink there is a special cabinet with an open rack at the bottom where dishes and glasses can be left to drip and dry. Dishes come in three shapes: a large flat one, a large deeper one (used for pasta and soups), and a smaller flat one for desserts. For everyday meals, the same glass is used for both wine and water, while for special occasions many households bring out their wine and champagne glasses. Wine lovers offer white and red wines in different glasses (the ones for the red being wider and deeper) and pour aged wines in decanters before serving. Forks, knives, spoons, and teaspoons are usually placed on the table near the crockery. Cups and small cups for milk, tea, and coffee are also a customary part of the eating utensils in every household.

Refrigerators are customarily smaller than the ones in the United States, although there is a trend to build them increasingly bigger. They are composed of a small freezer section and a larger cold section. The most advanced ones have areas with different temperatures and levels of humidity to imitate the environment of a cellar. Separate freezers have become common in many households, often kept outside or in the basement, if there is one. Most refrigerators do not have icemakers, but simply ice trays that need to be filled with water and placed in the freezing section. At any rate, Italians tend to use little ice in their drinks. This is a custom that puzzles many foreigners, especially in summer when the heat can be quite brutal. Dishwashers are quite common, especially in families where housewives work, and are also offered as wedding gifts.

Besides big appliances, lots of smaller ones have become current. First and foremost, in the past few years microwaves have invaded Italian kitchens, especially in younger households. Older people are still skeptical about them and even nurture doubts about the consequences that food cooked with waves can have on their health. Younger generations show none of those hesitations. It is possible to find cookbooks about how to cook anything with a microwave oven. At the very least, many use it to thaw and to warm up food. Most food lovers, though, find that dishes prepared in the microwave lack the texture and the hues of the food prepared in other ways. To address this objection, food companies are creating precooked single-portion dishes that can be kept in the freezer and popped in the microwave at the last minute.

Pressure cookers are much more popular in Italy than in the Unites States. As in the case of microwaves, there are cookbooks that teach how to use pressure cookers to prepare many dishes. Besides boiling soups or preparing stews, these appliances are even used to make such elaborate dishes as *risotto* and *polenta*.

Other common appliances are electric grills, coffee grinders, toasters, blenders, mixers, cheese graters, *salumi* slicers, and electric eggbeaters, all of which are also used by inexpert cooks. There are other machines that have become common wedding gifts but which end up being used quite rarely, such as deep-frying machines. These are composed of a main body that must be filled with frying oil, covered by a lid, and a sort of revolving metal wire basket inside it. The instrument, if well set and finely regulated, can actually give very good results, and it avoids the smell of frying oil in the kitchen, but it requires such large amounts of oil that the costs of operation are often quite high. Other contraptions are used to knead dough or to prepare ice creams. A quite common device used by those who enjoy making pasta at home is the pasta rolling machine. Operated manually or electrically, it consists of heavy metal cylinders that roll the dough to the desired thinness. Some of these machines also cut pasta in different shapes. There are many traditional instruments used to produce local cuts of pasta, like the *chitarra* in Abruzzo, made of thin wires tensed in a wooden frame. The sheet of pasta is placed over the wires and pushed through them with a rolling pin. Another contraption, similar to a small metal colander, is used to make *passatelli* from a mixture of eggs, grated cheese, bone marrow, and nutmeg.

Besides these specific instruments, pots and pans are commonly employed according to the different cooking methods. As in most European cuisines, these are steaming, boiling, blanching, stewing, simmering, sautéing, frying, deep frying, roasting, grilling, and baking.

Roasting is mostly done in the oven. In the past, it was customary to roast meat on a spit over a wood fire, and in the countryside this method is still used, giving the meat a special aroma. In certain areas of Sardinia, on the other hand, pig is traditionally roasted over coal in large holes dug in the ground, covered with rocks and wood. Meat and fish are often grilled, especially outdoors, but home barbecues have never become particularly popular.

The same cooking methods used at home are common in professional kitchens. What does change are the instruments available to cooks, who must be able to prepare food in large quantities and in limited time. Technological developments play a fundamental role in always providing new appliances that allow changes in the dishes proposed. Even the most traditional elements, like the pizza oven, have changed over time: besides the brick oven fueled with wood, satisfactory results can now be achieved with electric ovens that recreate the same cooking conditions. Nevertheless, in smaller establishments, the instruments and the techniques are often similar to those used in private homes.

THE TRANSMISSION OF CULINARY TRADITIONS

In the patriarchal society of the past, women were in charge of transmitting their knowledge and experiences in all culinary matters to the new generations. There was no desire for new recipes; the main task was to make the best of the limited resources available. Furthermore, food and dishes were connected with time and the cycle of life: Through them, the community was able to participate in and to mark changes in the seasons, the succession of crops, and the various phases in a person's life. These ceremonies and customs play a very important role in the construction of any society's identity. Recipes and techniques were transmitted orally and by practical example. Young girls were asked to help their mothers with the kitchen chores, starting from the easiest and less dangerous ones, to go onto more complex tasks. Socially relevant know-how was transmitted, while the inherited distinction of roles that sustained the patriarchal society was confirmed. Young girls were supposed to be able to prepare and cook food by the time they were ready for marriage. A woman with scarce culinary abilities was pitied and frowned upon.

In the countryside, even when women learned how to read and write, traditional dishes and procedures were mostly transmitted orally. There were no quantities, no weights, and no measurements, so everything was prepared following the cook's eyes, nose, hands, and taste.

Written recipes were at first the exclusive domain of professional chefs and cooks, mostly men, who had made a business out of food preparation and service. Only at the end of the eighteenth century, with the development of a literate and urban bourgeoisie, was the need to write down recipes felt. Many women enjoyed writing down the ingredients and the instructions to prepare their favorite dishes, especially when they needed to teach the recipe to a cook who was likely to come from another area with different traditions. The communication worked both ways, with bourgeois housewives taking notes on the new recipes learned from their staff. The habit of writing down recipes spread also to the countryside, especially in better-off households. Small notebooks, transmitted from mother to daughter, are still found among the beloved relics proudly owned by many Italian families. They are often pages soiled by sauces and juices, written with an old-fashioned hand, mentioning measurements and weights that are no longer used. Ounces, pounds, and other local measures puzzle modern readers, who often have to rely on their own experience and taste to re-create the recipe.

During the Fascist era and the world wars, women had to cope with scarce supplies. Women's magazines and recipe books insisted on dishes that would save money and resources, without leaving the family discontented. It was up to women to wage the daily confrontations with the black market (borsa nera).

When after World War II many families left their lands of origin, moved to the nearby cities or to other regions in their quest for a better life, and eventually joined the industrial or clerical workforce, the traditional system of transmission that had functioned for generations showed its limits. Most working women had no time to teach their children how to cook. Preparing the daily meals for the family was considered by many housewives as a chore that they hoped their daughters would not have to deal with when they had their own families. On the receiving end, young women did not want to perpetuate the patriarchal society that had forced their mothers into the kitchen, so they concentrated their energy on their studies and their careers. As a result, in the 1970s and 1980s many young people, especially those from urban families, did not learn how to cook. The chain of transmission seemed irremediably broken.

Fresh Anchovies with Escarole (*Aliciotti con l'indivia*)

- 2 pounds escarole
- 2 pounds cleaned fresh anchovies
- 6 cloves garlic, slivered
- 2 tablespoons dried bread crumbs
- 1 tablespoon extra-virgin olive oil
- salt
- pepper

Slice, salt, and drain the escarole in a colander for 2 hours. Wash and pat dry the fresh anchovies with paper towel. Rub a 9-inch round baking dish with extra-virgin olive oil. Arrange the anchovies in one layer. Salt and pepper to taste. Distribute a few slivers of garlic over the anchovies and some of the escarole. Repeat layers of anchovies, escarole, and garlic until all of the ingredients are used up.

Cover with the bread crumbs and drizzle with olive oil. Bake in preheated 400°F oven for 40 minutes. Serve tepid or at room temperature.

COOKBOOKS, MAGAZINES, AND TV

Then came the 1990s, with the renewed interest in food and wine, the latter finally considered a major component of the Italian culture and society. The economic value of many disappearing products became evident to many, who invested to save specialties that otherwise would have vanished. The artisans who were the depositories of precious know-how and techniques were treated with respect and admiration, and young people were again attracted to traditional professions related to food and wine, which not only ensured a decent living, but also enjoyed social respect and appreciation. Young professionals, who often lived by themselves, expressed their desire to follow recipes and learn dishes that their mothers had at times intentionally abandoned. It is now considered hip to be able to invite one's friends over and dazzle them with refined and complex preparations or to offer them unusual delicacies, mostly discovered from the almost endless legacy of local productions. The desire to emulate the hip section of society also inspired middle- and lower-middle-class youth to look at food and cooking in new ways.

However, there was a widespread and heartfelt need for guidance in culinary matters. Women's magazines have always had a recipe section, but those publications were considered too lowly and bleak, too connected with the image of a frustrated housewife, to be appreciated by many of these wannabe chefs. They searched for higher, more appealing authorities. For decades, food magazines like *La Cucina Italiana* had represented the high end of gastronomy, but their recipes, as well as those found on professional publications, were too complicated for people who were just starting out. Furthermore, some glossy magazines were perpetuating the *nouvelle cuisine* style that was going out of fashion, outdated by the renewed interest in traditional and local food. New publishers like La Gola first, and *Gambero Rosso* and Slow Food later, filled this void, offering magazines and books that spoke the language of the new generation of food lovers but at the same time were accessible and suggested doable recipes. A landslide of food and wine magazines has now invaded kiosks all over Italy, varying in graphic style, contents, and price. They cater to various sections of the public, from housewives who need a simple but creative recipe to vary their family menu, to weekend amateurs looking for dishes to surprise their dates, to proficient cooks who enjoy expanding their repertoires.

The next frontier for food is TV. Although from the 1970s personalities like Luigi Carnacina, Vincenzo Buonassisi, Luigi Veronelli, and actress Ave Ninchi have talked about food and wine on TV, in the 1980s some new shows concentrated on the culinary riches of the Italian provinces and countryside. The anchors often adopted lyrical tones that perpetuated the theme of the good old days. This approach to food is still prevalent. Now almost every TV channel has its own cooking shows, food documentaries, and even food news. In 1999 the first Italian food channel started broadcasting, as a joint venture between *Gambero Rosso* and Rai Sat, the satellite division of the public TV network.

The interest of the media in gastronomy has spurred a new generation of chefs who are comfortable in front of cameras and on the pages of magazines and newspapers. The new trend started with chefs who in the 1970s and 1980s were inspired by the changes brought by *nouvelle cuisine* in France, which required new presentations, smaller portions, lighter sauces, and fresh food.[2] The most famous of these revolutionaries was probably Gualtiero Marchesi, who dared to change traditional dishes without adhering to the classic international style of French *haute cuisine*.[3] His *risotto* topped by a paper thin gold leaf made history. The star chefs have added glamour to a profession that until a few years ago was not considered particularly desirable for a brilliant young person.

PROFESSIONAL COOKING

Many of the new chefs do not have formal professional training, which in Italy is almost solely provided by the Hotel Schools (*Scuola alberghiera*), at the high school level.

The most successful establishments are either family businesses, handed down from generation to generation, or in more recent times the enterprise of a single creative chef who starts his or her own restaurant.[4] In many cases, these chefs did other studies and then, spurred by the passion for food, took to cooking, learning from other chefs, and traveling all over Europe and the world to widen their perspectives. When they finally open their own place, they never stop creating original dishes and exploring old traditions and new trends. Quite often, their restaurants are located in small villages or provincial towns, particularly concentrated in northern and central Italy, with a few notable exceptions in Naples and Palermo. The choice of a rural or provincial environment can be explained by lower costs of the locations (rent and real estate), the closeness to the sources of fresh products, and the presence of older staff, usually women,

Chef in country restaurant, Tuscany. © Art Directors/Eric Smith

who still maintain the know-how to make time-consuming and complicated dishes. Needless to say, dining at these establishments is quite expensive, because of the food but also because of the elegant decors and
exquisite service. As a consequence, the clientele often come from the
cities, where gourmets always on the quest for the perfect meal also have
the means to afford high-priced restaurants.

Most of these star chefs are men, perpetuating a tradition that wants the
creative person in the kitchen to be a male, while the humbler duties are
reserved for women or young male apprentices. From the nineteenth century, the luxury restaurants and hotel chefs were always professionally
trained men, often educated in France. On the other hand, in family-run
trattorie and *osterie*, the cooks were prevalently women, while their husbands worked the tables and were in charge of the clients. It was, and still
is, common to find women preparing and selling food in stalls on the

street. Recently, young food lovers have been buying old *osterie* and trying to revive them by creating a relaxed and comfortable environment where clients can enjoy local wine and traditional recipes. Very often couples or groups of friends try their luck in these ventures. In this case, the gender division of roles is quite blurred, and whoever is better at cooking is in charge with the kitchen, often working with local staff.

The prevalence of family businesses and the rising tide of chefs and cooks without professional experience constitute a major challenge for professionally trained cooks, graduating from the Hotel Schools. Their style and the techniques they are educated in are often considered old-fashioned and unhip. After graduation, many of them prefer to start as apprentices in a restaurant of renown to acquire experience and create profitable contacts for future jobs. Some prefer to go and try their luck in foreign countries, usually in Italian restaurants. They have too little experience to become sous-chefs in popular restaurants, but they are too qualified to work in collective facilities like hospitals, schools, and company canteens, which prefer to hire less professional but cheaper staff, usually coordinated by some high-level professional. They often end up working in hotels, cruise ships, and other tourist facilities, with little claim to fame. The whole industry is undergoing major changes, just as Italian cuisine is enjoying widespread popularity all over the world.

NOTES

1. Piero Camporesi, "Il pane e la morte: alimentazione e rituali agrari," in *Alimentazione, folclore, società* (Parma: Pratiche Editrice, 1980).

2. Claude Fischler, *L'Homnivore* (Paris: Editions Odile Jacobs, 2001).

3. Gualtiero Marchesi and Luca Vercelloni, *La tavola imbandita: storia estetica della cucina* (Bari: Editori Laterza, 2001).

4. Alberto Capatti, *L'osteria nuova* (Bra: Slow Food Editore, 2000).

4

Typical Meals

While food and recipes have evolved dramatically over the centuries and vary according to different areas, mealtimes have not substantially changed since the late Roman Empire, although the amount of food consumed tended to differ along the centuries.[1] However, the triad of breakfast–midday meal–evening meal (in Italian, *colazione*, *pranzo*, and *cena*) marks daily life all over Italy.[2]

BREAKFAST

Breakfast in Italy is not as substantial as it is in the United States. Children usually have a slightly more structured meal, centered around a bowl of milk, often enriched with coffee (*caffellatte*), cocoa, barley, or industrial chocolate-derivative products such as Ovomaltina or Nesquik. Tea is definitely less common, being considered too light a drink to sustain children in the morning. Beverages are accompanied by plain or flavored cookies (*biscotti*), a slightly sweetened double-baked slice of bread (*fette biscottate*), or simple bread, all of them considered sufficient to ensure the necessary nutrients to get the day started, especially if eaten with jams, preserves, honey, or some kind of chocolate spread like Nutella. Sometimes croissants (*cornetti*, or so-called small horns) or slices of different kinds of cake can substitute for the usual foods. Cereals, which were considered extremely exotic until a few years ago, have found their way into the Italian breakfast. Most of the time, they are still used by a selected minority, either health-conscious consumers or people somehow influenced by the American way of life (or more precisely, by what the media covey to them of the American lifestyle).

It is common for adults to eat breakfast on their way to work. Before leaving home, they drink a small cup of coffee, which for most Italians is synonymous with breakfast. Coffee is invariably prepared with the stove-top coffeemaker, customarily called *moka* or *caffettiera*, that is a necessary fixture in every Italian household. This appliance is made of three metal pieces, usually stainless steel. The bottom piece, which always includes a security pressure valve, holds the water and a sort of funnel designed to contain the coffee grounds. A third piece is then tightened on top on the water container. When the coffeemaker is put on the stove and the water reaches the boiling point, pressure pushes the liquid through the coffee grounds in the funnel till it reaches the top piece. Most people never use soap to wash the *moka* coffee maker but just hot water and a rag to avoid the taste of chemical detergents that spoils the coffee aroma.

There are other kinds of coffeemaking appliances. Before this kind of *caffettiera* became popular after World War II, the use of the so-called Neapolitan coffeemaker was widespread. This contraption was also composed of three pieces, as in the case of *moka*, but the water never reached the pressure necessary to push it up through the grounds. When the water reached the boiling point, the whole appliance was removed from the flame and turned upside-down, so that the water percolated through the grinds by gravity and then gathered in the lower container. Nowadays, people often buy electrical machines that make coffee more similar to the espresso people can get in what are known as bars. They have become a popular wedding gift. Water, brought to boil by a heated coil, falls through a funnel containing the grounds directly into the cup.

Brunch is a new concept in Italy, borrowed from the United States and Great Britain. On weekends, it is mostly available in hotels that cater to a foreign clientele. Very few Italian restaurants have adopted this habit, usually consisting of a more substantial breakfast, quite similar to the American breakfast, with eggs, pancakes, waffles, and savory dishes. In private households, it is definitely unusual. During the weekend, if people wake up late, they prefer to limit themselves to coffee and wait till lunchtime for a more abundant meal.

MIDMORNING SNACK

Due to the scanty quantity of food consumed at breakfast, it is not uncommon to have a midmorning break, called *merenda o spuntino*. For adults, it often consists of another espresso or cappuccino, together with some pastry or a croissant. For the more health-conscious, some fruit or juice is also a viable option.

Classes at school stop at midmorning for a 15- to 20-minute recess, usually called *recreation (ricreazione)*. Children consume a more substantial snack, often brought from home: a small *panino*, a slice of pizza, a piece of cake, a fruit, or, more recently, a commercially produced snack. Some high schools now have in-house cafeterias where students and teachers can buy their snacks and drink their coffee during recess.

APERITIVO

Just before lunch, especially on weekends and vacation days, adults may go to a bar for a premeal drink or *aperitivo*. *Prosecco*, the light sparkling wine produced in the Veneto region, has become particularly popular, but also other slightly alcoholic drinks and mixed drinks are in high demand. *Aperitivo* is usually served with mixed nuts, crackers, potato chips, or olives.

MIDDAY MEALS

The midday meal *(pranzo)* usually takes place between 1 and 2 P.M. In the north, it is not rare to find people who prefer to have lunch as early as 12 P.M., while in the south the preference is for later meals.

Until not long ago, most Italians consumed their lunch at home, making it the biggest meal of the day. Nowadays, most kindergarten and elementary school children have lunch at the school canteen (older students usually finish their school day between 1 and 2 P.M. and go home for lunch). Similarly, all the people working from 9 to 5 have lunch in company canteens or in various kinds of eateries close to the workplace. Still, most people employed in public and government offices finish their working day at around 2 P.M., which allows them to go home for lunch. Also, most shops close more or less between 1 and 4, allowing enough time for shop owners and staff to eat lunch at home.[3]

In the past, the midday meal used to be much more substantial than now, when even people who can eat at home tend to eat less, mainly for reasons of health and fitness. The traditional midday meal was structured around two main courses, called *primo* (first dish) and *secondo* (second dish), a distinction that is still valid. *Primo* would usually be a pasta dish, or a soup; a *secondo* consisted of meat or fish, often served together with one or more side dishes called *contorni*, usually vegetables. Today most people have either a *primo* or a *secondo* at midday and have both courses in the evening. A complete meal with *primo* and *secondo*, often followed by substantial desserts, also mark weekends and special occasions.

Everyday meals usually end with some seasonal fruits, more rarely with a dessert, with the exception of ice creams or frozen desserts in summer. In hot weather, people fix very light meals, with a preference for salads or cold dishes. Even pasta and soups can be served cold in summer. The cold desserts, and lots of fruit, thus compensate for the lighter meal.

For many centuries, sweet dishes were not clearly separated from the savory parts of the meal. In fact, until the seventeenth century Italian cooks were still heavily influenced by medieval culinary traditions that freely mixed sugar and salt, often with generous additions of all kind of spices. The Muslim legacy, especially in Sicily and in the rest of southern Italy, played a paramount role in the development of these customs. Starting from the tenth century, preparation methods for jams and sweet preserves; the use of almonds, raisins, figs, and dates; and spectacular techniques to give sugar the most amazing shapes and colors spread through the Italian courts and invaded France and the rest of Europe during the Renaissance. Sugar is still present in some savory cooking recipes. Ground *amaretti* cookies and fruit-mustard preserve are added to make pumpkin *tortelli* in Mantova, Lombardy. In Naples salty fillings are baked in sweet dough to make savory pies. In Rome, chocolate is added to the most traditional versions of oxtail stew and to pig blood to make *sanguinaccio*, or blood cake. The very word that today means both "pastry" and "pastry shop" in Italian, *pasticceria*, derives from *pasticcio*, which used to designate any baked pie with a dough crust containing all sorts of stuffing, also of the sweet kind. The French expressions *pâté* and *patisserie* also derive from this word.

Spaghetti with Sicilian Pesto

- 2 tablespoons blanched almonds
- 2 tablespoons pine nuts
- 1/2 cup mint leaves
- 2 cloves garlic
- 1/2 cup extra-virgin olive oil
- 2 tablespoons freshly grated Romano cheese
- 1/2 pound ripe tomatoes, peeled, seeded, diced, and strained
- 1 pound spaghetti
- salt

Preheat the oven to 350°F. Place the almonds and the pine nuts on a sheet pan and toast them in the oven for 5 minutes. Remove from the oven and cool.

In a food processor, blend the toasted almonds and pine nuts, the mint, and the garlic, along with half of the olive oil. Blend in the grated cheese. Add the tomatoes, adjust the seasoning, and blend in the remaining oil. Process for half a minute more, until smooth, and transfer this mixture to a large bowl. Leave at room temperature.

Meanwhile, bring a large pot of salted water to a boil. Add the pasta and cook, uncovered, until *al dente*. Drain the pasta and place in the bowl with the tomato pesto. Toss, adjust the seasoning, and sprinkle with grated cheese.

LUNCH AT SCHOOL

School boards usually manage school canteens, so lunches vary according to places and local traditions, within general directives issued by the authorities responsible for education and health.[4]

Each school is now responsible for its own budget, which is formulated on the base of different requirements.[5] The board for each school formulates a document called "Educational Offer Plan," which states the goals and the management style for the institution, including extracurricular activities and all those aspects of school life that ensure the well-being of the children, such as the canteen operation. While each school should operate in the limits of its budget, thus trying to limit the expenses, a law on public services states that contracts must be attributed not according to the lowest bid, but on the base of the "most advantageous economic offer." Besides price, this includes elements such as quality, assistance, service, and even "esthetic and functional characters."[6] Furthermore, the same law imposes the use of organic, typical, and traditional products, including PDOs (Protected Designation of Origin), to school canteens in everyday food preparations to favor high quality and organic agricultural production. Even before that, a decision of the Highest Administrative Court *(Consiglio di Stato)* stated that elementary schools can limit themselves to choose the services of catering and food companies from its own province to consider the taste of local constituencies and to ensure effectiveness in communication between schools and catering companies.[7]

The structure of the courses in a school lunch tends to be similar to a complete homemade meal, with a *primo* and a *secondo* with *contorno*, followed by fruit or, more rarely, dessert. It is considered very important that children get enough food to guarantee an acceptable variety of nutritional elements for each meal, so the multiple course structure is maintained even if the portions are small. Since children are usually diffident toward food with which they are not familiar, school canteens try to serve quite bland and common dishes. *Primo* is customarily pasta seasoned with a simple tomato sauce, a dish that all of the students are supposedly used to. Soups are not particularly popular, and neither are vegetables, but French fries and potatoes in general are popular. Meat is served in the most unobtrusive fashions, such as grilled or pan-seared chicken breasts or sliced beef. The latter is known as *fettina*, or "thin slice," and when the budget allows it, veal is the meat of preference, considered as lighter and softer. Sliced meats can also be cooked in a light tomato sauce (*pizzaiola*) or breaded and fried (*fettina panata*). Meals are always supposed to end with fresh fruit that children usually have no problem eating, such as pears, apples, or bananas.

For both budget and hygiene reasons, school canteen meals are commonly precooked by specialized and authorized caterers and then warmed up in the school premises and served by the canteen staff. Very few schools can afford full-time cooks, although in smaller towns and villages it is still pretty common for the children to get meals prepared and cooked on the spot. Teachers take turns to ensure their presence during meals, to supervise discipline but also to provide children a less anonymous environment. It is often their task to introduce their students to unfamiliar dishes and to convince the children to at least try the food. Meals are customarily accompanied by water or fruit juice, while sodas are still frowned upon, even if children consume them at home. Milk, which still plays an important role in American school canteens, is not so common for lunch in elementary schools in Italy, while it is a common beverage in kindergartens.

High schools usually do not have canteens, because the school day ends by 2:30 at the latest. In case of schools that offer afternoon elective activities, such as music, sports, arts, or foreign languages, they might have small canteens such as those seen for adults. The same holds true for universities. Because in Italy there are no campuses, but students live with their families or in rented apartments outside the university compound, canteens are structured just like the ones in large business companies, offering meals at subsidized prices.

LUNCH AT WORK

Canteens are commonplace in large companies. When the number of full-time employees reaches a certain level, the unions that represent them usually negotiate meal deals with the company management. They include either a full-service canteen with subsidized prices, or, in case a canteen is not available, the monthly distribution of meal tickets (*buoni pasto*) that can be redeemed in shops, bars, and restaurants near the workplace. Most of the time, employees of smaller companies have to provide for themselves.

Company canteens, usually structured as self-service restaurants, offer a choice of a couple or more *primi*, a couple or more *secondi*, a few side dishes, fruit, and desserts. Also in this kind of canteen, meals are very often brought in by specialized caterers and only reheated on the premises. Many canteens now offer vegetarian or low-calories dishes, responding to a growing demand for healthier food.

When lunch is consumed outside the company premises, workers and employees can chose to sit down and have a meal in a local restaurant, often limiting themselves to a *primo* or a *secondo* (rarely both), or they can opt for lighter snacks. In this case they purchase a slice of pizza, a sandwich, or a *panino* in many bars and deli shops, and they consume them either on the spot, or outdoors, or even at their desk. Groceries and bakeries often prepare *panini* and pizza at lunchtime, especially if they are in the vicinity of offices and shops.

It is not uncommon for workers to bring their own lunches from home. They can consist of a cooked dish that does not need reheating or of a simple *panino*. Some companies are now providing refrigerators and microwave ovens for the use of their employees, who can then either reheat their cooked meals (at times leftovers from the previous night's dinner) or buy frozen meals that only need to be thawed. When lunches are consumed within the workplace, many opt for yogurt, fruit, and low-calorie meals and then have a larger meal at dinner.

When sitting down for a meal, many adults drink beer or wine, though in small amounts to avoid sleepiness in the afternoon. When they opt for a smaller meal, either eaten outdoors or at the workplace, a soda, a fruit juice, or just water is usually preferred. When meals are consumed at home, or during more formal meals, adults tend to consume more wine, but usually with moderation; looking tipsy at the table is considered improper. This said, most adults consider alcohol as part of a complete meal. They might settle for affordable wine during the week and then indulge in more expensive bottles on special occasions or for the Sunday meal.

After lunch, it is practically mandatory to take some time for another espresso. Many companies have warm beverage vending machines that sell espresso, cappuccino, hot chocolate, or tea. These machines are prevalent where adults work, while in colleges and universities soda vending machines have become common fixtures next to those distributing warm beverages.

AFTERNOON SNACKS

In the middle of the afternoon, most children are served another *merenda*, a light snack similar to what they consume at school during morning recess. When at home, they habitually get a larger choice of yogurt, fruit, cakes, biscuits, or commercial snacks to pick from. In the past few years, a certain diffusion of sweet prepackaged snacks is definitely noticeable, particularly for young children. New products are created and marketed specifically for the youngest consumers, advertised during cartoon shows or in children's comic books. Nevertheless, because it is parents who actually buy the snacks, marketers are usually careful to stress the nutritional value of their products: digestibility, energy provided, or pureness of the ingredients. When snacks are geared toward teenagers, their coolness or their pleasurable aspects are pointed out. Adults usually do not consume sweet snacks but would rather munch on smaller, often sugar-free candies. Savory snacks, like crackers or potato chips, are also popular and often less age-specific than sweet snacks. They are often offered with *aperitivi*.

When Italians receive guests in the afternoon, they tend to serve coffee, with a choice of sweet snacks. Some adults prefer tea to coffee on these occasions. Both at home and at bars, tea is usually preferred in prepackaged bags. Tea leaves are also sold by the pound in grocery shops or in specialty shops, but the lack of a tea culture in Italy makes them something quite special, mostly limited to aficionados. Very few people go through the hassle of brewing tea in a teapot. If they do, they tend to prefer teabags. Even fewer people choose the large Chinese-style tea leaves that are brewed in the individual cup, although the diffusion of Asian specialty shops makes these kinds of teas more accessible. Tea is customarily served with sugar and a slice of lemon. The habit of pouring milk in one's tea is considered foreign, specifically British.

Unlike the widespread American habit to stop for drinks or a beer after work, most Italians do not consume alcoholic beverages outside their meals or the premeal *aperitivo*, although after-dinner drinks are not uncommon. Nevertheless, even when beer is becoming increasingly ordinary, there is no bar or cocktail-bar culture comparable to that of the United States or northern Europe.

Zabaione Egg Cream

- 6 egg yolks
- 2 tablespoons sugar
- 2 tablespoons Marsala wine

Place the egg yolks in a small metal saucepan (better if it has a rounded bottom). Add the sugar and mix it with a whisk for a few minutes. When the mixture lightens in color and it starts making small bubbles, place the saucepan over a pot full of water simmering over medium heat. Make sure the water does not reach a boil. Keep on mixing with the whisk for 5 minutes, until it becomes a thick, smooth cream. Pour the *zabaione* in individual dessert cups, and serve with *biscotti*.

EVENING MEALS

The evening meal *(cena)*, which in the past tended to be lighter, is now acquiring more importance, because it is often the only time of the day where the whole family can sit together. Breakfast is a fast and often solitary meal, and the midday meal is often consumed away from home. The structure of a weekday evening meal is similar to midday: a *primo* (with a more pronounced preference for soups), a *secondo* with a side dish, and some fruit. Many opt either for a *primo* or a *secondo* or also prepare a single dish that includes more than one element. It is not unusual to keep some cheese and cold cuts in the refrigerator that can be used to fix a fast, light *cena*, together with a fresh tossed salad, tomatoes, or other vegetables. In recent years frozen meals have become increasingly popular, especially with younger people and singles. Frozen prepackaged *primi* and *secondi* are now available in most supermarkets and grocery shops, ready to be reheated in the microwave or simply sautéed in a pan, as in the case of pasta dishes. Although there is not a large choice of canned soups, precut vegetable mixes are sold frozen in bags. It is also possible to purchase some dehydrated soup and rice dishes that only need to be cooked in boiling water for a few minutes. If you are in a hurry, you can prepare your saffron *risotto* from a bag in 15 minutes. The result is obviously different from the real thing, but definitely acceptable.

As we have already mentioned, usually desserts are not part of everyday meals, with the exception of ice creams or other frozen desserts in summer. During weekdays, many adults would rather have fruit after their meals, while they customarily consume sweet food for breakfast or during breaks. Desserts are often perceived as festive elements, celebrating a Sunday meal, a holiday, a special occasion, or even a simple dinner with friends.

Evening meals, just as at midday, are accompanied by wine, beer, or nonalcoholic drinks, including sodas. After dinner, adults sometimes have some liquor. Many people love to drink digestive alcoholic drinks, usually herb- or vegetable-based and with a somewhat bitter taste, which for this reason are called *amaro*, or bitter.

Pasta and Bean Soup (*Pasta e Fagioli*)

- 10 ounces dried *borlotti* beans
- 3 tablespoon extra-virgin olive oil
- 1 clove garlic, finely chopped
- 1 teaspoon chopped fresh rosemary
- 1 teaspoon chopped fresh parsley
- 1 tablespoon flour
- 2 tablespoons fresh tomato puree
- 1/2 pound dried pasta (egg *tagliatelle*, cut into short pieces, or *ditalini*)
- 2 tablespoons grated *parmigiano reggiano*
- salt
- pepper

Cover the beans with cold water in a large bowl and let soak for at least 8 hours. Drain them and then place them in a heavy-bottomed pot with enough cold water to cover. Salt the water and bring to a boil over medium-high heat. Turn the heat to low and let simmer for 2 hours, until the beans are tender. Set aside; do not drain.

Heat the olive oil in a small pan. Sauté the garlic, rosemary, and parsley, and after half a minute add the flour. Stir continuously over low heat for 2 minutes. When the flour starts to brown, add the tomato puree and 1/2 cup hot water. Once this mixture comes to a boil, add it to the beans. Season with salt and pepper.

Meanwhile, bring a pot of salted water to a boil. Cook the pasta until still quite *al dente*, drain, and add it hot to the bean soup. Stir and let the soup come to a simmer, making sure that the pasta stays *al dente*. Serve hot in deep bowls, with a drizzle of extra-virgin olive oil and a sprinkle of grated *parmigiano reggiano*.

LATE-NIGHT MEALS

Especially in summer, after a night out, it is not uncommon for young people (but also for adults) to organize a so-called midnight spaghetti party (or *spaghettata di mezzanotte*). Because every household always has at least some pasta, olive oil, and garlic in the pantry, the most common dish on this occasion is pasta tossed in warm olive oil and garlic, often with the addition of some red-hot chili pepper *(pasta aglio, olio e peperoncino)*. There are various versions of this simple dish, ready in 15 minutes. Some people also fry dry bread crumbs with the oil and the garlic; others chop fresh parsley or even walnuts. Other people opt for a slightly complicated pasta dish, such as *carbonara* (with bacon and eggs) or *amatriciana* (with onion, bacon, and tomato).

Spaghetti all'amatriciana

- 1/2 pound *guanciale* (cured pig's cheek) or smoked bacon
- 2 tablespoons extra-virgin olive oil
- 1 teaspoon crushed hot chili pepper
- 1 tablespoon dry white wine
- 1 (28-ounce) can peeled tomatoes
- 1 pound spaghetti
- pepper
- 3 tablespoons coarsely grated Romano cheese

In a large pan, sauté the *guanciale* (or bacon) in the olive oil with the hot chili pepper. Add the white wine, and let it evaporate. Add the tomatoes. (Some people prefer to use the tomatoes whole, while traditionalists prefer the tomatoes crushed by hand.) Cook the sauce for 10 minutes, stirring frequently. Season with salt and a generous amount of ground black pepper. Meanwhile, cook the spaghetti until slightly undercooked. Drain the pasta and pour it in the pan with the hot sauce. Toss for one minute over medium heat to allow the pasta to absorb the sauce. Sprinkle with the Romano cheese and toss again.

NOTES

1. Massimo Alberini, *Storia del pranzo all'italiana* (Milan: Rizzoli, 1996).

2. P. Meldini, "A tavola e in cucina," in *La famiglia italiana dall'Ottocento a oggi*, ed. P. Melograni (Rome-Bari: Laterza, 1988).

3. Censis, *Rapporto sulla situazione sociale del paese 2003* (Milan: Franco Angeli, 2003).

4. Rosa Maria Finocchiaro, *La ristorazione scolastica: prospettive future* (Rome: Ministero delle Politiche Agricole e Forestali, n.d.).

5. Public Law on School Autonomy, D.P.R. 275 (8 March 1999).

6. Public Law 488, Article 59 (23 December 1999).

7. *Consiglio di Stato* V, n. 1375 (24 November 1992).

5

Eating Out

RESTAURANTS

Although Italians enjoy cooking and eating their meals at home and inviting friends and family for meals is a very common custom, restaurants constitute an important element in Italian social life. They are usually called *ristoranti, trattorie,* and *osterie.* The meaning of these words has changed over time. Now a *ristorante* is usually an establishment that offers nice décor, good service, and an upscale menu, but the word is also used for other kinds of eating places known as *trattorie* and *osterie,* providing simpler food and service at more affordable prices.

Restaurants are rarely patronized by persons eating by themselves, with the notable exception of businessmen from out of town or single men and women who prefer not to cook. Eating a complete meal by oneself is considered quite unsatisfying and psychologically depressing. Restaurants thus become places to celebrate birthdays, to have dates, and to mark holidays and special occasions

Most restaurants are independent enterprises. The hotel restaurants that until World War II set the pace of refinement and elegance are now usually anonymous, geared toward business clientele. The large facilities still existing in hotels are used for corporate dinners or wedding banquets, when guests receive all the same dishes. Most hotels only have a breakfast room.

With the renewed interest in traditional dishes and local ingredients, *osterie* and *trattorie* are undergoing a definite renaissance. It is not by

Piazza Navona restaurants and cafes, Rome. © Art Directors/TRIP/Bob Turner

chance that the guide to the Italian *osterie* published by Slow Food since 1990 has been a solid hit all along. Many small establishments have been sold to young entrepreneurs, who are often passionate about food and wine, who most of the time have little or no formal professional training, and who try to revive almost forgotten dishes at reasonable prices. At times, the new owners hire older local women or relatives to prepare dishes requiring know-how and long preparation time, as in the case of homemade pasta. Some *ristoranti* decide to offer traditional, regional, and local dishes in a more upscale environment. In this case there is a greater attention to the choice of ingredients, produce, and wine, with a tangible increase in prices.

Other establishments bet on new cooking styles, either by importing foreign models (such as *nouvelle cuisine* in the 1980s and, more recently, American steakhouses or Japanese-style sushi bars) or by adopting a creative approach toward Italian cuisine. Experiments in Italian-inspired fusion can result, of course, in either stimulating and really groundbreaking meals or in pretentious and short-lived forays.

Savory Sardines (*Sarde in Saor*)

- 2 pounds whole, cleaned fresh sardines
- 2 pounds (4 medium) white onions, thinly sliced
- 2 cups all-purpose flour
- 1 1/2 cups white wine vinegar
- 1 tablespoon raisins
- 1 tablespoon pine nuts
- frying oil

Rinse the sardines and dry them thoroughly with paper towels. Open them flat like a book, and then coat them with flour on both sides. Shake off any excess flour.

In a large frying pan, pour enough oil to cover the bottom and place over medium-high heat. When the oil is hot, fry the fish in batches until golden on both sides. Remove from the oil and drain on several layers of paper towel, sprinkling each batch with salt.

After sardines are fried, add a little more oil to the pan and slowly sauté the onions over low heat until soft. Season with salt and add a cup of the vinegar. Cook until the vinegar has evaporated.

On a large serving platter, layer half of the sardines, and then place half the onions on top. Add half of the raisins and the pine nuts. Layer the remaining fish and then the rest of the onions. Cover with the remaining raisins and pine nuts, and sprinkle with the remaining 1/2 cup of vinegar. Let marinate in the refrigerator for at least 1 day. Serve at room temperature.

THE HISTORY OF EATING OUT

The habit of eating out dates back to the Romans. While the higher classes preferred to eat in their abodes or to have slaves and servants cooking for them and bringing food along when they were traveling, the lower class was used to buying and consuming their meals outside their living quarters. Especially in the *insulae*, the large and tall buildings where many families were crammed into very small spaces, kitchens were generally absent because of the fear of spreading fires. When cooking at home, women resorted to small braziers or wood burners, which limited the dishes they could prepare. As a consequence, people often bought food from stalls on the street. The Latin author Seneca mentions them as *lixae*, selling drinks, sweets, and sausages.[1] These stalls could be protected from the sun and rain by some sort of awning (*tentoria*) or wood planks (*tabernacula*). The owner of these one-man enterprises often stocked goods in tiny cellars (*cellae*) under the surrounding buildings, which have been found during archeological excavations. Their business was regulated by law and controlled by city officials. The other option was to patronize taverns (called *taberna*, *caupona*, or *popina*) that, despite their popularity, were frowned upon because of their fame as places of sin. Taverns offered wine, often with a small choice of cooked dishes.[2] Other less legitimate activities like gambling, smuggling, and prostitution took place within their walls, in defiance of police control. In 363 C.E., the Church council of Laodicea forbade monks to enter them. Tavern keepers, who were accused of adulterating wine and conspiring against public decorum, were considered dangerous people, as low as gladiators and magicians. Taverns placed outside the urban centers and along the imperial post stations, offering board and lodging to travelers, were rather called *hospitium*, *diversorium*, or *stabulum*. Because respectable citizens also used them during voyages, they had a much better reputation than the city establishments did. However, the nobles and the rich Romans would go to their peers for hospitality instead of the taverns, adding to the low reputation of public eating and lodging places.

After the fall of the Roman Empire, urban centers suffered heavy depopulation, while self-sufficiency became the rule in the countryside. Most peasants would spend part of their time tending to animals, hunting, fishing, or gathering vegetables and berries from the woods, a set of activities that were considered by the Romans to be spending too much time with wildlife. Each family would gather and cook their own food, while taverns were found only along the main routes of communications. In the Middle Ages, it seems that the term *tavern* (*taberna*) was often used for private households that on occasion provided a roof and something to eat for the rare travelers, usually low-class merchants and, above all, pilgrims.[3] The nobles enjoyed hospitality from their peers or in monasteries.

The second half of the eleventh century marked the rebirth of the exchange economy, the development of markets, and the increase of commerce and trade. Merchants were traveling again all over Europe, demanding lodging and food when their hosts could not accommodate them, which was still the favorite arrangement even when they had to pay a small fee. In the growing cities, a legal and social distinction between places that sold food and drinks, marked again by a bad reputation, and those that also offered hospitality, became commonplace. Along the major commercial routes, the difference appeared definitely more blurred. The expression *albergum*, from which the Italian word *albergo*, meaning "hotel," appeared on documents around this time. These establishments become so profitable that the free communes and the lords started fighting to determine who had jurisdiction over them. At the beginning of the Renaissance, it was possible to distinguish between three different types: places where farmers sold the wine and the food they produced; taverns where professionals sold the products they bought on the market; and other establishments under direct control of the local political powers, be it a lord or a free commune.

For a few centuries, there were few developments in this field. Foreigners traveling in Italy would marvel at the use of forks and of porcelain and terra cotta crockery, at the refined table manners of their fellow guests, and, often, at the paucity of the portions.[4] Furthermore, the widespread use of vegetables and fresh fruit was unusual to northern travelers.[5]

From the seventeenth century, new drinks like chocolate, tea, and coffee become fashionable with the nobles and the developing bourgeoisie. Coffee was first introduced to Venice, which traditionally maintained close relationships with the Far East. Around the 1670s in Paris, travelers dressed in exotic Turkish clothes peddled the drink on the street. In the following decade, the Italian Procopio Coltelli opened the famous coffeehouse Procope starting a fashion that spread everywhere, including Italy. Coffeehouses, or *caffè*, become the meeting place for the budding bourgeoisie, especially in the northern regions under Austrian control. In the new public place, where tea and chocolate were also sold, professionals would discuss politics, culture, and the economy. One of the first political journals published in Italy, adopting the Enlightenment ideals, was actually called "Il caffè."

At the beginning, a new kind of establishment became fashionable in Italy, following the trend set in France: the restaurant, more often called *ristorante* or *trattoria* (from the French term *traiteur* indicating an establishment selling cooked food to take away). At first, the restaurant indicated restorative stocks that had become *à la mode* in Paris before the revolution. The places where these stocks were sold soon offered other warm courses that clients could choose from a list (*à la carte*), guaranteeing a more refined setting than common taverns and serving meals at any time to satisfy the different need of the clients. The service was more custom oriented than in taverns, and many establishments also had private dining rooms to protect the clientele's privacy.[6] Needless to say, the bill was higher than in taverns, but the growing bourgeoisie represented a viable market for the new enterprises. The fashion spread through Europe, reaching Italy in second half of the nineteenth century, while the country was being unified by the Savoy dynasty. Many cooks that had worked in noble households started their own businesses, opening *ristoranti* and *trattorie* in all the major cities and catering to the higher classes. At the end of the century, tourism became a major activity all over Italy, with many foreigners traveling and expecting the same amenities they had become accustomed to in other parts of Europe: grand hotels, good service, and elegant restaurants. Italy had no leading figures like César Ritz and Auguste Escoffier, but a great numbers of chefs started being professionally trained, working in so-called brigades following the French *haute cuisine* system.

Few could afford those establishments. People from lower classes kept on patronizing taverns, then called *osterie* (*oste* was the tavern keeper). Other common names for these establishments, which mainly sold wine and at times a few cooked dishes, were *bettola* (usually in a derogative sense), *gargotta* (from the French *gargotte*), and *mescita* (where wine was the main merchandise). Dialect terms were, for instance, *bacaro* in Venice, *crotto* in some areas of Lombardy, *fiaschetteria* in Tuscany, and *fraschetta* in Rome, indicating a place selling wine with a tree branch (*frasca*). The word *taverna* usually had better connotations, maybe because of the reputation of the British tavern. When these places were not part of a lodging facility (which was often the case in cities), many did not even have a kitchen. Clients brought their own food, buying wine from the *oste*, or bought some food on their way to the *osteria*, often close to bakers and grocery shops. When food was provided, the choice was usually limited, and meals were served at set hours. Wine was mostly bought in bulk and sold to the clients by the liter or the half liter. Special measurement bottles were available, so that the customers were sure about the quantity of wine received. They can still be found in restaurants and *trattorie*, and in fact they have made a comeback and are now used to serve the house wine.

Osterie were the gathering places for the men from the neighborhood, where they could play cards, rest, and discuss politics. *Osterie* became an important space for anarchists, socialists, and anybody in trouble with the law. The Socialist Party, nevertheless, was aware of the dangers connected with excessive consumption of alcohol and tried to fight the plague: Filippo Turati, a Socialist leader, was invited to exchange a liter (of wine) for a book, *libro contro litro*. There was an *osteria* for every 174 people in 1904 and 156 in 1913. They were more frequent in the urban centers of the north, where the recent industrialization was attracting many farmers, who were forced to live in small spaces and harsh conditions. In the south, where the warmer climate did not require closed spaces to spend time and gather with friends (a piazza would do), and where many farmers produced their own wines, *osterie* were less concentrated.[7] Particularly in the south, they were not considered proper places for women and children, because of the great quantities of alcohol consumed. The wine was often of very low quality but affordable to anybody. These establishments were mostly family businesses, where the woman tended to cook and the husbands took care of the clients, maintaining the gender division between roles and between private and public spaces.

The bourgeoisie discovered the *osterie* at the end of the nineteenth century when tourists, first on trains and then on bicycles and cars, took to traveling all over the country, especially in the countryside. Many train stations offered a simple restaurant often called a *buffet*, and *trattorie* and coffeehouses also catered to this new kind of client.

In 1908 a German, Hans Barth, wrote the first guidebook to Italian *osterie* in German. He had his book translated into Italian a couple of years later, with the help of the famous poet Gabriele D'Annunzio.[8] World War I put a stop to this development, while accustoming soldiers to get a daily ration of wine (250 grams) and even liquor like *grappa*, cognac, or rum when they were fighting in the trenches. During the Fascist era, the patriotic ideology positioned *osterie* as the quintessential expression of the Italian nature, and hence they were to be preferred to elegant *trattorie* or high-end *ristoranti*. The word *ristorante* itself was frowned upon because of its foreign origin. All of Italy was worthy of being discovered and appreciated. In this spirit, in 1931 the Italian Touring Club published the first *Guide to Italian Gastronomy*, which, overlooking the endemic poverty in many areas of the country, rhapsodized about the frugal nature of many populations and gave large space to festive foods that were often out of reach for many.[9] More ironic and connected with reality was the *Wandering Glutton* guidebook by Paolo Monelli, which gives us a good description of *trattorie* and *osterie* and their specialties all over the country. Italians were rediscovering their local roots just as the regime was working hard to instill the concept of a united motherland. The call for self-sufficiency launched by Benito Mussolini in 1936, followed by the hardships connected first to the World War II and then to the Nazi occupation, made eating out a luxury very few could afford.

It was not until the economic boom starting in the mid-1950s that dining out again became an activity available to many. The word *ristorante* now meant any place where any type of cooked food was provided. The less pretentious ones were called *trattoria*, usually implying a menu offering many local or regional dishes, and a simpler style of service. The word *osteria* was restricted to places that were dedicated to wine drinking, with or without food. The expression had derogatory overtones unless it was used ironically or was given a so-called good-old-time allure by being spelled *hostaria*. Rome was the place of the *dolce vita*, boosted by the 1960 Olympics and the film industry centered in Cinecittà. American stars enjoyed patronizing restaurants, bars, and modest *trattorie*. Some establishments owed their fame to foreign visitors. That was the case of Alfredo in via della Scrofa, whose fettuccine with triple butter (*al triplo burro*) acquired nationwide notoriety in the United States as fettuccine Alfredo but was quickly forgotten in Italy.

BARS AND COFFEEHOUSES

Starting in the 1950s, younger generations found a relaxed and laid-back place to gather in new "American-style" bars. Their fathers' *osterie* were considered old-fashioned and sleazy, carrying bad connotations related to poverty and alcoholism. Of course, these new bars had little in common with the American establishments of the same name. They were rather an evolution of coffeehouses, with a more modern decor and a less refined service, still serving coffee rather than alcoholic drinks and offering a choice of food, pastry, and ice creams. Many of them had a jukebox and a foosball (*biliardino*) table, a sort of billiard game modeled upon soccer. A pool table was less common, because it gave the bar a more adult ambience and a less respectable image. From the 1980s, video games were offered to attract younger clientele.

Despite the success of bars, many cities still boast elegant coffeehouses, usually more expensive than bars, offering great ambience and a nice choice of sweet-and-savory small bites of food. Many of the oldest establishments, like Caffé Greco in Rome or Caffè Florian in Venice, are now considered historical landmarks. These are places where clients sit down and take their time chatting with friends, reading, and having dates. In an urban environment, they ensure calm and privacy, while bars tend to cater to people on the go, who often consume their drinks and their snacks while standing. In smaller towns and in the countryside, nevertheless, bars often have tables and outdoor seating for the summer. Clients, who until a few years ago were mostly male, sit down to discuss politics and to gossip, to play cards, and to enjoy their drinks, making these establishments a modern equivalent of the *osteria* from the past.

The life of Italian bars revolves around coffee and other breakfast drinks, and not so much around liquor and alcohol, although the latter are regularly—and legally—sold in these places. Coffee franchising companies in the United States have adopted the terminology of the Italian bar: The staff members who make coffee are called *baristas*, just as in Italy, and often Italian words are used to indicate the different sizes of the beverage, such as *grande*. Besides this veneer of exoticism, nothing much is borrowed from the Italian bar culture.

The adults who prefer to have breakfast on the go make a quick stop in their favorite bar and have an espresso, often by itself but also accompanied by some croissant or pastry. Italian espresso is definitely different from anything called *espresso* in the United States. The portions are tiny, and the liquid is much denser and often bitter for an American palate. Nobody uses the word *espresso* when giving his or her order. Coffee in a bar cannot be but espresso, so people simply ask for their *caffè*, specifying how they want it. Coffee is consumed either in small cups *(tazzine)* or in small glasses. In this case you would ask for *caffè al vetro* (meaning "in the

Making espresso. © TRIP/H. Rogers

glass"). Espresso can also be *macchiato* when a little amount of milk is added. It is called *macchiato caldo* ("hot") or *freddo* ("cold"), depending on the temperature of the milk. In winter, some people like to add liquor to their espresso, commonly rum, *grappa*, or *sambuca* (juniper liquor). Coffee is then known as *corretto* ("corrected"). Another addition to coffee can be sweetened whipped cream (*panna montata* or just *panna*), and upscale bars sometimes offer small chocolates to the clients with their coffee. Espresso is usually served unsweetened. The clients can choose to drink it as it is or to add sugar (either white or brown) or other sweeteners. The only exception to this habit is found in Naples, where coffee is served sweetened unless the clients specify that they want it without sugar. In Naples, coffee cups are often kept upside-down in hot water at all times, so that when the espresso is served the cold crockery does not lower the drink temperature. Nevertheless, in summer coffee is also prepared in advance for the day, stored in the fridge and served cold as a refreshing drink. The lemon rinds that at times accompany espresso in restaurants and coffeehouses in the United States are quite rare in Italy.

Decaffeinated coffee is now available in most bars, and all major brands are producing increasingly better ground decaf coffee, also for domestic consumption. An old-fashioned but still common alternative to decaffeinated coffee is barley coffee (*caffé d'orzo*), with grounds obtained from roasted barley grains.

Espresso coffee is not the only breakfast drink consumed in bars. Besides tea, *caffellatte* (milk with some coffee) and *cappuccino* are extremely popular. *Cappuccino* takes its name from its brown color, similar to the frock of the capuchin monks. It differs from plain *caffellatte* because it contains a larger quantity of coffee and because the milk is warmed up with high-pressure hot vapors produced by the espresso machines themselves, creating a fluffy froth. Making good *cappuccino* is considered no less of an art than making good coffee. An expert *barista* is highly respected, and clients go out of their way to patronize his or her bar.

Other drinks are available all day long in a bar. Fresh-squeezed citrus juices, such as lemon, orange, and grapefruit, are in high demand. When fresh fruit is not available, customers can order bottled juices that come in all flavors: pear, peach, apricot, apple, and more recently exotic fruit such as mango and kiwi. Other drinks deriving from fruit are *orzata* (made from sprouting barley, sweet almonds, and sugar) and *latte di mandorla* (made from sweet and bitter almonds, sugar, and orange-flower water).

Mass-produced sodas have become popular in the past decades. Besides the brands that can be purchased all around the world, some local sodas have enjoyed uninterrupted success, such as Oransoda and Lemonsoda, bitter-orange soda (*aranciata amara*), citron-flavored soda (*cedrata*), and *chinotto*, a soft drink made from a kind of sour orange (Citrus aurantium) found in Liguria, Sicily, and Calabria.

Most bars sell candies over the counter but also offer pastries, ice cream, and a choice of savory bites. In this case the bar is known as a snack bar and, more recently, as bar *gastronomia*. The latter often offers cooked dishes at lunch, especially if it is located in urban centers near offices or other working places. The average bar displays *panini* (single-portion breads in different shapes, cut in two and filled with various ingredients), *tramezzini* (triangular, made of a sort of *pancarré*, a sort of upscale wonder bread), toasts, slices of pizza, pieces of *focaccia* with *salumi*, and sometimes salads and fruit salads.

KIOSKS AND STREET FOOD

Beside bars, there are plenty of ways to get food on the go. The tradition of street and market food, although dying, is still present. Nevertheless, people are increasingly more skeptical about hygienic conditions and have lost the taste for some of the most traditional foods the street stalls offer.

Every area has its own traditions, especially in the south, where the warmer weather facilitates street and outdoor life. Loitering is far from being considered a nuisance. Particularly in summer, piazzas, church steps, curbs, the tiniest patches of greenery, and even a simple bench become places to hang out, both for the young and the old. In small towns and villages it is still common to bring chairs out of the house and chat with the neighbors while enjoying the cool evening.

Street foods are the legacy of a past when hunger and poverty were common for many city dwellers who did not even have a kitchen at home. That is why many traditional street specialties are made with innards or the simplest ingredients, like bread, pulses, or fruit. In Florence, the most typical street food is *lampredotto*, bread with cow tripe. In Rome, watermelon stalls are extremely popular in summer, together with small booths selling *grattachecca*, shaved ice with fruit or syrup. All over central Italy, vans selling *porchetta* (roasted pork meat with garlic and other spices) are very common. In Naples, small pizzas can still be bought on the street, together with other fried foods; also *o pere e o musso* (small pieces of boiled pork feet and snout with lemon squeezed on top) is still popular. Along the coasts of Puglia, people swallow raw mussels and other crustaceans, often with just some lemon. In Sicily, Palermo is proud of *pane e panelle*, bread with chickpea fritters, and *guastedde*, spleen served in bread with sesame seeds and cheese. Street fairs are also occasions for selling lots of street foods, from roasted peanuts, to candies and fried pastries, *panini*, and fruits.

TAVOLA CALDA AND ROSTICCERIA

Some shops sell ready-made food to take out (home deliveries are still extremely rare). They are called *tavola calda* when they offer dishes that can also be found in any restaurant or made at home, and they often have small tables for the clients who want to eat on the premises. No service is provided; customers buy their dishes, often served in aluminum containers, at the counter and bring them to their tables. They are often required to clean up when they are finished.

Rosticceria specializes in fried or roasted foods that would take too long or be too annoying to prepare at home. These establishments always roast whole chickens on the spit, keeping them turning in special machines that allow customers to see them during the roasting process. Many shopkeepers place diced potatoes under the turning chickens so that the drippings fall on the vegetables. *Porchetta* is also a common specialty in *rosticceria*, particularly in central Italy. Among the fried foods, the most popular are large breaded olives stuffed with meat (*olive ascolane*), *supplì* (breaded balls of rice seasoned with tomato sauce and diced mozzarella), *arancini* (or *arancine*, breaded balls of rice stuffed with peas, ham, or other ingredients, sometimes seasoned with saffron), mozzarella pressed between two slices of bread and passed in beaten eggs (*mozzarella in carrozza*), meatballs (*polpette*), eggplant balls (*polpette di melanzane*), battered slices of vegetables (usually zucchini and eggplant), battered cod, potato fries, and zucchini flowers stuffed with anchovies and mozzarella (*fiori di zucchina*).

Rice Croquettes (*Supplì al Telefono*)

- 2 tablespoons butter
- 1 pound short-grain rice
- 4 cups hot beef broth
- 1/2 cup grated *parmigiano reggiano*
- 5 eggs
- 1 tablespoon minced parsley

- nutmeg
- 2 ounces boiled ham, diced
- 1/4 pound fresh mozzarella cheese, diced
- 1 cup flour
- 1 cup dry bread crumbs
- oil for frying
- nutmeg
- salt

Melt the butter in a saucepan. Add the rice and stir till it is translucent. Add a ladle of broth and simmer until absorbed, stirring occasionally. Keep on adding broth ladle after ladle, always waiting for the broth to be absorbed before adding more broth, until the rice is almost done. Add a third of the grated *parmigiano reggiano* and stir. Remove the rice from the heat, spread it on a wet marble surface (or a large cutting board), and let it cool completely. When it is cold, put it in a big bowl and mix it with the remaining *parmigiano reggiano*, the eggs, a pinch of nutmeg, the parsley, and salt. Make small, elongated balls with the rice mixture, inserting a piece of diced ham and mozzarella in the center of each. Beat the remaining 2 eggs in a small bowl. Dip the rice ball in the flour, then in the beaten eggs, and then in the bread crumbs. Fry in abundant oil and serve the *supplì* hot. They are called *al telefono* (on the phone) because when you bite them, the melted mozzarella will create long cheese strings like telephone wire.

PIZZERIAS

Many *rosticcerie* also use their oven to make pizza either in large metal pans or directly on the bottom of the oven. This kind of pizza, called *pizza al taglio*, is cut according to the customers' request and sold by the weight. Some shops specialize in *pizza al taglio*, adding very few fried items to their menu. In the past few years, pizza has also been sold by the slice, already cut and always having the same dimensions, in places similar to fast foods, where soda is also sold and tables are available to the clients. There are also restaurants that sell pizza à la carte. Customers can sit at their table, order their meal and their drinks from a menu, and be served by waiters. Usually the menu includes some *antipasti* like sliced *salumi*, cheese, or fried food, more rarely vegetables, and some desserts. These places are called *pizzeria*, a name also used for shops selling *pizza al taglio*. Until a few years ago, pizza was served at the table only in the evening. Many establishments now offer it also for lunch. Besides, many *trattorie* have diversified their menu adding pizza. A good pizza maker (*pizzettaro* or *pizzaiolo*) is a great asset, and until a few years ago he or she was highly appreciated. Recently many *pizzaioli* have been immigrants from northern Africa or southern Asia, who are willing to learn a new craft and ask for lesser wages than their Italian colleagues.

CATERING

Catered food is a growing segment of the market. Professional chefs and event planners hire cooks, wait staff, busboys, and cleaning staff to offer a complete package to their clients. The prevalent occasions for a catered meal are corporate events, when the food is brought directly to the company premises, and weddings. In that case, the couple rents an empty place, like a villa, garden, or historical building, and they ask the catering company to take care of everything else. Many of these venues have their own catering organizations. Formal catered meals are structured as in a restaurant, unless the company or the couple prefers a buffet dinner.

ENOTECHE AND WINE BARS

In the past 10 years, wine has become the object of a renewed interest both from connoisseurs and amateurs. Most grocery shops and even supermarkets now offer some choice of good wine, besides the cheaper products that still enjoy large popularity. Some specialized shops, called *enoteche* (sing. *enoteca*) cater to the needs of a growing public who are curious to taste new things and to know more about a world that until a few years ago was a realm reserved to few aficionados. *Enoteche* are the direct development of the wine shops that in the past used to sell bulk wine, pouring it into bottles provided by the clients.

The first occurrence of the word *enoteca* was registered in 1934 in the magazine *Enotria*.[10] At the end of the 1950s, the name was used for establishments centered around their cellar, offering a wide choice of high-quality wine, often from local producers, and at times serving cold dishes of bread, *salumi*, and cheese. *Enoteca* now mostly indicates a shop selling bottled wine, while the term "wine bar" is used for an establishment serving food to accompany the wine. Nevertheless, because they are considered as regular shops by law, *enoteche* often sell gourmet products such as jams, preserves, honey, and other prepackaged delicacies.

Many *enoteche* have an annexed wine bar, which operates under a different business license and is allowed to serve food to be consumed on the premises. Wine bars constitute an increasingly popular alternative to other types of restaurants, especially for high-end customers who are willing and able to spend a lot on a good bottle of wine and are knowledgeable enough to do so.

Partly to meet the burgeoning demand from their clients, partly to make them even more passionate about their products, some *enoteche*, but above all wine bars, organize tasting events and tasting classes. When they take place in wine bars, small bites of food are also provided, so that the clients can get more ideas for their food and wine pairings.

BIRRERIE, PUBS, AND *PANINERIE*

Wine is not the only alcoholic drink that is consumed by those who dine out. Beer is enjoying a growing success, especially among youth. It is less expensive than wine, served in larger servings, and it is refreshing in summer, with a lower alcohol content. New establishments have developed around this renewed passion for beer. They are called *pubs*, using the English word, or *birrerie* (sing. *birreria*) in Italian. The decor is usually quite different from that in other restaurants. Wooden tables and benches are prevalent. No tablecloth is provided, only paper towels. The service is minimal.

Non-Italian dishes are served, such as sauerkraut with boiled wurst sausages, hot dogs, hamburgers with French fries, potato salads, chili con carne, and baked beans. Some pubs also serve salads, pasta, and, above all, Italian-style *panini*, to satisfy all tastes. Some shops focus exclusively on *panini*, calling themselves *paninerie* (sing. *panineria*), a term that became popular in the 1980s before fast food became fashionable. In these shops, *panini*, filled with the most creative ingredients, are often served warm to give them a feeling of a real meal. This custom has spread to snack bars.

Some *birrerie* have introduced high-quality beers, along with the most common brands that can be bought either bottled or on tap. This has allowed some aficionados to become more knowledgeable, starting a new market. Monastery beers from Belgium, stouts from Ireland, red ales from Scotland, and wheat beers from Germany are no longer mysterious beverages.

FAST FOOD

Fast-food restaurants opened in Italy starting in the late 1980s, among heated public debates. Many considered that these shops signaled the demise of Italian tradition and a confirmation of American imperialism.

They first attracted all kinds of clients, including adults curious to taste the novelty. With time, fast-food restaurants have become the province of children, teenagers, and very young adults. The advertising campaigns are clearly geared toward those sectors of the population. Some parents take their children to fast-food restaurants as a treat or to mark special occasions, reinforcing the positive image of a place where normal table manners can be overlooked. Also, the decoration is clearly designed to attract young clients.

However, fast-food restaurants had to adapt themselves to the local taste. They added pasta salads and vegetable salads to their menus. Furthermore, they decided to offer beer and wine.

Some Italian entrepreneurs found the concept appealing and created chains that operate like foreign fast foods but serve only Italian dishes and pizza. These kinds of shops are now quite common in and around train and bus stations, airports, and service areas along the highways.

SERVICE AREAS

Most of the Italian transportation system developed along the highways that the government started building in the 1960s, boosting the development of the national car industry, which guaranteed thousands of jobs. Along the highways, service stations were created to allow drivers to rest and eat. While some of them are simple snack bars selling food, many have become large facilities, including a snack bar, Italian-style fast-food shops, a more formal restaurant, and a supermarket often selling local products. Many Italians enjoy long lunch breaks, especially during long trips.

PICNICS

In summer, but also in spring and autumn when the climate allows it, many Italians enjoy outings on the mountains, walks in the countryside, or hours just spent lying in the sun on a beach. People tend to bring simple *panini* and drinks (including wine) when out for a walk in the country or a hike on the mountains. On the other hand, if they organize a picnic to a place where they can drive, the amount of food brought along increases drastically. It is not uncommon to see whole families unpack folding tables and chairs, coolers, and pots and pans full of cooked food like *lasagna*, fried breaded slices of beef (*fettine impanate*), eggplant *parmigiana*, and rice-filled grilled tomatoes. Until a few years ago similar scenes were

Outside meal, Rome. © TRIP/P. Rauter

also common on the beach. Now people tend to buy light *panini* (with tuna fish, mozzarella, fresh tomatoes, and such) directly from the concessions on the shoreline, together with fruit salads and ice creams. The big lunch on the beach is considered low class and tacky. Many concessions also operate as restaurants. They offer cooked meals, especially at night, allowing clients to dine right on the beach while admiring the sunset and enjoying fresh seafood dishes.

Clam Soup

- 4 pounds clams
- 6 tablespoons extra-virgin olive oil
- 3 cloves garlic
- 2 tablespoons bread crumbs

- 1 tablespoon finely chopped parsley
- 4 slices grilled country bread
- pepper
- salt
- pinch of saffron

Using a stiff brush, carefully clean the clams and soak them in lightly salted water for 24 hours. Remove the clams from the water, and place them in a large pan. Cover the pan with a lid and set it over medium heat, until the clams open, about 7 minutes. Discard any clams that remain closed. Reserve the clams and filter the liquid left in the pan through a fine sieve to eliminate all traces of sand.

Chop the garlic and, in a deep pan, sauté it in the olive oil, together with the bread crumbs. Add the clams and the filtered water, adding enough additional warm water to make a liquid soup. Season with salt, pepper, and a pinch of saffron. Let simmer briefly, until the soup acquires a reddish-gold hue. Serve in a bowl with a slice of grilled bread.

AGRITURISMI AND VIE DEL VINO

New forms of high-end tourism focusing on food and wine as expressions of local culture and traditions have developed in the past 20 years.

An *agriturismo* is an enterprise run by a farmer who offers food and lodging to tourists on his property, using the products from the farm and at times organizing recreational or cultural activities. National and regional authorities promoted this new type of tourism, hoping that it would entice farmers to stay on their land at a time when Italian agriculture was undergoing a major crisis, and many local and traditional productions were at risk of disappearance.

According to the law that regulates this kind of business, farming and animal breeding must remain the main activity, with tourism as an additional source of income.[11] Hence only farmers can start an *agriturismo*. It is not enough to own a farm or a property in the countryside; the land must actually be cultivated. Besides, only preexisting structures can be renovated to provide lodging to the tourists. With a few exceptions determined by local regulations, new constructions are not allowed. Small patches of unproductive land can be dedicated to camping sites for a limited number of tents.

These new establishments enjoyed instant success, responding to the growing interest for rural life, local traditions, and disappearing food products. They offered lodging and meals at very convenient prices, often also selling the products from the farm to the tourists. *Agriturismi* have actually played a very important role in attracting urban dwellers to the country-side, including remote areas that otherwise would have remained un-touched by tourism.

It soon became clear that an *agriturismo* was a good investment. Finan-cial groups that had no connection to the local life and traditions bought abandoned properties, often resuscitating farming activities that had been discontinued decades before. Using the loopholes in the local regulations, many *agriturismi* focused on the real source of money: tourism, using farm-ing as a sort of cover-up. Upscale facilities offering tennis courts and swimming pools started sprouting all over the place, also providing refined dining experiences with a veneer of rural charm. Some establishments even bought the products used in their kitchen from neighboring farms. However, the role of *agriturismi* in bringing new life to the countryside and greater fascination with local food cannot be denied.

The same kind of interest generated another movement, the Towns of Wine (*Città del Vino*), an association formed by 526 townships that give their names to a particular wine; that produce DOC wines on their terri-tory; and whose history, tradition, and culture are connected to vineyards and vine growing. These towns organize frequent events to entice tourists to visit their wine producers and to discover their culinary treasures.[12] In 1993 the Movement for the Wine Tourism (*Movimento Turismo del Vino*) was founded, including more than 900 wine producers that welcome tourists on their premises. Local authorities, wine and food producers, ho-tels. and *agriturismi* soon started cooperating to create enticing offers and packages to attract high-end visitors who were interested in the unique mixture of culture, traditions, and good food of a specific area. In 1999 a national law regulated these activities, now called Wine Routes (*Strade del Vino*), defined as "signaled routes marking natural, cultural and envi-ronmental points of interests, vineyards, and wine producing farms open to the public."[13]

ETHNIC RESTAURANTS

A relatively new phenomenon, often limited to urban centers, is the growth of ethnic restaurants. Until the 1970s very few immigrants chose Italy to start a new life, with the exceptions of some North Africans and Middle Easterners. From the 1980s, a large wave of arrivals from China marked the beginning of a more noticeable immigration from all over the world: southern Asia, the Philippines, South America, and many African countries. With the fall of the Berlin Wall, great numbers of Eastern Europeans started trickling into Italy. The massive arrivals of Albanians crammed in tiny boats and the frequent shipwrecks along the coasts made Italians realize that the demographics of their county were changing. Despite the growing xenophobia and the widespread fear of loss of identity, the percentage of foreigners living in Italy is still pretty low, compared with that in other European countries. The immigrant communities are so small that, with the exceptions of big cities like Milan, Turin, or Rome, they do not have restaurants that cater to their needs. On the other hand, stalls and shops selling exotic products have become common in the public markets of most large towns, wherever immigrants need specific ingredients to cook their food at home.

Chinese restaurants are definitely the most visible and numerous. Curiously enough, the owners of many of these establishments tend to come from southern China. Specifically, the county of Wenzhou in the province of Zhejiang appears to be the homeland of many Chinese cooks working in Italy. Some believe that Chinese organized crime is at the root of this phenomenon, allowing the exploitation of the newly arrived immigrants and an uninterrupted flux of cheap labor from the motherland.[14] Many cooks are not professionally trained but have the most diverse backgrounds. As a consequence, the average level of food in Chinese restaurants is pretty low. Nevertheless, they have adapted their food to the Italian taste and eating habits. Menus are divided into appetizers, *primi* (rice and noodles), *secondi* (meat and fish), *contorni* (mostly vegetarian and tofu dishes), and desserts. Also the flavors and the ingredients have often changed to meet customers' preferences. Such flexibility, together with very low prices, has determined the success of Chinese restaurants, now considered a perfectly viable solution for low-budget diners.

Besides the Chinese, not many other ethic restaurants are available: a few "African" establishments (mostly from Ethiopia and Somalia), some Moroccan or more vaguely "Arab," some Japanese, Mexican, very rare Brazilian, some scattered Turkish, German, Spanish, Persian, Thai, and Vietnamese.

Curiously, French restaurants are a rarity, confirming the attachment of Italians to their food traditions, especially against their eternal rivals in culinary matters, the French. Furthermore, French food tends to be expensive because of its ingredients, the service, and the dining style. Instead, in the current mentality, with the exception of Japanese restaurants because of the fresh fish, ethnic restaurants are supposed to be cheap.

NOTES

1. Seneca *Epistulae* VI.56.2.

2. A. Dosi and F. Schenll, *Pasti e vasellame da tavola* (Rome: Quasar, 1986).

3. Hans Conrad Peyer, *Von der Gastfreundschaft zum Gasthaus* (Hanover: Hahnsche Buchhandlung, 1987).

4. Fynes Moryson, *An Itinerary* (London: n.p., 1617).

5. Antoni Maczak, *Viaggi e viaggiatori nell'Europa moderna* (Bari: Laterza, 1994), 80.

6. Rebecca Spang, *The Invention of the Restaurant* (Cambridge, MA: Harvard University Press, 2000).

7. Alberto Capatti, *L'osteria nuova* (Bra: Slow Food Editore, 2000).

8. Hans Barth, *Osteria, Guida spirituale delle osterie italiane da Verona a Capri* (Rome: Voghera, n.d.).

9. Touring Club Italiano, *Guida gastronomica d'Italia* (Milan: Touring Club Italiano, 1931).

10. Marescalchi Arturo, "Enoteca Italica," in *Enotria* (October 1934), 599.

11. Public Law 730 (5 December 1985).

12. Riccardo Pastore, *Il marketing del vino e del territorio: istruzioni per l'uso* (Milan: Franco Angeli, 2000).

13. Public Law 268 (27 July 1999).

14. Francesco Sisci and Dionisio Patrizia, *Piovra Gialla* (Pavia: Liber Internazionale, 1994).

6

Special Occasions

Italians tend to find plenty of excuses to make a meal a special occasion. As is the case everywhere in the world, food is at the center of all kinds of events, both private and public. Italians love both cooking at home and going out to eat. Sharing meals at home with friends and family is common, also in urban environments. Close friends and family feel free to drop by unannounced or on very short notice. In fact, this is an element that characterizes close social relationships; on the other hand, invitations ahead of time denote that the guests are from an outer circle of friends and family. Also, coffee time after lunch is a favorite time to pay a visit and have a good chat over a steaming cup of espresso.

SUNDAY MEALS

Any festive occasion or visit is an excuse for more elaborate meals. Sunday dinners (*pranzo della domenica*) still maintain their character of special meal, a legacy of a time of scarcity when, especially in the countryside and in the proletarian urban neighborhoods, most families could afford to eat a little more only once a week. Furthermore, Sunday was the day when families would go to church, the day of the Lord, to be marked also by the relative abundance of food consumed. The reasons behind the survival of the Sunday meal are no longer related to economic constraints or religious meanings, but rather to the need of reinforcing family and social ties that risk growing weaker under the stress of everyday life.

On Sundays, the main courses, *primi* and *secondi,* usually become more elaborate, and cooks make an effort to prepare more side dishes. Some hosts offer more than one *primo* and more than one *secondo* to prove their cooking abilities and to show appreciation for their guests.

The meal often starts with some hors d'oeuvres, or *antipasto,* which is usually finger food such as olives, sliced salami, small pieces of cheese, and *sottaceto* vegetables. The food is served on small plates or bowls for the guests to pick while they are still standing, before the actual meal starts. For important events, the antipasto can become a real course, with more elaborate delicacies: marinated raw anchovies, vegetable relishes, and meat *carpaccio.* In this case, *antipasto* is served as a first course, when all the guests are already sitting around the table. Nevertheless, antipasto portions are much smaller than the appetizers in the United States.

Sunday meals, or any kind of festive meals, continue with *primi* that the hosts do not habitually enjoy during week days, either because they require a long preparation time, because they are expensive, or simply because they belong to another regional tradition and are hence considered special. All over the country, families frequently choose filled pasta, such as *tortellini* and *ravioli, cannelloni,* and *lasagna,* or at least fresh pasta (either bought or homemade), to mark a special occasion. Food lovers prepare more elaborate sauces, such as meat *ragù* or fish-based condiments, or choose expensive ingredients, such as mullet-cured roe (*bottarga*) or truffle.

Tagliatelle with Ragù

- 1/3 cup extra-virgin olive oil
- 1 medium onion, finely minced
- 1 stalk celery, finely minced
- 1 medium carrot, finely minced
- 1/2 pound *pancetta,* minced
- 1 pound lean ground beef
- 1 cup medium-bodied red wine
- 2 pounds ripe tomatoes, peeled, seeded, and diced
- 1 pound fresh *tagliatelle*
- 1/2 cup freshly grated *parmigiano reggiano* cheese
- salt
- pepper

In a large saucepan, heat the oil over medium heat. Add the onion, celery, and carrot, and sauté until the vegetables soften. Add the *pancetta* and stir until it becomes translucent. Add the ground beef, raise the heat, and cook for 5 minutes, stirring occasionally. Add the red wine and cook until it evaporates. Add the tomatoes, turn the heat down to low, and let simmer, covered, for 1 hour. Uncover, add salt and pepper, and simmer for 15 minutes longer. Meanwhile, bring a large pot of salted water to a boil. Add the *tagliatelle* and cook, uncovered, until *al dente*. Drain the pasta and place in a serving bowl. Pour the *ragù* on top and toss. Sprinkle with the grated cheese.

BUSINESS MEALS

Much business is also done around the table. Italians do not have a relevant bar culture in the American sense, and meetings over drinks are quite rare, although now wine bars are often the place to meet coworkers or potential clients after work. Nevertheless, lunch is the prime time for business meals. Because culturally a long meal intrinsically conveys meanings of conviviality and familiarity, sharing a long elaborate lunch is considered conducive to ease tensions between coworkers or to facilitate business between companies. This kind of meal generally takes place at a restaurant, usually chosen by the person or the company that sends the invitation. The restaurant tends to be upscale or well known; these are hip places where most people would certainly like to go. If the hosts want to surprise their guests with their wit or worldliness, they might invite them to some unusual place, like a little greasy spoon that serves tasty local or traditional dishes. Other choices may include new restaurants that the host feels will become popular soon, or exotic restaurants, if the host considers his guests adventurous enough. At any rate, once the place is decided, the host or hostess tends to leave his or her guests free to choose what they prefer, limiting himself or herself to suggest some dishes that are particularly good in that establishment. More rarely a set menu is decided in advance. Wine and sparkling wine are served with the meal, usually selected by the host or hostess, who can thus exert a certain control over the final bill. Conversations are held at all times, but usually the interval between courses allows more freedom to talk. Italians are not afraid to spend a lot of time around a table for business; it is considered working time, after all.

CELEBRATIONS FOR RELIGIOUS INITIATIONS

Many ceremonies are connected to specific moments in the initiation to the Catholic religion, which is still dominant by far. Even many non-religious people do not renounce these celebrations.

Christening (*battesimo*) is the first occasion to mark most children's lives. When a baby is first born, friends and family send presents, sweets, and chocolate, often to the hospital room where the mother is recovering from the delivery. More substantial presents are offered when the baby is brought home and, for families celebrating the baby's christening, on the occasion of the ceremony.

In the days preceding the rite, families send out *bomboniere*, little souvenirs often made of ceramics, glass, or metal: a small dish, a tiny vase, a key ring, a cute box, anything to mark the occasion. Together with these objects, families parcel up smooth confectionery with sugar-coated almonds called *confetti* (from the Latin *confectus*, which means "finished," or "polished"). They are usually pink for girls and light blue for boys. At times, a chocolate core substitutes for almonds. These little candies are supposed to represent good fortune and abundance. *Confetti*, usually in the number of five, less frequently three, come with a tiny card with the name of the newborn and the date of the christening. Nonreligious families also send out *bomboniere* with *confetti* to announce the birth of their offspring. In this case the card only has the baby's name and the date of birth.

After the christening ceremony in the church, families invite relatives and friends to join them to celebrate the occasion. In the past, a full lunch in a restaurant or at home, offered by the family, was the rule. Most young couples, especially in urban environments, now prefer a catered buffet in a rented place or some refreshments at home. The menu varies, but there is always a big cake, offered with *spumante* or champagne to make a toast to the baby's health and lucky future and to congratulate the parents. The hosts distribute *confetti* again, often with different *bomboniere*.

First communions and confirmations are also marked by family celebrations, generally big lunches after the ceremony, held at home or at a restaurant. For many children, the presents and the big lunch offered in their honor are more impressive than the religious ceremonies themselves.

A festive lunch is also organized when a young person takes religious vows as a priest, a monk, or a nun. If the families are not happy with the career choice, the religious institution usually welcomes the neophyte with the meal.

BIRTHDAYS

Even when children turn a year old, big parties are thrown to celebrate their birthdays. Often parents limit themselves to an afternoon event, where they serve hors d'oeuvres, sandwiches, and small pieces of pizza and other finger food, accompanied by soft drinks. One specific element marks these events: the birthday cake. Mothers who can cook pride themselves on baking the cake at home, but more and more often they order it from pastry shops, in which case they might look like American cakes, with whipped cream, icing, and some writing on top. From some reason, soft, layered cakes are preferred, including delicacies such as a *tiramisù* or a *torta millefoglie* (layers of puff pastry filled with different-flavored creams). The act of slicing the soft cake is somehow fundamental to the celebration. While the cake is served, a bottle of sparkling wine *(spumante)* is noisily uncorked. The wine is then served to all of the participants, who make a toast together, often clinking the glasses and wishing happy birthday *(buon compleanno)*, good health *(salute)*, or simply *cin cin* (a word that supposedly reproduces the sound of clinking glasses). The cutting of the birthday cake and the consumption of sparkling wine are the central elements when the celebration includes a full dinner, which includes dishes that are often the favorites of the birthday person. At the end of the meal the cake and the sparkling wine are served.

According to Catholic tradition, every day is dedicated to a specific saint, and the people who carry his or her name are supposed to solemnize that day to honor the saint. These celebrations are called *onomastico*, when a special cake and some sparkling wine, if not drinks at a bar, are often offered to family members, friends and co-workers. As the saying goes, "The saint pays" *(il santo paga)*.

Cialda Wafers Filled with Orange-Flavored *Mascarpone* Cream

- 4 egg whites
- 4 ounces durum flour
- 4 ounces honey
- 4 ounce butter
- 3 egg yolks
- 1/4 cup sugar
- 1/2 pound *mascarpone* cheese
- 1 tablespoon grated orange rind
- 1/4 cup of freshly squeezed orange juice
- 3/4 cup whipped cream
- 1 tablespoon icing sugar
- 1 blood orange, cut into sections

In a large bowl, mix the egg whites, the flour, the honey, and the butter into a smooth dough. Roll out the dough 1/8-inch thick and cut out 4-inch circles. Preheat the oven at 350°F. Place the disks on a pan and bake them in the oven for 5 minutes. Remove from the oven and let cool.

In another bowl, whisk the egg yolks with the sugar, and then slowly stir in the *mascarpone*, the orange rind, and the orange juice. Blend in the whipped cream.

Place half of the wafer disks on a serving tray, put some cream filling on them, and top with the remaining disks. Sprinkle icing sugar and decorate with orange wedges.

ACADEMIC AND PROFESSIONAL ACHIEVEMENTS

Italians do not have proms or official graduation ceremonies when students complete high school or college. However, the occasion is always celebrated privately, with friends and family. Students customarily organize a meal or a picnic on the 100th day before the beginning of the exams that mark the end of high school (*maturità*). This occasion, called "the hundred days" (*i cento giorni*), is often celebrated out of town, either in a restaurant or at a student's summer home. If students pass their final exams, their families throw a party or a meal to celebrate the accomplishment.

Until the late 1990s, it was mandatory for all male citizens to join the army for one year, to do the so-called military service (*servizio militare* or *servizio di leva*). The end of this period (*congedo*) was also often celebrated with a big family meal.

College and university graduations (*laurea*), achieved at the end of a long period dedicated to the writing of a final dissertation (*tesi*), are often celebrated with one or more meals, from the more formal, when members of the extended family are invited, to the most relaxed, with friends and other students. Many still mark the occasion with *confetti*, the colors of which depend on the type of *laurea*: a color for humanities, one for sciences, one for law, one for medicine, one for architecture, one for engineering, and so on. Curiously, Italians receive the title of doctor (*dottore*) by defending their final *laurea* dissertation, and not with the Ph.D., usually after four or five years if they keep up with their studies.

Many professional categories have a sort of entrance exam, taken after a period of apprenticeship. These occasions, as well as new jobs and promotions, are celebrated with special meals. Professionals are at least expected to invite friends and co-workers for an *apertivo* to mark the moment.

ROMANTIC DINNERS

Romantic dinners are particularly important. Couples are supposed to go out when they are dating, with a preference for nice, discreet spots, although at times crowded but hip and trendy places are chosen. Quite often, because the single population is growing in Italy, dinners take place at the apartment of one of the partners. As it is often portrayed in movies, and especially in commercials, great importance is given to the setting and the mood: candles, flowers, good music, and all the other paraphernalia that are now shared by pop culture in Western countries. Menus tend to be simple, centered on a dish that the host or hostess is sure to master in order to impress the partner. If one of the partners is a good cook, then it is likely he or she will want the other partner to know and to appreciate that fact. After all, especially for women, being a good cook is still considered a plus; more and more often, though, single men who live alone learn how to cook. Many young people, nevertheless, tend to live with their parents until they get married, because it is hard to find jobs and it is expensive to live alone. In that case, romantic dinners will take place at a restaurant, unless the relationship has become more established and the partners are introduced to the families. It is quite normal, even considered polite, for dating or engaged people to have meals at their partner's parents' home. When the couple goes out for dinner, especially at the beginning of the relationship, it is good form for the male to pay the restaurant bill. Sometimes a lunch or a dinner is organized to celebrate the engagement, which usually coincides with the announcement of the wedding's date.

WEDDINGS

Before a wedding, it has become common for the friends of the couple to organize one party (*festa di addio al celibato*) for the bridegroom and one for the bride. It is usually an informal and quite raucous get-together. A buffet of finger food is provided, rather than a meal, because both the bride and her future husband are often busy trying to lose weight in order to be able to fit into their wedding clothes and to look good in the ceremony pictures and videos. However, these parties are occasions when it is absolutely acceptable to drink more than usual and even to get drunk, frequently on sparkling wines and liquors.

There is no rehearsal dinner before the ceremony. There are neither bridesmaids nor groomsmen wearing all the same clothes. At any rate, no self-respecting Italian would wear the same outfit as anybody else at the same ceremony. Whether the function takes place in a church or in the city hall (as it happens for nonreligious weddings), couples only pick two to four persons as witnesses (*testimone*), without whom the ceremony would not have legal validity. Witnesses are allowed to dress as they please.

After the ceremony, while the newly married couple disappears to take the inevitable pictures, guests are invited to precede them to the place where the wedding supper or dinner takes place, usually either a restaurant or a rented place where food is prepared by a catering company. In the past, especially in the countryside, it was common to hold the wedding meal at the home of the bride (it was often the bride's father who paid for most of it). This custom has virtually disappeared, with the exception of couples that decide to organize a very small ceremony, limited to the closest family and friends.

The more formal meals start with finger food and drinks, enjoyed outside if the place and the weather allow it. When the couple arrives, all the guests are invited to take their assigned place, often written in big billboards, where a name or a number is given to each table, and the names of all the guests are listed under the corresponding table. The bride and the groom usually sit with their parents at a central table, and from time to time they visit the different tables, thanking the guests for attending and for sending gifts. The number of guests varies, but it is not uncommon to attend weddings with more than 100 guests. In the countryside, especially in the south, where social relationships are closely knit because many people live in the same village or small town, guests can number in the hundreds. Many families invite even more guests, to display their wealth and their social status. In urban environments, the number of guests is definitely lower.

The meal starts with one or two appetizers, continuing with a couple of *primi*, if not three, and two or three *secondi* accompanied by several *contorni*. All the dishes are served one after the other, so that guests do not choose between the two or three *primi*, or between the two or three *secondi*, but have a portion of each. Of course they can skip any dish, but usually they would at least get a tasting portion to honor the table. After the main courses, desserts are served. At the end, the wedding cake is brought; the couple is supposed to cut the first slice, while the guests toast to their future happiness with sparkling wine. The cake is taken back to the kitchen, sliced, and served to the guests. The meal ends with liquors and coffee.

The whole meal can last a few hours. Especially in the south and in the country, families tend to outdo each other by displaying their wealth with a long series of courses. In cities and larger towns, any exaggeration in the quantity of food provided is often perceived as vulgar.

Wedding meals can become quite noisy and boisterous, with frequent invitations addressed to the couple to get up and kiss in front of the guests. Sometimes a band plays between courses or at the end of the meal, while guests dance. The banquet ends after the bride has thrown her bouquet to the single women who have attended the wedding.

FUNERALS

Funerals can also be an occasion to eat, although that is no longer a common custom. Especially in the south, family and friends were expected to bring food to the home of the deceased, who was usually kept at home until the funeral. It was a way to express one's sympathies with the family of the deceased, supposedly too crushed by grief to even think about eating. In fact, particularly right after the death, many manifested their mourning by abstaining from food, so it was up to the family and friends to insist that they nourish themselves. After the funeral, there was a big meal, called *consolation* or *cunsòlo* in many southern areas, when all the people participating in the funeral provided some dishes, often with lavish abundance.

CHRISTMAS

Catholicism being the traditional religion in Italy, liturgy and religious festivities were often connected with specific foods and meals.[1] One of the most important holidays was Christmas, celebrating the birth of Jesus. The date of December 25 was chosen because it was already a holiday in pre-Christian Rome, dedicated to the sun, at the end of a few festive days, called Saturnalia, around the winter solstice. The date was symbolic, representing the coming of the light to the world.

At the vigil (*Vigilia*), before the midnight mass, families gather for a so-called lean supper (*cena di magro*), that does not include meat courses. However, the dishes are still numerous, abundant, and, above all, delicious, usually pretty much the same year-in and year-out, changing according to the area. *Primi* include pasta both with vegetables and fish. Among the most traditional dishes, there is pumpkin ravioli (*tortelli di zucca*) in Mantova, ricotta and herbs ravioli (*tortelloni* or *ravioli di magro*) in Bologna and other areas in central Italy, anchovy spaghetti (*spaghetti con le alici*) in Rome, and clam vermicelli (*vermicelli con le vongole*) in Naples. More recently, some families also have pasta with tuna fish sauce and with salmon or *bottarga* (dried mullet roe). The most traditional families prepare vegetable soups such as the chickpea and chestnut soup in central Italy or the series of seven-vegetable soups in Sicily, a dying custom.

Among *secondi*, eel *(anguilla)* is probably the fish more closely connected with Christmas. It is called *capitone* in Naples when it is bigger and *bisato* in Veneto when it is smaller. Depending on the area, eel can be roasted, grilled, fried, served with a tomato sauce, or *in carpione* in Rome (floured and fried, with vinegar and other ingredients poured on top). Close second is salted codfish *(baccalà)*, prepared in many different ways. Vegetables are usually served in a salad, or sliced, battered, and fried. In Rome the mixed fried dish *(misto fritto)* includes cauliflower, codfish, mushrooms, cardoon, artichokes, and many other delicacies.

Desserts served during the Vigil supper were supposed to be fat free, to keep the lean character of the meal. Nowadays all kinds of Christmas desserts are served. While in some families it is still customary to make some desserts at home, most of the Christmas delicacies are commercially made, some of which can also be bought from bakeries and pastry shops. Because bread, the symbol of eternal life and of God's love, seemed to play a very important role in the Christmas meals of the first Christian communities, many desserts are actually derived from bread, which for the holidays was rich, round, tall, and well leavened. The origin of many desserts is evident in their names: *pandoro* from Verona (*pan d'oro* means "bread of gold"), *panettone* from Milan (*pan di tono*, or "important bread"), *pan speziale* from Bologna ("spiced bread"), *panforte* from Siena ("strong bread"), *pan pepato* from Ferrara ("peppered bread"), *pan nociato* from Umbria ("bread with nuts"), *pan giallo* from Rome ("yellow bread") *parrozzo* from Abruzzo (*pan rozzo*, or "rough bread"). As the names reveal, in time different ingredients were added to the bread to make it more festive, such as spices, nuts, raisins, candied and dried fruits, chocolate, and honey. All these desserts, mostly from northern and central Italy, were prepared in the shape of loaves and sliced to serve. In the south, on the other hand, there is a prevalence of single-portion desserts, more similar to cookies in concept. The most widespread are *mostaccioli*, or *mustaccioli*, square or diamond shaped, with different ingredients according to the area of provenance, but usually quite hard, made of flour, spices, sugar, almonds, or other nuts, and baked and covered with chocolate or jam. *Caggionetti* (in dialect, *caggiunitte*), *ravioli*-shaped pastries filled with a chickpea flour and chocolate mixture, are typical from Abruzzo. In Naples one of the traditional desserts is *struffoli*, small balls of fried dough, dipped in honey, and arranged in a wreath, often decorated with colored spangles. In Puglia we find *cartellate* (or in dialect, *cardeddate*), indented ribbons of sweet dough made of flour, white wine, and olive oil, rolled on themselves, fried, and topped with honey or cooked must. Nougat candy, or *torrone*, is widespread all over Italy; it can be soft or hard, it can contain hazelnuts or almonds, and it can be covered in chocolate or have some liquor.

Christmas Day dinner, which is customarily served in the early afternoon, is dominated by meat. Meat stocks and broth are very common *primi*, usually with *pasta ripiena* (or "filled") with meat-based fillings, such as *ravioli*, *tortellini* from Bologna, the ring-shaped *anolini* from Parma, and the square *cappelletti* from Reggio Emilia. In some areas of Abruzzo, a sort of savory *pandispagna* with pieces of ham and salami is baked, diced, and soaked in broth. Whatever it may be, the *primo* (or *primi*, if more than one are provided) must be rich and abundant. Very rich *lasagna* is quite common, together with tall pasta pies called *timballo*. Made famous by the movie *Big Night*, *timballo* is filled with more pasta, meat, vegetables, eggs, diced *salumi*, and served sliced. Similar dishes are *sagne chine* in Calabria and *pastizzu di Natali* in Sicily.

The favorite meat for a Christmas *secondo* was capon, now commonly replaced by turkey (big but cheaper and easier to find), even chicken. Capon was often boiled and stuffed, and the resulting broth was used for the *primo*. Pork is also a common choice. The dinner ends with the same desserts that are served during the Vigil supper. Many leftovers are served on December 26, the day dedicated to Saint Stephen, also a holiday with no specific religious meaning.

Fried Zucchini (*Zucchine Impanate*)

- 2 pounds small zucchini, ends trimmed
- 2 large eggs
- 2 cups extra-virgin olive oil
- 2 cups all-purpose flour
- salt
- pepper

Wash and dry the zucchini well. Cut them into thin 1/8-inch thick slices. Place the slices on a kitchen towel to get rid of any extra moisture. Beat the eggs and season with salt and pepper.

Pour the oil into a deep frying pan and place it over medium-high heat. Using a fork, and being careful not to puncture the zucchini, dip each zucchini slice into the beaten egg and then coat it with flour on both sides. Shake off any excess flour. Slip the zucchini slices into the hot oil, making sure to leave space between them, and fry until they are golden brown on both sides.

Remove from the oil and drain on several layers of paper towel, seasoning each batch with salt as they are done. Serve immediately.

Whipped Salt Cod (*Baccalà Mantecato*)

- 2 pounds boneless salt cod
- 1 cup milk
- 1/2 cup extra-virgin olive oil
- 3 cloves garlic, finely minced
- 2 tablespoons finely chopped parsley
- salt
- freshly ground pepper

Soak the salt cod in water for 2 days, changing the water occasionally, till the cod softens. Drain the cod, place it in a saucepan, and add the milk and enough water to cover. Place over medium heat and bring it slowly to a very gentle simmer. Cook for about 15 minutes, until the cod is soft. Drain the cod from the milk and flake it with your hands, removing any bones or fragments of skin.

Place the fish in a food processor and process to a fine puree, gradually adding the olive oil while the machine is running. If the puree is too salty, add some warm milk. Add the garlic and parsley and season with black pepper.

The whipped cod, a traditional dish of Venice, is usually eaten with grilled slices of *polenta*, but you can also spread it on crackers or grilled slices of country bread.

CAPODANNO

Capodanno, or New Year's Eve, is celebrated all over Italy with parties and late suppers. The menu varies, but it is quite common to eat *zampone* or *cotechino* with lentils. *Zampone* is minced pork meat with spices, stuffed into the skin of a pig's foot. *Cotechino*, stuffed into pig's intestine, is made with minced pork meat, lard, and skin (called *cotica*, hence the name). Both *zampone* and *cotechino* are boiled and served with mashed potatoes or boiled lentils, symbolizing abundant money. At times the lentils are stewed in tomato sauces, and slices of *zampone* or *cotechino* are added to it. Another tradition requires that bottles of sparkling wine be opened at midnight on the dot, while hundreds and hundreds of firecrackers (and often more dangerous fireworks) explode outside. In the past it was customary to throw old stuff out of the window to signify renewal. Many families also have a New Year's Day dinner, with rich and abundant dishes that vary from family to family.

EPIFANIA

On January 6, the Catholic Church celebrates the Three Kings presenting gifts to Jesus, an event considered as the first public appearance of the Son of God (hence called *epifania*, meaning "epiphany"). In time, the name *Epifania* was corrupted to *Befana*, which is also the name of an old ugly lady riding a broom, but not considered a witch, who brings sweets, candies, and little presents to the good children and just coal to the bad ones. Just as Santa *(Babbo Natale)*, who brings gifts on Christmas, does the *Befana* comes down the chimney. Children would hang socks and stockings from the hearth (the cowl over the stove in modern kitchens), while leaving some food in the kitchen to thank her and to let her get some rest. On that day, all over Italy there are street fairs selling gifts and, above all, all kinds of sweets. It is also possible to buy hard sugar made to look like coal, to put in the *Befana's* stockings as a joke. There are no typical foods for this holiday, with the exception of *pinza* in Veneto and Friuli, a *focaccia* made of wheat or maize flour, lard, and dried fruits.

CARNEVALE

Carnevale, or Mardi Gras (*Martedì grasso,* or "fat Tuesday") is the holiday celebrating the last days before the beginning of Lent, the period of preparation for Easter that starts with Ash Wednesday (*mercoledì delle ceneri*). The name may come from the Latin expression *carnem levare,* which means "to take away meat." Lent was in fact a "period of lean" (*tempo di magro*), because no meat was allowed until Easter. As an anticipated compensation for the 40 days of Lent, Carnevale was a time of excess, when social order went topsy-turvy, and wild parties, balls, and parades were organized, often with participants wearing masks in all kinds of disguises. Large meals were prepared, but there are not many *primi* and *secondi* typical of this holiday, with the exceptions of *gnocchi* in Veneto. On the other hand, many desserts are prepared exclusively for Carnevale, especially fried ones. *Frittelle,* lumps of wheat or rice-based dough, made puffy by frying, date back to the sixteenth century, mentioned by Bartolomeo Scappi under the Venetian dialect term *fritole. Frappe, cenci,* or *chiacchiere* are long stripes of crunchy fried dough powdered with sugar,

Carnival masks with *ciambelle*.

widespread all over Italy with different names. In Emilia, we find many *ravioli*-shaped fried pastries, filled with jam, chestnuts, pumpkin, candied fruits, and many other ingredients. *Castagnole* in central Italy and *sfinci* in Sicily are small balls of fried dough covered in honey. Also in Sicily, *cannoli* are very popular on this holiday.

Frappe

- 2 cups all-purpose flour
- 1/3 cup sugar
- 2 eggs
- 2 tablespoons rum
- 2 teaspoons finely grated orange zest
- 3 tablespoons extra-virgin olive oil
- oil for frying
- confectioner's sugar

Mix the flour, sugar, eggs, rum, orange peel, and olive oil in a bowl to make a soft dough. Add a little milk if the dough is too stiff to roll out. Let rest for half an hour. Roll out the dough on a lightly floured work surface as thin as possible without breaking it. Cut the dough into one-inch-wide, five-inch-long strips. Fry the strips in hot oil until they expand and become light golden brown. Drain from the oil and place on paper towel. When they are cool, sprinkle with confectioner's sugar.

Fried Cream (*Crema Fritta*)

- 1 quart (4 cups) whole milk
- zest of 1 lemon (in one stripe)
- 2/3 cup cornstarch
- 5 eggs, 4 of them separated
- 1 1/2 cups sugar
- 2/3 cup all-purpose flour
- 2 cups dry bread crumbs
- frying oil

Boil the milk with the lemon zest. In a bowl, beat 4 egg yolks (save the whites for another purpose) and the sugar with a whisk until the mixture becomes whitish. Add the cornstarch and the warm milk. Pour the mixture back into the pot and keep on mixing over medium heat for about 10 minutes. When the cream thickens and starts detaching from the walls of the pot, remove it from the heat. Discard the lemon zest, and pour the cream over a pastry board or on a sheet pan. Let it cool off for 3 or 4 hours until it hardens. With a long, sharp knife, cut the cream in 1-inch squares. Beat the remaining egg. Coat the squares in the flour, in the beaten egg, and then in the bread crumbs. Fry them in sizzling oil for a few minutes until they are brown on all sides and drain on paper towel. Serve hot.

LENT

Ash Wednesday marks the beginning of the 40 days of Lent, called in Italian *Quaresima*, from the Latin *quadragesima*, meaning the "40 days," or more literally the "40th day." The number 40 recurs in the Bible (the days of the Flood, the years the Jews spent in the desert, the days Jesus fasted) carrying a meaning of repentance, atonement, and punishment. Lent was a period of fast (*digiuno*) and abstinence (*astinenza*) from certain foods, particularly meat. Many Catholics still avoid meat on Ash Wednesday, Lenten Fridays, and Holy Saturday.

As early as the fifth century, some Church Fathers supported the view that this 40 days' fast had been instituted by the Apostles, but in the documents from the first three centuries, we find considerable diversity on the issue of practices and duration for the fast before Easter. It is only in the

fifth canon of the Council of Nicea (325 C.E.) that we find the first mention of the Greek term *tessarakoste*, modeled on the older word, *pentekoste*
(Pentecost), indicating the 50th day, that had come to represent the
whole period between Easter Sunday and Whit-Sunday. Traditions varied
all over the Mediterranean. In Rome, in the fifth century, Lent lasted six
weeks but there were only three weeks of actual fasting, when some ab-
stained from all living creatures, while others ate fish and birds, and others ate only fish.[2] In time, it was required that the faithful fast not only
sometimes during the 40 days, but every day for that whole period, when
the rule was to take only one meal a day in the evening. Eggs and milk and
its derivatives, which were allowed in the first century, were successively
forbidden until a few centuries ago.[3] In the past, Lent was interrupted on
a Thursday, considered halfway through the period *(mezzaquaresima)*,
when meat was allowed and parades were organized. A big wooden pup-
pet of an old woman dressed in rags, representing the harshness of Lent
and with her belly full of dried fruits, chestnuts, and nuts, was disembow-
eled, sawed, and finally burnt. Although this custom has disappeared,
some remnants may be identified with the game of piñata.[4]

In order to respect the abstinence from meat, cereals, vegetables, and
fish constituted the main options. Fresh fish being a luxury, many would
opt for dried fish (salted cod fish or herring), freshwater crawfish, frogs,
and even snails.[5]

EASTER

Easter *(Pasqua)* was established in 325 C.E. by the Council of Nicea, on
the first Sunday following the first full moon after the equinox of spring.
For this reason its date varies between March *(Pasqua bassa* or low) and
April *(Pasqua alta* or high). The holiday, the name of which is connected
to the Hebrew Pesach (the flight from Egypt), celebrates the resurrection
of Jesus. Everything in this holiday, which takes pace at the beginning of
spring, is traditionally connected with rebirth and renovation, with the
cycle of nature. For this reason Easter was more meaningful than Christmas in traditional rural environments, while Christmas was stronger in
cities and with the bourgeoisie. Easter desserts originated in the countryside are more horizontal than the Christmas desserts; they have shapes re-
minding one of breasts and pregnant wombs.[6]

The most evident symbol of the theme of fertility is the egg, which
plays a very important role at Easter, to the point that boiled eggs to be

eaten on the day of Easter were brought to church to be blessed at the midnight mass. Boiled eggs were painted in bright colors by boiling them with different ingredients (parsley for green, red beets for red, yellow for ashes) or using crayons. When chocolate became fashionable, pastry chefs took to shaping it into empty eggs (*uova di Pasqua*) containing little presents. Now most chocolate eggs are mass-produced and they vary in price depending on the present inside them. Boiled eggs are also used to decorate sweet and savory cakes, like *casatiello* in Naples, *scarcella* in Puglia, *angulis* in Sardinia. In Sicily, they make little figures with dough (*pupi cull'ova*) decorated with boiled eggs. Eggs are also the main ingredients in many pies, such as the multilayered *torta pasqualina* in Genoa and the cheese pies (*torta al formaggio*) widespread all over central and southern Italy. Beaten eggs are part of the mixture made of various types of cheese, diced *prosciutto* and *salami* that fill the *caniscione*, a sort of Easter *calzone* in Naples.

Lamb meat is another important element in the Easter meal, the lamb being a symbol of Christ sacrificed for the good of mankind and a reference to the flight from Egypt, when according to the Bible all Jews were required to butcher a lamb. All over Italy lamb is served roasted or grilled. In Abruzzo it is prepared with a sauce of eggs, cheese, and lemon (*agnello cacio e ovo*), while in Tuscany it is *pilottato*, cooked on the spit with tiny pieces of lard and herbs under the skin. In Lazio, people tend to favor the very young lamb that has not started grazing yet, called *abbacchio*, probably from the Latin word *baculum*, indicating the pole to which young lambs were tied to keep them from getting lost. In some areas kid meat is roasted for the holiday.

In many areas, there is still a tradition of an Easter breakfast, where boiled eggs, *salami*, savory and sweet pies, and chocolate are served, together with wine. In this case, the Easter lunch takes place a bit later than a usual Sunday dinner, around 2 P.M. The menus vary, with eggs, lamb, and the various pies being the most characteristic dishes.

Among the desserts, *colomba* (a leavened bread shaped like a dove and covered with a sugar and almond glaze) and chocolate eggs are present all over Italy, produced commercially or bought from pastry shops. Many desserts are still homemade. Besides the already-mentioned cakes with whole boiled eggs in them, we can mention *pastiera* in Naples (a cake filled with boiled wheat grains, ricotta, candied fruits and flavored with orange flower water) and *cassata* in Sicily (the sweet *ricotta* cheese cake), where making little lambs out of marzipan (*marzapane*) is still a living tradition.

MAY DAY

May Day is a holiday in Italy, and many take advantage of the spring weather to do their first outing and picnic. Around Rome, typical elements of these picnics are fresh fava beans and *pecorino* cheese.

FERRAGOSTO

Ferragosto, celebrated on August 15, is connected with the ancient Roman custom to honor Consus, the god protecting the harvest. With the beginning of the empire, this holiday became a festival dedicated to the first emperor, Augustus, and it was called *feriae augustales*, from which the word *Ferragosto* derives. The Catholic Church celebrates on that same day the Assumption to Heaven of the Holy Virgin. The holiday is just another occasion for celebration and big meals, with no particular dish representing it.

LOCAL FAIRS

Between March and October, but especially in summer to attract tourists, many cities, towns, and even small villages organize street fairs (*fiera*), often dedicated to a product or a dish typical of that place.[7] The celebrations are then called *sagra*, usually backed by the local authorities and having some sort of cultural and traditional value. In fact, these events are almost always a recent creation connected with the desire of reconstructing a vanishing past and to promote a local product. It is impossible mention them all: The themes range from artichokes to watermelons, from different types of pasta to wine.

THE DAY OF THE DEAD

The day of the dead (November 2) was not an occasion of mourning, but rather a holiday to celebrate the connection with the ancestors and the dead member of the social group. Fava beans were the main ingredients for many dishes. Since Roman times, they were connected to the dead, and they were supposedly able to chase away the bad spirits. Small cookies are prepared in the shape of fava beans, called *fave dei morti*. They are made of flour, sugar, almonds, egg whites, and some liquor. The bones of the dead (*ossi di morto*) were small, white, hard cookies baked on that day.

Rigatoni with Artichokes, Peas, and Fava Beans

- 4 medium artichokes
- juice of 1 lemon
- 4 tablespoons extra-virgin olive oil
- 2 cloves garlic, minced
- 1 pound rigatoni
- 1 cup shelled fresh fava beans
- 1 cup shelled fresh peas
- 2 tablespoons grated Romano cheese
- salt
- pepper

Discard the external leaves of the artichokes until you reach the softer, inner leaves, trim the tips, and scoop out the fluffy choke in the center. Thinly slice the artichokes and soak them in a bowl of water acidulated with the lemon juice (to keep the artichokes from turning dark). Drain the artichokes and sauté them in a large, deep pan with 2 tablespoons of the olive oil and the garlic over medium heat for 12 to 15 minutes. Add the fava beans and the peas, and cook until done but still *al dente*. If necessary, add some warm water to keep the vegetables moist.

Meanwhile, bring a large pot of salted water to a boil. Add the rigatoni and cook, uncovered, until *al dente*. Drain the pasta and toss it in the pan with the vegetables and their juice. Stir, add the remaining 2 tablespoons of olive oil, adjust the seasoning, and sprinkle with the grated cheese. Serve immediately.

PROTECTOR SAINTS

Many holidays are dedicated to Catholic Saints (*patrono*) who are supposed to protect a specific place or a specific category of people. Every Italian city or town has its own *patrono* or *patrona*, and usually his or her celebration is also a civil holiday. However, a few saints enjoyed a deep devotion in rural societies, and their holidays are still celebrated all over Italy.

Saint Anthony (*Sant'Antonio*, January 17) was a hermit who spent long times in the desert and was tempted by the devil in the form of a pig. The saint is often represented with a pig, embodying the defeated evil, and he is considered the protector of animals. In the past, on his holiday, farmers would bring their animals in front of churches to be blessed. For the animals that could not be brought over, the farmers would have some bread blessed, which they would feed to the animals afterward. Because he had won over the devil, Saint Anthony is also venerated as the protector of fire and hearths. A few special dishes are prepared on the occasion, such as beans with pork rinds (*fagioli con le cotiche*) and *cassoeula* in Lombardy, a stew made of cabbage and all kinds of pork cuts: sausages, little *salami*, ribs, feet, ears, and skin.

Saint Valentine (*San Valentino*, February 14) is considered the protector of lovers. The holiday has become a big affair for the candy industry, because lovers give candies and chocolates to their partners. It is also a day for romantic dinners.

Saint Joseph (*San Giuseppe*, March 19) is a celebration day that breaks the Lent abstinence. The new vegetables of the spring season are served, and many fried desserts are prepared, often filled with custard, such as *zeppole* in Naples, *bigné di san Giuseppe* in Rome, *raviole* in Emilia, and *crispeddi dolci* in Sicily.

On the day of Saint John (*San Giovanni*, June 14), huge bonfires were lit in the country, to keep away the pests from the harvest and to celebrate the beginning of summer. All over Italy, snails were the dish prepared to honor the Saint. In Rome fresh-snail vendors and little stalls selling cooked snails made a fair out of the occasion.[8]

The day of Saint Lucy (*Santa Lucia*, December 13) is traditionally considered the shortest of the year. In Veneto, children used to receive small gifts and sweets. Since the legend tells that the Saint tore her own eyes out so as not to see the man who wanted to take advantage of her, all over Italy little cakes in the form of eyes are prepared. In Sicily *cuccìa dolce* is the main dessert, made of wheat grains boiled in water with pumpkin, chocolate, ricotta cheese, cinnamon, sugar, and must.

NOTES

1. A. Lancellotti, *Feste tradizionali* (Milan: SEI, 1951).

2. Eusebius, *Historia Ecclesiae* V, 24.

3. P. Zaccia, *Il vitto quaresimale* (Rome: n.p., 1636).

4. Carlo G. Valli, *Belle feste* (Padova: MEB, 1992).

5. A. R. Borzini, *Ricchezza del mangiar povero* (Rome: Accademia Italiana della Cucina, 1975).

6. Piero Camporesi, *La terra e la luna* (Milano: Garzanti, 1995), 291.

7. T. Capuozzo and M. Neri, *Feste e sagre dei paesi italiani* (Milan: Mondadori, 1985).

8. Livio Jannattoni, *La cucina romana e del Lazio* (Rome: Newton Compton, 1998).

7

Diet and Health

Since World War II, Italians have witnessed radical changes in the level of their food consumption and in its composition. Many now perceive the old dietary theories and the folk concepts about food and eating, although still quite strong, as insufficient to confront the changes brought about by the fast-paced industrialization that has swept the country, the success of mass distribution, globalization, and new scientific breakthroughs in the fields of biology and genetics.

THE RISE AND GLORY OF THE MEDITERRANEAN DIET

For centuries populations around the Mediterranean Sea, including Italy, had to strive against food scarcity, toiling soils that were often less than generous and making do with what they could grow around them.[1] Finally, starting from the end of World War II, even the less well-off became able to afford a more diverse and abundant diet. Nutrition patterns changed under the influence of new packaging and conservation techniques, industrial mass production, and more sophisticated systems of distribution. A widespread economic development that let to the actual boom in the 1960s allowed many to lead better lives and enjoy a more regular intake of food, even though that often meant severing the ties to their traditional ways of life, including culinary habits. The daily energy intake passed from slightly more than 2,000 calories in the 1950s to almost 3,500 nowadays.

Italians were finally able to consume more meat and sugar, but because of fattier and more caloric diets, coronary diseases were affecting more people than at any time before in Italy. At the same time, the whole world seemed to realize that the way Mediterranean people had eaten for centuries in their effort to fight hunger actually constituted a very healthy diet. In the 1950s, American epidemiologist Leland Allbaugh, sponsored by the Rockefeller Foundation, and later scientist Ancel Keys, who had spent time in Naples, noticed that in many regions bordering the Mediterranean Sea, people boasted very low rates of heart disease and relatively long life expectancies. The research that followed seemed to show that Italian southern diets were very low in fat and high in carbohydrates from grains. This fact and the consequent low concentration of blood cholesterol in large sections of the population were thought to account for this reduced coronary risk among southern Italians. Another study, commissioned in the 1960s by the European Atomic Energy Commission (Euratom), allowed a better description of the dietary patterns that seemed to underlie these phenomena. However, the American public became aware of these findings in the late 1980s, when Ancel Keys and a group of researchers published the results of the survey work they had conducted in seven countries. Then, in 1990, the U.S. Department of Agriculture issued dietary guidelines for Americans that become the basis for the 1992 Food Guide Pyramid, clearly shaped after the findings by Keys in southern Italy back in the 1950s. Nevertheless, the popular concept of a Mediterranean diet as we know it received unprecedented international publicity when in 1993 it was promoted by a conference organized by the World Health Organization together with the Harvard School of Public Health and the Oldways Preservation and Exchange Trust. Interestingly, the connections of this last organization to olive oil, wine, and other food industries has been pointed out.

The international media fell in love with the Mediterranean diet, which not only promoted healthy and palatable food, but also allowed people to lose weight, especially if adopted together with a less sedentary style of life. While these assumptions proved to be quite correct, it is nevertheless useful to analyze the Mediterranean diet as a cultural artifact that heavily influences the attitude of many foreigners, including Americans, toward the food of southern Europe, namely Italy. What is the Mediterranean diet after all? Because of the way the media describe the Mediterranean diet, it is unclear whether it is considered as a cultural and historical construction, as a selection of specific foods, or, more scientifically, as a nutrient profile. The three elements appear interwoven in magazines and popular literature, so that if the focus is on nutrients and food selections, little space is given to the deep connections between a specific nutritional pattern and the society that created it as a part of its culture. At any rate, it is not easy to pin down what the Mediterranean diet is in terms of sheer nutrients, because it varies in time and space. The exclusive attention on food, however, suggests a change from diet to cuisine, which is particularly alluring to readers always looking for authenticity and prone to adopt foreign foods as a sign of distinction. Likewise, if the main stress is on the Italian way of life as expressed in eating, the public will tend to concentrate its attention on the social aspects of communal consumption of food and traditional cooking, often oblivious of what is served in the dishes.

CONTEMPORARY DIET

Despite the modification in their dietary patterns over the past 50 years, and the regional differences, Italians tend to eat more carbohydrates, pulses, and vegetables than do Americans. The distribution within these categories has changed too. From the 1950s, the growing availability of bread and pasta marked a decrease in the consumption of other cereals, considered less desirable, such as barley or rye. Rice and maize maintained a certain acceptance in northern regions. At the end of the 1970s, wheat derivatives showed a clear flexion. The southern regions traditionally consume larger quantities of carbohydrates and vegetables than the northern ones. Among the vegetables, potatoes and legumes, which have scarce at times, have been less popular, while other produce, such as tomatoes, different kinds of salads, peppers, eggplants, mushrooms and zucchini, entered everyday diets. Fruit is always considered indispensable; in this category, citrus and exotic fruits, such as bananas, pineapples, and coconuts, are becoming increasingly widespread. In past decades many urban dwellers, especially young people, lost any sense of what the seasonal fruit would be. The diffusion of mass distribution in supermarkets and the increasing success of frozen food had provoked a loss of contact with the realities of productions and, hence, seasons. In recent years a new interest for food, culinary traditions, and organic produce has caused many consumers, especially in the most affluent strata of the population, to become more conscious about the freshness and seasonal availability of what they buy.

Among the consumption of different kinds of meat, beef increased until the 1970s, reaching a constant level that suddenly decreased at the end of the 1990s, due to the mad-cow-disease scare and other health-related anxieties. On the other hand, consumption of chicken, pork, and rabbit is growing because of the lower prices of these meats and the fact that Italians now consider them as nutritious as beef. Mutton, goat, and horse meat were and still are consumed in limited amounts, mostly for the preparation of traditional dishes. In the past few years, ostrich was introduced in Italy, although its popularity is still extremely circumscribed. When it comes to meat, northern regions show higher rates of consumption, compared to southern regions. Furthermore, beef is more popular in the north, while in the south, pork and mutton are preferred. Chicken is a favorite all over the country.

Despite the extension of Italian coasts, Italians have never consumed large amounts of fish, mainly by reason of its high prices and the difficulty buying it when far from the coasts (with the exception of large cities). For this reason, fish was relatively more accessible in the southern regions. Also, dried fish like salted cod and stockfish have lost acceptance, probably because of the long preparations they require and their rising cost.

While lard and *pancetta* were traditionally the most accessible fats, and butter in the north and olive oil in the south were common but definitely more expensive, in the past few years other kinds of oil (sunflower and peanut above all) have occupied large sectors of the market. Margarine enjoyed a certain popularity in the 1970s and 1980s, marketed as the light and easy alternative to butter and oil. Recently, consumers have become more and more skeptical about it, also because it has been deemed related to the increase of cholesterol levels in the blood. As a general rule, Italians all over the county make use of many more fats than 50 years ago. The same happened with sugar, the consumption of which has more than doubled since the 1950s.

As for wine and other alcoholic drinks, wine has roughly maintained the same levels of consumption, with a traditional prevalence in the northern regions, while beer has become a favorite for the younger generations.

As in any other Western country, these are general trends that change drastically with differences in the number of family members, income, level of education, age, sex, and location. For instance, lower-income families and families with many members tend to consume relatively more bread and pasta than families with a higher income and fewer members (the two factors often coincide).

Table 7.1
Daily Wine Drinkers Aged 15 Years and Over by Sex, Age Group, and Geographical Area—Year 2001 (rates per 100 people)

	Age Groups					
Geographical areas	*15–34*	*35–44*	*45–54*	*55–64*	*65 and over*	*Total*
Males						
Northwest	21.2	45.8	57.0	63.4	72.1	48.1
Northeast	23.7	41.4	59.6	67.9	67.9	47.7
North	22.3	44.1	58.1	65.2	70.4	47.9
Central	25.1	49.1	59.5	62.4	65.2	48.9
Continental South	25.9	54.1	62.9	66.1	62.5	48.1
Islands	20.1	41.1	48.8	55.0	47.8	37.6
South	24.0	50.1	58.4	62.4	57.6	44.7
ITALY	23.5	47.0	58.5	63.8	65.2	47.0
Females						
Northwest	7.0	14.1	25.7	30.0	30.3	20.4
Northeast	7.1	18.5	30.4	29.7	31.3	21.9
North	7.0	15.8	27.6	29.9	30.7	21.1
Central	8.5	21.4	28.1	33.2	28.2	22.5
Continental South	7.8	20.8	22.7	27.7	22.2	17.8
Islands	5.7	12.7	14.5	16.1	10.1	10.5
South	7.1	18.3	20.1	23.7	18.2	15.5
ITALY	7.3	17.8	25.3	28.5	25.3	19.4
Total						
Northwest	14.2	30.5	40.8	46.9	47.2	33.8
Northeast	15.5	30.2	44.8	48.8	46.2	34.4
North	14.8	30.4	42.4	47.7	46.8	34.0
Central	16.8	35.5	44.3	47.0	43.7	35.2
Continental South	16.9	37.2	42.5	46.4	39.2	32.4
Islands	12.9	26.4	31.5	34.5	26.2	23.5
South	15.6	33.8	39.0	42.4	34.9	29.5
ITALY	15.5	32.6	41.6	45.9	42.4	32.7

Source: ISTAT—Unità "Struttura e dinamica sociale."

THE EVOLUTION OF DIETARY CONCEPTS

Faced with epochal changes in their dietary patterns, many Italians seem to become more and more interested in questions regarding their eating habits. However, concerns about food, health, and diet are not an exclusively contemporary phenomenon. Until the seventeenth century, people living in Italy, just like those in the rest of Europe, based their health and diet beliefs on the theories elaborated by famous physicians from the past. The most influential were Hippocrates of Cos (between the fifth and the fourth century B.C.E.), Celsus (first century C.E.), and, above all, Galen (second century C.E.).[2] According to their assumptions, a healthy human body was the result of the balance of four fluids, also called *humors*: blood, choler (yellow bile), phlegm, and melancholy (black bile). Each of these fluids manifested different physical qualities: heat, cold, moisture, and dryness. In this theoretical system, blood was considered hot and moist, choler was hot and dry, phlegm was cold and moist, and melancholy was cold and dry. The predominance of any of the four humors conditioned the health and the character of each individual, his or her so-called complexion, in the language of the time. A prevalence of blood determined a sanguine disposition, an excess of choler provoked an outburst of anger, and so on. Different foods were also supposed to have their own complexions, which were assimilated by the bodies that ate them. In this framework, sickness was considered an unbalance of humors, due to the excess of a certain fluid. The naturally healthy balance differed for each individual and was ensured by the ingestion and the digestion of elements that presented opposite qualities to the surplus fluid. For instance, if a person suffered from melancholy, losing weight and showing sunken eyes, the excess of the cold and dry humor was to be counterbalanced by the consumption of hot and moist ingredients, such as onions. As a consequence, there were no general cures that worked for everybody. Doctors were supposed to determine the natural complexion of their patients and to interpret all symptoms in terms of surplus of certain fluids. Based on the resulting diagnosis, they would advise the assumption of specific foods or substances. Furthermore, digestion was considered as a form of cooking that took place in the stomach and the intestine, where food was the fuel providing energy to the body.

With the fall of the Roman Empire and the arrival of Germanic tribes from the north, this medical wisdom was basically lost, maintained only vaguely in the monasteries, which continued to cultivate the Greek and Roman traditions. Galen's approach to diet survived in the Byzantine Empire and Persia. When the Islamic Caliphate conquered these territories, Arab- and Persian-speaking scholars translated the ancient texts in their languages and absorbed all the available knowledge. Ibn Sinna, also known as Avicenna, who lived between the tenth and the eleventh centuries, reorganized the theories received from Celsus and Galen in his Canon (Qanun), which for centuries became the authority in the field.[3] This medical wisdom reached Italy when the Arabs conquered Sicily, and it was successively adopted in the Norman reigns in southern Italy. In the eleventh century, a medical school was founded in Salerno, near Naples, where scholars translated a landslide of texts and compiled a famous dietary known as Regimen Sanitati Salerni, which upheld humoral physiology and made it popular all over Italy.[4] The establishment of the University of Naples by Frederick II in 1224, an emperor who gave protection to Muslim science, the proximity of Amalfi, a seaport open to Arab drug dealers and whose ship traded in all kind of Oriental products, had an unfavorable influence on the school in Salerno. The rise of universities in Montpellier, Padua, and Bologna—the latter particularly renowned for the studies in human anatomy—determined the decadence of Salerno.

In the second half of the fourteenth century, many scholars such as the famous Frances Petrarch fought against the influence of religion and scholastic philosophy over medicine and other sciences, using their knowledge of Greek to access the original texts from antiquity. The terrors of the 1348 plague convinced many of the powerlessness of current medicine. After the fall of Constantinople in 1453, numerous Greek scholars came to Italy, giving a further boost to the cultural movement known as humanism. Endowed with a better knowledge of the Hellenistic masterpieces, many scholars showed interest in classical Latin, originating a diligent and enthusiastic search for original manuscripts. The West could get acquainted with the works of the pre-Aristotelean philosophers and physicians in their original tongue. From the 1470s to the first half of the seventeenth century, a great number of dietary volumes were published, stimulated by the invention of the printing press. The first works were still deeply influenced by Muslim teachings and were mainly geared toward the courts. With the development of Greek studies, many authors turned to the classic sources, often criticizing the courts for their excess in food consumption, labeled as gluttony. The spreading Reformation embraced the critique of life in royal and noble households, including the lavishness of the Papal court in Rome, and undermined traditions connected with Catholicism such as Lenten fast and abstinence. From the end of the sixteenth century, scientific endeavors were characterized by the intense activity of the translators, by the critical treatment of sources from the Greek-Roman antiquity, and by independent investigation especially in the field of botany. Scholars such as Andreas Vesalius and Gabriele Falloppio, who taught in Padua, demonstrated the weakness of the anatomical concepts in the Galenic theory by dissecting corpses. Numerous authors, among them Gerolamo Cardano, Alessandro Petronio, and Giovanni Domenico Sala, opposed widespread nutritional concepts, basing their critique on local habits and traditions and on personal observation.⁵ A traveling German doctor, Theophrastus Bombastus of Hohenheim, known as Paracelsus, elaborated a new theory of the causes of disease (etiology), introducing chemical therapeutics. Furthermore, he strongly upheld the usefulness of mineral waters and native botanical drugs from which he distilled so-called essences and tinctures that were meant to replace folk remedies. Neglecting anatomy and physiology, he thought that all diseases could be explained not by fluids but by entities, which he divided into *ens astrorum* (cosmic influences that included elements such as climate and country), *ens veneni* (toxic matter in the food, the actual cause of contagious diseases), *ens naturale et spirituale* (any defects in physical or mental constitution), *and ens deale* (any adversity cast by Providence). He also maintained that for each disease there existed a specific remedy. Developing the theories put forth by Paracelsus, some chemists and alchemists noted that many natural substances, when heated, separated in a volatile fluid that they equated with mercury; an oily substance, or sulfur; and a solid residue, or salt. While mercury determines smells, sulfur induces sweetness and moistness, and salt controls the taste and texture of foods.⁶

While the theory of fluids was attacked by the developments of chemistry, the idea that digestion was similar to cooking slowly became obsolete. The discovery of blood circulation by English physician William Harvey of Folkstone (1578–1657), published in 1628, and Marcello Malphighi's research on blood corpuscles using the microscope dealt the final blow to Galen's theories. These findings were at the base of the efforts by many scientists, called *iatrophysicists*, to explain all physiological processes according to the laws of physics. Opposing their views, other doctors, known as *iatrochemists*, maintained that chemistry was sufficient to account for all medical facts. Among these, the Belgian Jan Baptista van Helmont (1577–1644), famous for his studies on gas, conjectured that many processes of the living body, like digestion, nutrition, and even movement, are due to fermentation that converts dead substances such as food into living flesh. Franz Sylvius (1614–1672) also sought to explain physiological processes by suggesting fermentation (molecular motion of matter) and "vital spirits" as moving forces. A few years before, the Croatian Santorio Santorio (1561–1636), born as a nobleman from Friuli in the service of the Venetian republic, had studied the human body by weighing its solid and liquid intakes and excretions.

The new research and theories of food fermentation in the body changed the way food was perceived and prepared. Ingredients that fermented easily, like fresh vegetables and fruit, became more popular than in the past, when they had been considered dangerous. In the kitchen, sauces rich in butter and oil were considered useful to bind salts and solid ingredients to substances with a high content of mercury, or volatile fluids, such as wine and spirits. These theories remained prevalent until the nineteenth century, when scientists like Jakob Moleschott (1822–1893) and Justus Freiherr von Liebig (1803–1873), who also had the first intuition to divide nutrients in carbohydrates, proteins, and fats, developed the modern concept of metabolism.

OBESITY, SLIMMING DIETS, AND FOOD-RELATED PATHOLOGIES

The old wisdom and the traditional concepts of food and eating are often not able to make sense of the evolution of the Italian consumption habits. With the drastic changes in dietary patterns due to the increase of consumption levels, problems such as hearth diseases, high blood pressure, and obesity have become urgent.

Obesity, especially in children, has become a main concern for the Ministry of Health, which has launched public campaigns finalized to educate the parents and the children themselves to eat in a more correct way. Almost 25 percent of children and teenagers between the ages of 6 and 17 are overweight, with a definite prevalence in the south. The region with the highest rate is Campania, with 36 percent, while the one showing the lowest figures is Val D'Aosta, closely followed by Trentino Alto Adige and Sardinia. Children between ages 6 and 9 are those with the highest rates, around 33 percent, a figure that is causing much concern at the social and political level.[7] These data are consistent with the poor propensity to regularly practice physical activity and the high amount of free time habitually spent in watching television observed in the sample. The number of obese children is less impressive, about 4 percent, but nevertheless worrisome. Youth between 15 and 24 seem less prone to obesity, with the highest rates in the age range between 45 and 64.

The expansion of the overweight (with a body mass index between 25 and 30) and obese population (with a body mass index above 30) clashes with the increasing diffusion and the widespread preference for body images that favor fitness and slim figures. As in other Western countries, the stark contrast between their actual bodies and the models proposed by media and culture often originates nutrition-related pathologies such as anorexia and bulimia, especially in adolescents and young adults, with a prevalence in females. Also, adult women now show a different attitude toward their bodies. In the past, until the 1960s, a shapely and full-bosomed

Table 7.2
Obese People Aged 15 Years and Over by Sex, Age Group, and Region—Years 1999–2000 (rates per 100 people)

Regions and Geographical Areas	Age Groups					
	15–24	25–44	45–64	65 and over	Total	Standardized rate[a]
Males						
Northwest	10	57	117	97	80	71
Northeast	19	66	147	113	96	87
North	14	61	130	104	87	78
Central	12	55	124	110	83	74
Continental South	18	79	164	124	103	98
Islands	31	79	146	131	101	97
South	22	79	158	126	103	97
ITALY	17	66	138	113	92	84
Females						
Northwest	21	32	112	110	76	69
Northeast	18	43	111	125	82	75
North	20	37	111	117	79	72
Central	0,6	32	111	118	76	68
Continental South	18	59	173	176	112	109
Islands	14	35	136	159	89	87
South	16	51	161	171	104	101
ITALY	16	41	128	134	87	81
Total						
Northwest	15	45	115	105	78	70
Northeast	19	54	129	120	89	81
North	17	49	121	112	83	75
Central	0,9	44	117	115	79	71
Continental South	18	69	168	154	108	103
Islands	22	57	141	147	95	91
South	19	65	159	152	104	99
ITALY	16	54	133	125	89	82

[a]Standardized rates have been calculated using Italian resident population aged 15 years and over—Census 1991.

Source: ISTAT—Unità "Struttura e dinamica sociale."

woman was considered desirable. It is enough to see that among the popular movie stars of that time were Gina Lollobrigida and Sophia Loren. From the 1960s on, a slim figure became the standard of female beauty, with skinny fashion models as symbols. Since the 1990s a reevaluation of curvaceous women has been under way, as the success of actresses like Francesca Cucinotta and Sabrina Ferilli seems to indicate. As to men, the prevalent image of desirable and trendy masculinity is related to a fit, if not muscular, body, epitomized in the so-called six-pack abdominals (*addominali a tartaruga*). If many young adults and adults opt for sports and exercise in the gym as a solution to their weight problems, others prefer to resort to slimming diets. The common trait of these alternative dietary patterns is that they entice with extreme solutions in short periods of time instead of a constant and long-term transformation of the subject's everyday diet. Against all Mediterranean customs, some diets suggest the drastic reduction of carbohydrates while increasing the protein intake. The most famous Italian version of this approach is the so-called jockey diet (*dieta del fantino*), which is based on consuming meat almost exclusively. Other diets (*dieta dissociata*) consider eating carbohydrates and meat in the same meal as the cause of excess weight. For instance, it is harmful to eat pasta seasoned with a meat-based sauce, like *ragù*, or with seafood, while it is acceptable with a simple tomato sauce. Other schools of thought considers food intolerance (*intolleranze alimentari*) as the source of extra fat. Because the human body is supposedly unable to assimilate substances that it cannot tolerate, these ingredients would automatically become fat. The solution is to find all the substances to which each subject is intolerant, usually a lengthy list of foods that, when eliminated, limits the daily calorie intake and causes a certain loss of weight, giving the impression that the diet actually works. At times the solution is found in collective action, as in the case of diets based on group therapy and mutual help to resist the temptations of the table. Some theories propose the elimination of all unnatural and nonorganic products, while others, based on the Chinese concepts of *yin* and *yang*, refuse certain vegetables such as tomatoes or peppers, for being too *yin*. Vegetarians and vegans usually reject these excesses and reach a healthier and more complete diet. Last but not least, hundreds of products in the forms of pills and meal substitutes lure the consumers into the illusion that it not even necessary to change one's dietary patterns to lose weight.[8] Faced with these phenomena, the Italian government and the state institutions responsible for public health are assuming a very active attitude to educate Italians about nutrition.

The National Research Institute for Food and Nutrition or INRAN (*Istituto Nazionale di Ricerca per gli Alimenti e la Nutrizione*) is in charge of research, information, and promotion in the field of food and nutrition in order to protect consumers and to enhance the quality of food production. Under the supervision of the Ministry for Agriculture and Forests, INRAN periodically publishes a booklet called *Guidelines for a Healthy Italian Diet*, with the last edition issued in 2003. Each edition tries to in-

corporate the changes in habits and culture and to explain the most recent scientific findings in accessible language. Together with the High Institute of Public Health (*Istituto Superiore della Sanità*), INRAN promotes
research on food quality and food security in the field of certifications, labeling, and enhancement of the specific traits of national products, and it
cooperates with the development and application of biotechnologies.
Since 1977, the Italian Society for Human Nutrition (*Società Italiana di
Nutrizione Umana*), founded in 1963, has periodically issued a document
called "Levels of Recommended Absorption of Energy and Nutrients for
the Italian Population" or LARN. In addition, the Institute of Food Sciences (*Istituto Scienze dell'Alimentazione* or ISA), a branch of the National
Research Council (CNR), studies the composition and nutritional quality of foods and researches the characterization and enhancement of foods
typical of the Mediterranean diet.

NEW TRENDS IN CONSUMPTION

Consumers are increasingly concerned about the quality of the products
that they purchase in shops, supermarkets, or even fresh fruit and vegetable outdoor markets.

In 1962 the military Corps of Carabinieri founded a special section
called the Antisophistication Squad (NAS, or *Nucleo antisofisticazioni*) to
eliminate frauds connected with food, such as the sale of expired or unsafe
products and the addition of illegal ingredients to food. From 1979, NAS
also controls food in military barracks, hospitals, schools, and retirement
homes. In 1986 Carabinieri also started an Ecological Squad (NOE, or
Nucleo Operativo Ecologico) to protect the environment from illegal pollution, a key factor for organic agriculture. Veterinarians under the direction of each city council are supposed to control the quality of meat and
fish sold everywhere, while city policemen investigate the cleanliness of
shops and markets.

To respond to growing concerns about food security, the Italian government has issued laws regulating both the quality control of fresh produce
and what can be sold under the definition of organic (*biologico*), in compliance with the decisions handed down by the European Union. To have
their products recognized as deriving from organic agriculture (*agricoltura
biologica*), farmers have to grow them without employing artificially syn-
thesized chemical agents or genetically modified organisms. Furthermore,
they have to adopt culture rotation to prevent parasites and diseases, and
they have to fertilize the soil only with organic substances or natural min-

erals. Farmers receive the official recognition from the agencies responsible with controlling their activities only after meeting the above-mentioned requirements for at least two years previous to the sowing or, in case of perennial cultures, for three years before harvest. Before the entire period of conversion has elapsed, produce can be certified as "in conversion to organic agriculture." Both certifications must clearly appear on labels and wrapping.

The organic sector is constantly growing, a result of popularity among youth and parents of small children. Besides, politically aware consumers have recently shown an increasing interest in products distributed and sold by shops belonging to the so-called commerce for equity and solidarity *(commercio equo e solidale)*. The income from these products is certified to be redistributed to the producers, usually located in developing countries. Coffee, tea, chocolate, rice, and spices are grown on land still belonging to the local farmers, outside the control of large multinational companies. The farmers are organized in cooperatives that sell their crops directly to organizations that distribute to European markets, thus skipping all middlemen and distributors, who often end up exploiting the farmers by allotting them a tiny fraction of the final earning.

All these phenomena are changing the eating habits of large sections of the population. Quality-conscious and politically conscious consumers are now likely to be prepared to spend more to purchase products designated as PDO (Protected Designation of Origin) or PGI (Protected Geographical Indication), organically grown vegetables and fruits, and items from the network of the commerce for equity and solidarity. Furthermore, they would not blink if they had to drive quite a few miles to get their meat or vegetables from a farmer in the county whom they can trust or to reach that specific producer in the next town. Computers help too, since many purveyors of high-quality products now offer their goods over the Internet, especially if they are cured or somehow conserved. Of course, these consumers are likely to be more educated and to have a larger income than the average person. The majority of Italians, even if sensitive to these issues, keep on buying in bulk at the local supermarket, and on a day-to-day basis at their corner store or at the closest outdoor market, which usually provides fresh produce at reasonable prices. Even in these outlets, nevertheless, consumers tend to prefer products that give a certain guarantee of their quality and their safety within a reasonable range of cost. Frozen food, especially vegetables and fish, are perceived to be safe; their sales, also boosted by their convenience, are constantly increasing. Truth be told, most frozen-food companies are putting huge efforts and investments into creating products that ensure better quality and a growing similarity to traditional homemade dishes. It is not unusual to find frozen fish soups, pasta with seafood, or even more complicated meals. They are not quite the same as the originals, but they are acceptably close if people do not have the time or the inclination to spend an evening in the kitchen.

PREGNANCY, BIRTH, AND BREASTFEEDING

Dietary rules change during each individual's lifetime. A very special period for many women is pregnancy. Gaining weight in the months preceding the birth of a baby is considered not only acceptable but is even recommended. "Pregnant women have to eat for two," went the old saying. Nowadays, although women are urged to eat healthfully, excess weight is considered unnecessary and dangerous at the moment of the delivery. Future mothers are supposed to eat regularly, increasing the daily intake of calories, especially if they plan to breastfeed. In the first months of pregnancy, when nausea is frequent, women are cautioned to eat less and more often and to choose those foods that bother them less. It is expected that pregnant women will have so-called whims (*voglie*), related to food. Their husbands and the whole family usually try to satisfy these sudden cravings to avoid the baby showing birthmarks the same color of the desired food. For instance, a reddish birthmark could be called a strawberry whim and a brownish one would be a "coffee whim," due to the unsatisfied desire in the mother.

Food containing high levels of protein, calcium, and iron is usually prescribed. An old saying warned that a woman might lose "a tooth for each pregnancy." In the popular wisdom, meat is considered paramount for the regular development of the fetus. In fact, red meat, as well as liver, is high in protein and iron content. Meat and wine are believed to "make blood," thus helping the woman to prepare herself for the delivery, when loss of blood is highly likely. Nevertheless, raw and cured meat (such as *prosciutto*) is avoided, for fear it might transmit anything dangerous to the fetus. Despite physicians tending to discourage the use of any kind of alcohol, a half glass of wine with meals is commonly considered healthy, after the first months of pregnancy and at the end of the related nausea. Drinking too much wine or liquor, instead, is deemed dangerous.

Women are also advised to rest and to drink lots of water to help kidneys do their job especially when the mother is close to the birth, which is also when intestinal constipation is quite common. To help with this problem, women are often given vegetables and cooked fruit.

Most women opt for breastfeeding, which is considered better for the child, because it creates a closer connection to the mother and provides the baby with all necessary nutrients and protection against infections and diseases. For this reason, breastfeeding is much more socially accepted than in the United States. In fact, mothers are often extremely upset if they are not able to produce enough milk and they have to resort to formula. In the past, the mother would let a wet nurse breastfeed her baby, a second-best solution, with formula less desirable. The approach to formula is exemplified also by the fact that formula producers are required by law to indicate on the box of their product that breastfeeding is superior and that at any rate the formula cannot be used without express indications from physicians, pharmacists, or dieticians. In fact, the law now bans definitions of formula as "adapted milk" (latte adattato), "maternalized milk" (latte maternizzato), or "humanlike milk" (latte umanizzato), which were used in the past. The current denomination is now "artificial milk" (latte artificiale), which clearly has negative connotations. Formulas are divided in two categories: the ones designed for babies up to six months old and the ones for older babies, also called "continuation formula" (latte artificiale di proseguimento). Only the second kind can be advertised. Formulas are sold in pharmacies and not in drugstores, which make them much less desirable and acceptable.

It is still absolutely normal for women to breastfeed in social situations and public places like buses, trains, or even restaurants. It was even more so when it was a common belief that babies were supposed to be fed at fixed hours. In recent years, pediatricians tended to advise mothers to feed their babies regularly but with flexibility. For instance, they are now urged not to wake up their babies from their naps to feed them, within reasonable limits. When they breastfeed, women are advised to avoid food that can give a bad taste to the milk, such as garlic, onion, cabbage, asparagus, or substances usually considered as allergenic, like chocolate, strawberries, peaches, cherries, crustaceans, clams, mussels, and fermented cheese. Coffee and tea are supposed to make the child nervous. Doctors now advise women who breastfeed to increase the intake of milk and cheese for calcium, olive oil for oleic acid, and fish for omega-3 acids. Oleic and omega-3 acids are considered necessary for the healthy development of the baby's nervous system. If the mother decides to use formula, she is urged to go back to her usual diet as soon as possible.

Maternity leaves usually last until the beginning of the weaning, when babies are able to get milk from mother a couple of times a day when she is home from work.

BABIES AND CHILDREN

Up to 5 months of age, babies are fed exclusively milk or formula. From 5 to 12 months, babies are weaned, and new flavors and foods are introduced into their diet. Between 1 and 3 years, the babies are supposed adapt their diet to the adults' habits.

The first foods given to babies during the weaning are usually finely mashed fruit given in a teaspoon to teach babies to swallow. The next step may consist of cereal-based flours (*pappa*), often reinforced with vegetables and fruit, cooked in a light vegetable broth. It is quite common to add some olive oil or grated *parmigiano reggiano* to these mixtures. Plain *parmigiano* is considered highly digestible, while in the case of olive oil parents are advised to buy special products for babies, especially in the first phase of the weaning. *Pappa* can be substituted by some very thin pasta, called "little sand" (*sabbiolina*), always cooked in vegetable broth, and later lyophilized meat and fish are added to the mixture, to accustom babies to new flavor. In time, commercial homogenized foods are introduced, together with bigger cuts of pasta, like little stars (*stelline*). Homogenized foods are sold in various flavors, including trout, flounder, rabbit, and lamb, which would not be thought of as baby-friendly in the United States. The goal is to let babies get used to the taste of real food, because there is no concept of "baby food" per se. When they are about 10 months old, babies are supposed to be ready for so-called real food: Fish and meat are served in tiny pieces, and increasingly big shapes of pasta are prepared. When babies turn a year old, foods that are considered heavy or less digestible are added to their diets, such as eggs or tomato sauce. At this point, babies are usually more than happy to start eating what their parents and other adults eat, especially at social occasions when many people are gathered around the table.

The following years are the period when children are socialized in their food manners, learning to eat by themselves and using glasses, dishes, spoons, and forks in the proper way. Besides, they are taught to eat any food that may be served, with some exceptions like fried foods or *salumi* usually added to the children's diet later. For these reasons there are no baby menus in restaurants. Children are supposed to eat small portions of the same dishes the adults are having. Children are often curious to taste adult food, and in many families it is acceptable to serve them even tiny drops of coffee in their milk or a few drops of wine, often diluted in lots of water. Of course, when it comes to food, every child tends to have his or her own preferences. But it is quite usual to see a certain taste for pasta, potatoes, and fruit, while meat, fish, and vegetables are often refused, especially if served in unfamiliar ways. School canteens deal with these problems by serving bland and unthreatening food, and teachers, busy with keeping discipline, often give up when children do not even try new dishes.

Children are not supposed to be eating all the time, consuming snacks that are often high in calories and poor in nutrients. It is common to see toddlers walking around with a bottle that usually contains unsweetened fruit juice, milk, or even plain water. If the children get whiny, the usual solution is the pacifier, not some food or snack. Also, when they are taken to grocery stores with their mothers, children are used to the fact that they are not getting any food to eat while in the store, but rather they amuse themselves with little toys.

Of course, food industries are trying to get parents to buy sweet food for their children, so it is not uncommon to see a rack with little snacks or candies near the checkout in most stores and supermarkets. Commercials for those foods run frequently during children's programs on TV. As a consequence, rates of overweight and obese children in the population are rising.

A new phenomenon is fast food. Introduced at the end of the 1980s, it provoked a debate about the nutritional value of this kind of food, especially when Italians started realizing the benefits of the so-called Mediterranean diets. Fast food was and still is thought to be fattening, difficult to digest, and addicting. At any rate, it is the first introduction to flavors that are totally foreign to Italian cuisine, like ketchup.

Nevertheless, one of the favorite snacks for children and teenagers is still pizza, which is usually served in smaller portions than in the United States (bought by the weight, not by the precut slice) and has a smaller content of fat, because it is covered with much less cheese.

Depending on the family, teenagers between the ages of 15 and 20 are allowed by their parents to drink some wine with meals. Because the regulations about drinking age are basically absent or ignored, it is up to the adults to keep teens from drinking in excess. By the time they reach college age, young adults are over any curiosity about alcohol, so it is unusual to see the college beer binge parties that are quite common in other countries.

SENIOR CITIZENS

The percentage of seniors in the Italian population is growing more quickly than in most Western countries, due to a low birthrate, which in the 1990s was among the lowest in the world. The change in demographics is affecting the way senior citizens are thought of, because now they constitute an actual social force with a certain voting power. In general, people live longer than in the past, although with many health problems due to lack of activity, the absence of a culture that urges older citizens to exercise, and nutritional habits that are not attuned to their actual needs. There is no concept of food for the elderly. Senior citizens are supposed to eat the way they always did, unless they have specific ailments or suffer from loss of teeth. They continue to drink wine with their meals, to have their coffee in the morning, to season their dishes with large quantities of salt, and to consume fried food and sweets. Since the calorie intake does not decrease, while retirement implies a less active style of life, it is quite common for older people to gain weight and to suffer from problems connected with high levels of cholesterol in the blood, high blood pressure, and diabetes. The change in the dietary patterns of the populations as a whole, with a larger intake of meat, fat, and sugar, has often negatively affected older generations, which grew up on a totally different diet. Heart problems, strokes, and other traumatic events have become routine.

Only recently has a certain concern for menopausal women and their problems due to lack of calcium become widespread. As a consequence, older women are urged to consume more milk and cheese, preferably skim milk and cheese with a low fat content.

FOOD FOR THE SICK

Italian physicians are not particularly interested in matters of nutrition, unless foods affect some specific ailments. With the exception of pediatricians, who are definitely more involved in the subject because of the pressure from mothers, many of them do not even study that subject during their professional training. For this reason, the advice some medical doctors give is quite vague, often based more on common sense than on study and research. If patients have high levels of cholesterol in their blood, they are advised to cut out fatty foods. If their blood pressure is high, they are urged to consume less salt, and so on. Nutritionists and dieticians are considered only in case of chronic ailments that need a controlled diet (diabetes, high levels of triglycerides, ulcers, and intestinal problems) or if patients want to lose weight.

Most of the knowledge people get about their food and their nutritional needs come from less reliable sources, namely, the media. Most TV channels, newspapers, and magazine have a section on health, which often deals with food-related issues. As a result, people act on a mix of popular wisdom, medical advice, and personal taste. For colds, liquids are not the first things that come to mind. People would rather think about specific drinks: tea with honey, warm milk with cognac, and hot wine boiled with orange zest, a dry fig, a slice of apple, and spices. Orange juice, which is rich in vitamin C, is considered a good solution. For a case of flu, but also for any kind of minor illness of the stomach and the intestine, the preference is for a light diet. In this case, the favorites are always boiled rice and pasta with olive oil and a little *parmigiano reggiano* (but with no sauces), chicken or vegetable broth, boiled vegetables, boiled fish, and cooked fruit. When the sick person is recovering, some meat cooked with no fat and drizzled with extra-virgin olive oil, along with *prosciutto crudo*, are added to the diet.

In hospitals, professional nutritionists take care of deciding the diet for each patient, according to his or her needs. Nevertheless, hospital cooks often limit themselves to reheating or thawing dishes that are prepared in external facilities, already in prepackaged portions. Only small or private hospitals actually cook food on the premises. The result is that hospital food is considered more like a punishment than a tool for recovery. Patients complain that it is bland, tasteless, overcooked, or plain disgusting. The patients' relatives usually smuggle in the hospital dishes that they know their loved ones like, even when those dishes are not indicated or might even be dangerous. At times, the patients' diet is negotiated between the physicians, the dietitians, and the relatives. Many believe that if the patient enjoys his or her food, the recovery process is faster.

MINERAL WATERS

Cleanness and purity, and a quest for a healthier style of life, find peculiar expression in Italians' growing passion for mineral water, which now constitutes a huge market. The Romans already knew most of the modern Italian watering places, but their curative properties were too little valued during the Middle Ages. About 1336, Petrus de Tussignana wrote about the famous thermae of Bormio; in 1340, Giacomo de Dondi about Abano. The impulse to study mineral springs was in modern times given by Paracelsus. Starting from the Renaissance, many sources were highly praised for their curative effects on various ailments.

Cold-water therapies became fashionable in the nineteenth century. As in contemporary spas, around the most celebrated sources hotels, swimming pools, and other facilities were built, including restaurants catering to the dietary requirements of the guests. Expressions like "to do the waters" (fare le acque) and "to pass the waters" (passare le acque) entered the common language, although these therapies were limited to the higher strata of society.

The importance of water is now widely acknowledged. Public health authorities actively campaigned to save water and to integrate it the daily diet. The last edition of the Guidelines for a Healthy Italian Diet, published in 2003, includes a chapter about water and all the misconceptions about its consumption.[9] The report explains that citizens can drink water during meals without fear of a difficult digestion; that water neither makes you gain weight nor provokes liquid retention; and that waters with a lower mineral content are healthier than others. The document specifically tackles the problem of tap water with a high calcium content. It reassures people suffering from kidney stones that drinking water with calcium does not worsen their problem; on the other hand, it affirms that the human body can absorb as much calcium from water as from milk.

On a daily basis, many Italians buy and consume bottled mineral water, considered purer than tap water (usually potable all over the country) and therapeutic to keep a healthy body, responding to the different needs of every individual. According to the total content of salts (called fixed residual or residuo fisso), the law classifies mineral waters in minimally mineralized (minimamente mineralizzate, with a fixed residual of less than 50 mg/l), scarcely mineralized (oligominerali, 50–500 mg/l), medium mineral waters (mediominerali, 500–1500 mg/l), and highly mineralized (fortemente mineralizzate, more than 1500 mg/l). These data must be clearly indicated on the label of the mineral water, together with other information about the biological analysis and the specific minerals found in it. Nevertheless, labels cannot refer to specific properties that might prevent or cure any specific ailment; they must limit themselves to general properties favorable to health, such as "it may have diuretic effects," "it may have laxative effects," or "it stimulates digestion."[10]

There is also a growing market for the so-called source waters, which differ from mineral waters in that the levels of salts must be within the limits imposed for tap water and that they cannot boast properties favorable to health.

GENETICALLY MODIFIED ORGANISMS, MAD COW, AND OTHER FEARSOME MATTERS

Italy and the European Union consider food safety a very important issue. Recent events provoked a widespread wave of panic throughout Europe, causing citizens to adopt very strict attitudes about what should make its way to the table.

It all started in November 1986, when the first official case of Bovine Spongiform Encephalopathy, or BSE (the so-called mad cow disease) was detected in British cattle. The cause of the epidemic was identified in the feed made from animal carcasses and offal, especially sheep. The epidemic had actually originated in the late 1970s when pro-business government policies introduced deregulation in the meat-rendering industry, allowing many usable parts of dead animals to become supplements for livestock diet without being steamed at high temperatures or being sterilized using organic solvents.[11] The result was that the infectious agents—in this case prions—could survive in the fodder and be transmitted to cows and humans eating their meat (when it affects humans, the disease is called Creutzfeld-Jakob disease). The first cases of BSE in cows were observed as early as 1984, but in the following years the British government tried to cover it up to support the beef industry. It did not work.

In 1989, the European Union imposed an embargo on the exportations from Britain of veal aged more than six months, and in 1994 it banned the use of fodder deriving from livestock. In 1996 the Union voted for a total ban of beef from the United Kingdom, forcing the British government to kill any cow older than 30 months. Nevertheless, British beef was still being smuggled all over Europe, and the scandal exploded in the summer of 1997. After two years, the situation seemed to ease and the European Union lifted the embargo on beef from the United Kingdom. Nevertheless, France and Germany refused to comply. At the end of 2000, Italy, a country that so far had considered itself basically untouched, passed a law imposing a BSE test on all cattle older than 30 months. The first official case of an infected animal was detected at the beginning of 2001, pushing Italy to the threshold of a full-fledged mad-cow-disease scare. At the same time, another epidemic, the so-called foot-and-mouth disease, started affecting cattle, sheep, and pigs all over Europe, increasing the general panic even if this virus only rarely makes humans sick. In July 2001, the European Union enforced new regulations that allowed only the use of chickens and pigs to produce cattle feed. At the same time, all the meat imported from other countries was to be inspected and certified. Italy implemented BSE tests to be run on all cows older than 24 months, and at the end of 2001 the government adopted a labeling system that allows consumers to know where the beef comes from, what the animal ate, where it was butchered, and other reassuring pieces of information. Nevertheless, the discovery of many violations against the new laws made the consumption of beef plummet, increasing the sales of fish and unusual livestock like horse, ostrich, or kangaroo.

Many traditional dishes became less popular or were officially banned, and the hard-line aficionados had to conspire with local butchers or courageous restaurant owners to keep on eating their favorites. For some time, in Rome, fried cow brains, ox tail, and *pajata* (suckling veal intestines) were virtually a memory. In Florence, the famous thick steak known as *bistecca alla fiorentina* was outlawed, and so was the consumption of marrow, fundamental for dishes such as *risotto alla milanese*. More recently, people have been going back to their local food, but the meat market will probably never fully recover from the blow, because the eating habits have deeply changed. Beef consumption is still decreasing due to its high cost, right when Italy is struggling against an economic crisis that has been associated by the popular wisdom with the implementation of the Euro currency in January 2002. The media also connected this drop in beef consumption (and of meat in general) to health concerns and even to the raise of global temperatures. In fact, during the 2003 summer heat wave, meat sales plummeted in Italy.

It was partly because of BSE that the European and namely Italian attitude toward GMOs (genetically modified organisms) has been so radically different from that in the United States. Because there is no definitive proof that GMOs are not harmful to humans, most Europeans prefer to stay on the safe side, refusing to ingest anything that could remotely be identified as genetically modified. In July 2001, the European Union adopted a legislative package that established a system to trace and label GMOs, regulating the diffusion on the market of food and feed products derived from genetically modified elements when there is a content above 1 percent, considered a reasonable level of so-called accidental presence. The new regulation requires traceability of GMOs from the field to the table, carried out by the European Food Security Authority, which is in charge of providing consumers with all the necessary information to make their choices.

In the spring of 2003, the Italian Senate approved the project for a law that, implementing the European regulation 178/2002, allows biotechnologies to be patented as long as they are "not contrary to human dignity, public order, the protection of the health and the life of persons and animals, to the preservation of plants and biodiversity, and to the prevention of damages to the environment." Among other measures, experimentation will have to be approved by a National Committee that will implement a ban on tests carried out near protected zones or areas dedicated to organic agriculture. Furthermore, strict controls will be applied to any genetic manipulation of products protected by the registration as PDO or PGI.

PARMA, EMILIA ROMAGNA: THE DEBATE ON THE EUROPEAN FOOD AUTHORITY

While the new regulations are being implemented, and all the member states are rushing to get as many registrations as possible, a silent battle was waged over food safety and the establishment of a European Food Authority. In a "White Paper of Food Safety" issued by the Commission in January 2000—the executive body of the European Union—the establishment of an independent European Food Authority was proposed as the most appropriate response to the need to guarantee a high level of food safety. The mad cow scare and other worries had become so important to the public opinion that European institutions felt they had to take a clear stand.

Immediately, the political debate focused on where to locate the new Authority, creating a conflict between different countries that each proposed to host the new body: Italy recommended the city of Parma, while Finland offered Helsinki. In the Mediterranean states, public opinion immediately labeled the second candidate as a laughing stock, since Finns are not continentally renowned for their cuisine and their famed products. The issue, nevertheless, lay elsewhere. It embodied the struggle between different perceptions of what food is and what security might entail. Northern European citizens have a sense of what is edible that is much closer to the general understanding in the United States: Cheese made of unpasteurized milk and aged in natural caves, for example, does not immediately register as safe. Cured pork fat seasoned and kept in marble vats, as in the case of the *lardo* from Colonnata, is immediately perceived as unhealthy. Beyond the immediate concerns about mad cow disease and the debate about the GMOs, it became clear that Italy would accept food policies that value traditions and local habits, while their northern counterparts would push for a more scientific approach.

The result was that when regulation no. 178 passed in January 2002, establishing the European Authority for Food Security, no decision was made about the whereabouts of the new body. The Authority, the regulation states, constitutes an independent scientific point of reference in evaluating risks and guaranteeing the regular functioning of the internal market. It will also formulate pronouncements about scientific matters that are sources of controversy and help to manage any future emergency crisis at the Union level. The Authority is not supposed to have any enforcement authority, but it would pass its recommendations to the European Commission. Nevertheless, it is granted an autonomous right of communication in order to provide information directly to the public, although in case of emergency it has to coordinate its communication with the commission and the member states. Although the internal organization, the staff, and the finances were all laid out in the 2002 regulations, it was not until December 2003 that a meeting of the heads of member states, held in Brussels, assigned the offices of the newly created Authority to the city of Parma.

NOTES

1. Stefano Jacini, *I risultati dell'inchiesta agraria* (Turin: Einaudi, 1976).

2. Hippocrates, *De Diaeta,* trans. W. H. Jones (Cambridge, Mass.: Cambridge University Press, 1967); Aulus Cornelius Celsus, *De Medicina*, trans. W. G. Spencer (Cambridge, Mass.: Cambridge University Press, 1938); Claudius Galen, *Opera Omnia*, ed. C. G. Kühn (Hildesheim: Georg Omls Verlags, 1965).

3. Nancy Siraisi, *Avicenna in Renaissance Italy* (Princeton: Princeton University Press, 1987).

4. *Regola Sanitaria Salernitana,* trans. Bianca Romagnoli Gigliotti (Rome: Napoleone, 1972).

5. Ken Albala, *Eating Right in the Reinassance* (Berkeley and Los Angeles: University of California Press, 2000), 36–47.

6. Rachel Laudan, "Birth of the Modern Diet," *Scientific American* 283, no. 2 (2000): 62–67.

7. S. Brescianini, L. Gargiulo, and E. Gianicolo, *Eccesso di peso nell'infanzia e nell'adolescenza* (Rome: Convegno Istat, 2002).

8. Cristina Barbagli, "Mangio poco eppure ingrasso," *Gambero Rosso* 28 (1994): 47–52.

9. Ministero per le Politiche Agricole e Forestali, Istituto Nazionale di Ricerca per gli Alimenti e la Nutrizione, *Linee guida per una sana alimentazione Italiana*, 2003, http://www.INRAN.it.

10. Cristina Barbagli, "Per non perdersi in un bicchier d'acqua," *Gambero Rosso* 129 (2002): 34–51.

11. Marion Nestle, *Safe Food* (Berkeley and Los Angeles: University of California Press, 2003), 251.

Glossary

Antipasto (plural, Antipasti)   Appetizer.

Aperitivo   Premeal drink, usually served with mixed nuts, crackers, potato chips, olives, and other finger food.

Baccalà   Salt-dried cod.

Bruschetta   Slices of grilled bread with different toppings, often served as an appetizer.

Caffellatte   Warm milk with espresso coffee.

Caffettiera   Coffeemaker, usually one that sits on a stove top.

Cappuccino   Steamed frothy milk with espresso coffee.

Cena   Evening meal.

Colazione   Breakfast.

Companatico   Anything eaten with bread, often referring to the filling of a panino.

Contorno (plural, Contorni)   Side dish.

Dolce   Literally, "sweet," referring to desserts in general.

Fagiolo (plural, Fagioli)   Bean.

Frittata   From the verb *friggere* (to fry), referring to omelets or other fried flat pies.

Frittella   Lumps of wheat- or rice-based dough, made puffy by frying.

Fritto/Frittura   Fried food.

Gelato   Egg custard-based ice cream.

Guanciale   Cured pork cheeks.

Insaccato (plural, Insaccati)   Cured pork meat wrapped in a piece of pig intestine, skin, or other kind of artificial wrappers, such as sausages or *salami*.

Lardo   Cured pork fat.

Merenda   Midmorning or midafternoon snack.

Minestra (plural, Minestre)   Vegetable soup with pasta.

Pancetta   Meat obtained by curing the ventral region of the pig with salt and spices or through a smoking process following the spicing phase.

Polenta   Thick porridge obtained by cooking ground maize (including the kernel) in boiling water.

Pranzo   Midday meal.

Primo (plural, Primi)   First course, usually a pasta or a soup.

Prosciutto   Ham cured raw (crudo) or cooked (cotto).

Salame (plural, Salami)   A particular category of salume made of ground pork meat and spices.

Salume (plural, Salumi)   General term for cured pork meat.

Secondo (plural, Secondi)   Second course.

Sfoglia   Thin sheet of dough.

Soffritto   Cooking base in many dishes and sauces, made of garlic, onion, and celery, thinly chopped (sometimes with lard added) and slowly browned in either olive oil or butter.

Spuntino   General term for snack.

Stoccafisso   Stockfish.

Strutto   Lard, or rendered pork fat.

Torta (plural, Torte)   General term for a round pie, both sweet and savory.

Zabaione   Egg-yolk cream cooked in Bain Marie together with sugar and sweet wine.

Zuppa   Vegetable soup.

Resource Guide

WEB SITES

General Web Sites on Italian Food

italianfood.about.com
www.agraria.org/prodottitipici.htm
www.italiancookingandliving.com/
www.italianfoodforever.com
www.made-in-italy.com/winefood/food/

Magazines and Publishers

Bibenda
www.bibenda.it
Cucina e Vini
www.cucinaevini.it
Gambero Rosso
www.gamberorosso.it
Gola Gioconda
www.golagioconda.it/
La Cucina Italiana
www.cucinait.com/World/Home_We.asp
Sale & pepe
home.mondadori.com/salepepe/
Veronelli editore
www.veronelli.com/

Viaggi e sapori
www.viaggiesapori.it/

FILMS

Accattone (1960) by Pier Paolo Pasolini

Albero degli Zoccoli, L' (1941) by Ermanno Olmi

Americano a Roma, Un (1954) by Steno

Camerieri (1995) by Leone Pompucci

Cena, La (1998) by Ettore Scola

Fellini—Satyricon (1969) by Federico Fellini

Ferie d'Agosto (1995) by Paolo Virzì

Festa di Laurea (1984) by Pupi Avati

Filomena Marturano (1951) by Eduardo Di Filippo

Gattopardo, Il (1963) by Luchino Visconti

Giornata particolare, Una (1977) by Ettore Scola

Grande abbuffata, La (*La grande bouffe*, 1973) by Marco Ferreri

Italian Fast Food (1986) by Ludovico Gasperini

Ladri di biciclette (1948) by Vittorio De Sica

Lamerica (1994) by Gianni Amelio

Lingua del Santo, La (2000) by Carlo Mazzacurati

Maccheroni (1985) by Ettore Scola

Macellaio, Il (1998) by Aurelio Grimaldi

Mediterraneo (1991) by Gabriele Salvatores

Minestrone, Il (1981) by Sergio Citti

Miseria e nobiltà (1954) by Mario Mattoli

Mortadella, La (1971) by Mario Monicelli

Napoli milionaria (1950) by Eduardo Di Filippo

Novecento (1977) by Bernardo Bertolucci

Paisà (1946) by Roberto Rossellini

Pane amore e fantasia (1954) by Luigi Comencini

Pane e cioccolata (1973) by Franco Brusati

Questi fantasmi (1954) by Eduardo Di Filippo

Ricotta, La (1963) by Pier Paolo Pasolini

Riso amaro (1949) by Giuseppe De Sanctis

Rocco e i suoi fratelli (1960) by Luchino Visconti

Roma (1972) by Federico Fellini
Roma città aperta (1945) by Roberto Rossellini
Sette chili in sette giorni (1986) by Carlo Verdone
Soliti ignoti, I (1958) by Mario Monicelli
Terra Trema (1948) by Luchino Visconti

ORGANIZATIONS

Altro mercato
Association for the Promotion of Commerce for Equity and Solidarity
www.altromercato.it

Associazione Città del Vino
Association of the Cities of Wine
www.cittadelvino.com

Associazione Italiana Dietisti
Italian Association of Dieticians
www.asid.it

Associazione Italiana Disturbi dell'Alimentazione e del Peso AIDAP
Italian Association for Food Related Pathologies
www.positivepress.net/aidap

Associazione Italiana Sommelier AIS
Italian Sommelier Association
www.sommelier.it/

Autorità Europea per la Sicurezza Alimentare
European Food Security Authority
www.parmafoodauthority.org

European Union (EU)
europa.eu.int/

Food and Agriculture Organization of the United Nations (FAO)
www.fao.org/

Istituto Commercio Estero
Italian Trade Commission
www.naturalmenteitaliano.it

Istituto di Scienze dell'Alimentazione (ISA)
Institute of Food Science
www.isa.av.cnr.it/

Istituto Nazionale di ricerca per gli alimenti e la nutrizione (INRAN)
National Research Institute for Food and Nutrition
www.inran.it
Istituto Nazionale di Statistica (ISTAT)
Italian National Institute of Statistics
www.istat.it

Istituto Studi Ricerche e Informazione sul mercato agricolo ISMEA
Istitute for the Research and Information on the Agricultural Market
www.ismea.it

Istituto Superiore della Sanità
High Institute of Public Health
www.iss.it/

Ministero della Salute
Ministry of Health
www.ministerosalute.it

Ministero delle Politiche Agricole e Forestali
Ministry of Agriculture and Forest Policies
www.politicheagricole.it

Movimento Turismo del Vino
Wine Tourism Movement
www.movimentoturismovino.it

Oldways Preservation and Exchange Trust
www.oldwayspt.org/

Parlamento Italiano
Italian Parliament
www.parlamento.it/

Presidenza del Consiglio
Italian Head of Government Office
www.governo.it/

Slow Food
www.slowfood.com
www.slowfoodusa.org

Società Italiana di Nutrizione Umana
Italian Society for Human Nutrition
www.sinu.it

World Trade Organization (WTO)
www.wto.org

Selected Bibliography

Many Italian sources were used in the writing of this book, and some of them can be found in the notes section at the end of each chapter. This bibliography contains sources in English only, and they are also recommended for further reading.

GENERAL WORKS

Beardsworth, Alan, and Keil Teresa. *Sociology on the Menu*. New York: Routledge, 1997.

Beauchamp, Gary K., and Bartoshuk, Linda, eds. *Tasting and Smelling*. San Diego: Academic Press, 1997.

Charles, Daniel. *Lords of the Harvest: Biotech, Big Money, and the Future of Food*. Cambridge, Mass.: Perseus Publishing, 2001.

Counihan, Carole M. "Food." In *The Anthropology of Food and Body*. New York: Routledge, 1999.

Curtin, Deane, and Lisa Heldke. *Cooking, Eating, Thinking*. Bloomington: Indiana University Press, 1992.

Douglas, Mary. *Implicit Meanings*. London: Routledge, 1975. 2nd ed., 1999.

———. *Purity and Danger*. London: Routledge and Kegan Paul, 1969.

———. "Standard Social Uses of Food: Introduction." In *Food in the Social Order*. New York: Russell Sage Foundation, 1984.

Elias, Norbert. *The Civilizing Process*. Oxford, England: Blackwell, 1994.

Fine, Gary Alan. *Kitchens: The Culture of Restaurant Work*. Berkeley: University of California Press, 1996.

Finkelstein, Joanne. *Dining Out: A Sociology of Modern Manners*. New York: New York University Press, 1989.

Goody, Jack. *Cooking, Cuisine and Class*. Cambridge, England: Cambridge University Press, 1982.

Johnson, Hugh. *Story of Wine*. London: Mitchell Beazley, 1996.

Kurlanski, Mark. *Cod*. New York: Penguin, 1998.

———. *Salt: A World History*. New York: Walter and Company, 2002.

Lambrecht, Bill. *Dinner at the New Gene Café*. New York: St. Martin's Press, 2001.

Lupton, Deborah. *Food, The Body and the Self*. London: Sage, 1996.

MacCannel, Dean. *The Tourist: A New Theory of the Leisure Class*. Berkeley: University of California Press, 1976. 2nd ed., 1999.

McGovern, Patrick. *Ancient Wine: The Search for the Origins of Viniculture*. Princeton, N.J.: Princeton University Press, 2003.

McGovern, Patrick, Stuart Fleming, and Solomon Katz. *The Origins and Ancient History of Wine*. Amsterdam: Gordon and Breach Publishers, 1996.

Mennell, Stephen. *All the Manners of Food*. Urbana: University of Illinois Press, 1985. 2nd ed., 1996.

———. *The Sociology of Food: Eating, Diet and Culture*. London: Sage, 1993.

Murcott, Anne. "Talking of Good Food: An Empirical Study of Women's Conceptualizations." *Food and Foodways* 40 (1995): 305–318.

Pence, Gregory, ed. *The Ethics of Food*. Lanham, Md.: Rowman & Littlefield, 2002.

Salaman, Redcliffe. *The History and Social Influence of Potato*. Cambridge, England: Cambridge University Press, 1985.

Stearns, Peter. *Fat History*. New York: New York University Press, 1997.

Symons, Michael. *A History of Cooks and Cooking*. Chicago: University of Illinois Press, 2000.

Verblen, Thorstein. *The Theory of the Leisure Class*. New York: Macmillan, 1899; New York: The Modern Library, 2001.

Visser, Margaret. *The Rituals of Dinner*. New York: Penguin, 1991.

Warde, Alan, and Lydia Martens. *Eating Out*. Cambridge, England: Cambridge University Press, 2000.

Young, Carolin C. *Apples of Gold in Settings of Silver: Stories of Dinner as a Work of Art*. New York: Simon & Schuster, 2002.

REFERENCES

Bastianich, Joseph, and David Lynch. *Vino Italiano: The Regional Wines of Italy*. New York: Clarkson Potter, 2002.

Clark, Martin. *Modern Italy, 1871–1925*. London: Longman, 1984.

Dalby, Andrew. *Dangerous Tastes: The Story of Spices*. Berkeley: University of California Press, 2000.

Dolamore, Anne. *Olive Oil Companion*. London: Grub Street, 1988.

Flandrin, Jean-Louis, and Massimo Montanari. *A Culinary History of Food*. New York: Penguin Books, 2000.

Ginsborg, Paul. *A History of Contemporary Italy: Society and Politics, 1943–1988*. London: Penguin, 1994.

Gundle, S., and S. Parker, eds. *The New Italian Republic: From the Fall of the Berlin Wall to Berlusconi*. London: Routledge, 1995.

Hughes, Spike. *The Pocket Guide to Italian Food and Wine*. New York: Simon & Schuster, 1986.

Kiple, Kenneth, and Kriemhild Conée Ornelas. *The Cambridge World History of Food*. Cambridge, England: Cambridge University Press, 2000.

Mariani, John. *The Dictionary of Italian Food and Drink*. New York: Broadway Books, 1998.

Root, Waverly. *The Food of Italy*. New York: Vintage Books, 1971.

Rosenblum, Mort. *Olives: The Life and Lore of a Noble Fruit*. New York: North Point, 1996.

Tannahill, Reay. *Food in History*. New York: Three Rivers Press, 1973. 2nd ed., 1988.

Toussaint-Samat, Maguelonne. *History of Food*. Malden, Mass.: Blackwell, 1992.

Unwin, Tim. *Wine and the Vine: A Historical Geography of Viticulture and the Wine Trade*. London: Routledge, 1991.

Woolf, Stuart. *A History of Italy, 1700–1860*. London: Methuen, 1979.

HISTORICAL OVERVIEW

Albala, Ken. *Eating Right in the Renaissance*. Berkeley: University Press of California, 2002.

———. *Food in Early Modern Europe*. Westport, Conn.: Greenwood Press, 2003.

Artusi Pellegrino. *Science in the Kitchen and the Art of Eating Well*. 1897. New York: Marsilio, 1997.

Baránsky, Zygmunt, and Robert Lumley, eds. *Culture and Conflict in Postwar Italy: Essays on Mass and Popular Culture*. New York: St. Martin's Press, 1990.

Barzini, Luigi. *The Italians*. New York: Atheneum, 1964.

Biasin, Gianpaolo. *The Flavors of Modernity: Food and the Novel*. Princeton, N.J.: Princeton University Press, 1993.

Black, Maggie. *The Medieval Cookbook*. London: British Museum Press, 1992.

Black, William. *Al Dente: The Adventures of a Gastronome in Italy*. New York: Bantam Press, 2003.

Bober, Phyllis Pray. *Art, Culture and Cuisine: Ancient and Medieval Gastronomy*. Chicago: University of Chicago Press, 1999.

Braudel, Fernand. *The Mediterranean and the Mediterranean World in the Age of Philip II*. Vol. 2. 1966. Berkeley: University of California Press, 1995.

———. *The Perspective of the World: Civilization and Capitalism, 15th to 18th Century*. Vol. 3. 1966. Berkeley: University of California Press, 1992.

Brothwell, Don, and Patricia Brothwell. *Food in Antiquity*. London: Tames and Hudson, 1969; Baltimore: Johns Hopkins University Press, 1998.

Burke, Peter. *The Historical Anthropology of Early Modern Italy: Essays on Perception and Communication*. Cambridge, England: Cambridge University Press, 1987.

Camporesi, Piero. *The Anatomy of the Senses*. Cambridge, England: Polity Press, 1994.

———. *Bread of Dreams: Food and Fantasy in Early Modern Europe*. Chicago: University of Chicago Press, 1989.

———. *Exotic Brew: The Art of Living in the Age of Enlightenment*. Cambridge, England: Polity Press, 1990.

———. *The Land of Hunger*. Cambridge, England: Polity Press, 1996.

———. *The Magic Harvest: Food, Folklore, and Society*. Cambridge, England: Polity Press, 1999.

Cento Bull, A., and P. Corner. *From Peasant to Entrepreneur: The Survival of the Family Economy in Italy*. Oxford, England: Berg, 1993.

Cernilli, Daniele, and Marco Sabellico. *The New Italy*. London: Mitchell Beazley, 2000.

Crosby, Alfred. *The Columbian Exchange*. Westport, Conn.: Greenwood Press, 1972.

Dalby, Andrew. *Siren Feasts: A History of Food and Gastronomy in Greece*. New York: Routledge, 1996.

Dalby, Andrew, and Sally Grainger. *The Classical Cookbook*. London: British Museum Press, 1996. 2nd ed., 2000.

Dalle Vacche, Angela. *The Body in the Mirror: Shapes of History in Italian Cinema*. Princeton, N.J.: Princeton University Press, 1992.

Davidson, James. *Courtesans and Fishcakes*. New York: St. Martin's Press, 1998.

Diamond, Jared. *Guns, Germs, and Steel*. New York: W. W. Norton, 1997.

Dickinson, Robert. *The Population Problem in Southern Italy: An Essay in Social Geography*. Syracuse, N.Y.: Syracuse University Press, 1955.

Diner, Hasia. "Black Bread, Hard Bread: Food, Class, and Hunger in Italy." In *Hungering for America*. Cambridge, Mass.: Harvard University Publishers, 2001.

Duggan, Christopher. *A Concise History of Italy*. Cambridge, England: Cambridge University Press, 1994.

Feeley-Harnik, Gillian. *The Lord's Table: The Meaning of Food in Early Judaism and Christianity*. Washington, D.C.: Smithsonian Institution, 1994.

Gilbert, Mark. *The Italian Revolution: The End of Politics Italian Style*. Boulder, Colo.: Westview Press, 1995.

Gramsci, Antonio. *Selections from the Prison Notebooks*. New York: International Publishers, 1971.

Grimm, Veronika. *From Fasting to Feasting, the Evolution of a Sin: Attitudes to Food in Late Antiquity*. New York: Routledge, 1996.

Hearder, Harry. *Italy: A Short History*. Cambridge, England: Cambridge University Press, 2001.

Hobsbawn, Eric, and Terence Ranger. *The Invention of Tradition*. Cambridge, England: Cambridge University Press, 1983.

King, Russell. *Land Reform: The Italian Experience*. London: Butterworths, 1973.

Leitch, Alison. "The Social Life of *Lardo*: Slow Food in Fast Times." *The Asia Pacific Journal of Anthropology* 1, no. 1 (2000): 103–228.

Levi, Carlo. *Christ Stopped at Eboli: A Story of a Year*. New York: Farrar, Straus, 1947.

Levy, Carl. *Italian Regionalism: History, Identity, and Politics*. Oxford, England: Berg, 1996.

Livi Bacci, Massimo. *Population and Nutrition: An Essay on European Geographic History*. Cambridge, England: Cambridge University Press, 1991.

Lumley, Robert, and Jonathan Morris. *The New History of the Italian South: The Mezzogiorno Revisited*. Exeter, England: University of Exeter Press, 1997.

Marinetti, F. T. *The Futurist Cookbook*. London: Trefoil Publications, 1989.

Montanari, Massimo. *The Culture of Food (The Making of Europe)*. Oxford, England: Blackwell, 1996.

Montanari, Massimo, and Alberto Capatti. *Italian Cuisine: A Cultural History*. New York: Columbia University Press, 2003.

O'Connor, Maura. *The Romance of Italy and the English Political Imagination*. London: St. Martin's, 1998.

Nicolau, Antoni, and Simon Zimmermann. *Sacred Foods: Bread, Wine, and Oil in the Ancient Mediterranean*. Barcelona: Institut de Cultura—Museu d'Historia de la Ciutat, 2001.

Orlando Consort. *Food, Wine & Song: Music and Feasting in Renaissance Europe*. Los Angeles: Harmonia Mundi France, Production USA, 2001. Compact disc.

Parasecoli, Fabio. "Postrevolutionary Chowhounds: Food, Globalization, and the Italian Left." *Gastronomica* 3, no. 3 (2003): 29–39.

Petrini, Carlo. *Slow Food (The Case for Taste)*. New York: Columbia University Press, 2003.

Polo, Marco. *The Travels of Marco Polo*. New York: Viking Press, 1958.

Rebora, Giovanni. *Culture of the Fork*. New York: Columbia University Press, 2001.

Redon, Odile. *The Medieval Kitchen: Recipes from France and Italy*. Chicago: University of Chicago Press, 1998.

Robb, Peter. *Midnight in Sicily: On Art, Food, History, Travel, and La Cosa Nostra*. Boston: Faber and Faber, 1998.

Sarti, Roland. *Long Live the Strong: A History of Rural Society in the Apennine Mountains*. Amherst, Mass.: University of Massachusetts Press, 1985.

Scholliers, Peter, ed. *Food, Drink and Identity: Cooking, Eating and Drinking in Europe since the Middle Ages*. Oxford, England: Berg, 2001.

Thorne, John, and Matt Lewis Thorn. "Mangiamaccheroni." In *The Outlaw Cook*. New York: North Point Press, 1992.

Verga, Giovanni. *Cavalleria Rusticana and Other Stories*. New York: Penguin USA, 2000.

Wright, Clifford. *A Mediterranean Feast*. New York: William Morrow, 1999.

MAJOR FOODS AND INGREDIENTS/COOKBOOKS

Anderson, Burton. *Treasures of the Italian table: Italy's Celebrated Foods and the Artisans Who Make Them*. New York: Morrow, 1994.

Andrews, Colman. *Flavors of the Riviera*. New York: Bantam Books, 1996.

Bastianich, Lidia. *La Cucina di Lidia: Recipes and Memories from Italy's Adriatic Coast*. New York: Broadway Books, 2003.

———. *Lidia's Italian Table: More Than 200 Recipes from the First Lady of Italian Cooking*. New York: William Morrow, 1998.

Behr, Ed. "Emilia Romagna: Stories from the Region Whose Cuisine Has Always Been Called Italy's Riches and Best." *The Art of Eating* 54 (2000): 1–22.

———. "In Tuscany." *The Art of Eating* 41 (1997): 1–11.

Bugialli, Giuliano. *Bugialli on Pasta*. New York: Stewart, Tabori and Chang, 2000.

———. *Bugialli's Italy: Traditional Recipes from the Regions of Italy*. New York: William Morrow, 1998.

———. *The Fine Art of Italian Cooking*. New York: Clarkson Potter, 1990.

———. *Food of Naples*. New York: Stewart, Tabori and Chang, 2003.

———. *Foods of Sicily & Sardinia and the Smaller Islands*. New York: Rizzoli, 1996.

———. *Giuliano Bugialli's Classic Techniques of Italian Cooking*. New York: Simon and Schuster, 1982.

———. *Giuliano Bugialli's Foods of Italy*. New York: Stewart, Tabori and Chang, 1984.

———. *Giuliano Bugialli's Foods of Tuscany*. New York: Stewart, Tabori and Chang, 1992.

Caggiano, Biba. *Biba's Taste of Italy: Recipes from the Homes, Trattorie and Restaurants of Emilia Romagna*. New York: Morrow, 2001.

Cantarelli, Corrado, and Ch. Mercier, eds. "Pasta and Extrusion-Cooked Foods: Some Technological and Nutritional Aspects," Proceedings of an International Symposium, Milan, Italy, March 25–26, 1985. New York: Elsevier, 1986.

De Blasi, Marlena. *The Regional Foods of Northern Italy*. New York: Three Rivers Press, 1997.

Downie, David. *Cooking the Roman Way*. New York: HarperCollins, 2002.

Field, Carol. *Celebrating Italy*. New York: William Morrow, 1990.

———. *Italy in Small Bites*. New York: William Morrow, 1993.

———. *In Nonna's Kitchen: Recipes and Traditions from Italy's Grandmothers*. New York: HarperCollins, 1997.

Goldstein, Joyce. *Cucina Ebraica: Flavors of the Italian Jewish Kitchen*. San Francisco: Chronicle Books, 1998.

———. *Enoteca: Simple, Delicious Recipes in the Italian Wine Bar Tradition.* San Francisco: Chronicle Books, 2001.

Granof, Victoria. *Sweet Sicily: The Story of an Island and Her Pastries.* New York: HarperCollins, 2001.

Hazan, Giuliano. *Every Night Italian.* New York: Scribner, 2000.

Hazan, Marcella. *The Classic Italian Cookbook.* New York: Knopf, 1973.

———. *Essentials of Classic Italian Cooking.* New York: Knopf, 1002.

———. *Marcella Cucina.* New York: HarperCollins, 1997.

———. *Marcella's Italian Kitchen.* New York: Knopf, 1995.

———. *More Classic Italian Cooking.* New York: Knopf, 1978.

Jenkins, Nancy Harmon. *The Essential Mediterranean.* New York: HarperCollins, 2003.

———. *Flavors of Puglia.* New York: Broadway Books, 1997.

———. *Flavors of Tuscany.* New York: Broadway Books, 1998.

———. *The Mediterranean Diet Cook Book.* New York: Bantam, 1994.

Kasper, Lynn Rosetto. *The Splendid Table: Recipes from Emilia Romagna.* New York: William Morrow, 1992.

La Place, Viana. *La Bella Cucina: How to Cook, Eat, and Live Like an Italian.* New York: Clarkson Potter, 2001.

Lo Monte, Mimmetta. *Classic Sicilian Cookbook.* New York: Simon and Schuster, 1990.

Machlin, Edda Servi. *The Classic Cuisine of the Italian Jews.* Croton on Hudson, N.Y.: Giro Press, 1992.

Negrin, Micol. *Rustico: Regional Italian Country Cooking.* New York: Clarkson Potter, 2002.

Petroni, Paolo. *The Complete Book of Florentine Cooking.* Florence: Il Centauro, 1995.

Plotkin, Fred. *Italy for the Gourmet Traveler.* Boston: Little Brown, 1996.

———. *Recipes from Paradise: Life and Food on the Italian Riviera.* Boston: Little, Brown, 1997.

———. *La Terra Fortunata: The Splendid Food and Wine of Friuli Venezia Giulia.* New York: Broadway Books, 2001.

Roden, Claudia. *The Food of Italy.* London: Chatto and Windus, 1989.

Sacerdoti, Mira. *Italian Jewish Cooking.* London: Robert Hall, 1992.

Scicolone, Michele. *A Fresh Taste of Italy.* New York: Broadway Books, 1997.

———. *Savoring Italy.* New York: Time Life Books, 1999.

Sidoli, Richard Camillo. *The Cooking of Parma.* New York: Rizzoli, 1996.

Simeti, Mary Taylor. *On Persephone's Island: A Sicilian Journal.* New York: Knopf, 1986.

Simeti, Mary Taylor. *Pump and Sustenance: Twenty-five Centuries of Sicilian Food.* Hopewell, N.J.: Ecco Press, 1989.

Tasca Lanza, Anna. *The Heart of Sicily.* New York: Clarkson Potter, 1993.

Tornabene, Wanda, and Giovanna Tornabene. *Sicilian Home Cooking.* New York: Knopf, 2001.

Willinger, Faith. *Eating in Italy: A Traveler's Guide to the Hidden Gastronomic Pleasures of Northern Italy*. New York: William Morrow, 1998.

———. *Red, White, and Greens: The Italian Way with Vegetables*. New York: HarperCollins, 1996.

Wright, Clifford A. *Cucina Paradiso: The Heavenly Food of Sicily*. New York: Simon & Schuster, 1992.

Zanini de Vita, Oretta. *The Food of Rome and Lazio*. Rome: Alphabyte Books, 1994.

COOKING

May, Tony. *Italian Cuisine: Basic Cooking Techniques*. New York. Rizzoli, 1992.

TYPICAL MEALS

Goddard, V. A. *Gender, Family and Work in Naples*. Oxford, England: Berg, 1996.

Ketzer, David. *Family Life in Central Italy*. New Brunswick, N.J.: Rutgers University Press, 1984.

EATING OUT

Carter, Donald. *States of Grace: Senegalese in Italy and the New European Immigration*. Minneapolis: University of Minnesota Press, 1997.

Fant, Maureen. *Trattorias of Rome, Florence, and Venice*. Hopewell, N.J.: Ecco Press, 2001.

Fast Food in Europe: Quick Service Catering in West Germany, United Kingdom, France, Italy, Spain, Netherlands and Belgium. New York: Economist Intelligence Unit, 1990.

Herbach, Andy. *Eating and Drinking in Italy: Italian Menu Reader and Restaurant*. Open Road Pub. Guide. Cold Spring Harbor, N.Y.: Open Road Publishing, 2001.

SPECIAL OCCASIONS

Bianchi, Anne. *Italian Festival Food*. New York: MacMillan USA, 1999.

Bonino, Maddalena. *The Festive Food of Italy*. Boston: Little, Brown, 1991.

Scicolone, Michele. *Italian Holiday Cooking*. New York: William Morrow, 2001.

DIET AND HEALTH

Crotty, Patricia. "The Mediterranean Diet as a Food Guide: The Problem of Culture and History." *Nutrition Today* 33, no. 6 (1998): 227–232.

Keys, Ancel, Flaminio Fidanza, Vicenzo Scardi, Gino Bergami, Margaret Haney Keys, and Ferruccio di Lorenzo. "Studies on Serum Cholesterol and Other

Characteristics of Clinically Healthy Men in Naples." *Archives of Internal Medicine* 93 (1954): 328–336.

Nestle, Marion. "Mediterranean Diets: Historical and Research Overview." *American Journal of Clinical Nutrition* 61 (1995): 1313S–1320.

Pagano, Romano, Carlo La Vecchia, Adriano Decarli, Eva Negri, and Silvia Franceschi. "Trends in Overweight and Obesity among Italian Adults, 1983 through 1994." *American Journal of Public Health* 87, no. 11 (1997): 1869.

Schard, David, Bonnie Liebman, and Stephen Schmidt. "Going Mediterranean." *Nutrition Action Health Letter* 21, no. 10 (1994): 5–9.

Zizza, Claire, and Shirley Gerrior. "Trends in Availability of Foods and Nutrients: A Comparison Between the United States and Italy, 1961–1992." *Family Economics and Nutrition Review* 12, no. 1 (1999): 26–42.

Index

About the Author

FABIO PARASECOLI, based in Rome, writes on and teaches about Italian food and food history and represents the Italian media firm Gambero Rosso in New York City.

Recent Titles in
Food Culture around the World

Food Culture in Japan
Michael Ashkenazi and Jeanne Jacob

Food Culture in India
Colleen Taylor Sen

Food Culture in China
Jacqueline M. Newman

Food Culture in Great Britain
Laura Mason